Also by Fausto Vicarelli

KEYNES: THE INSTABILITY OF CAPITALISM

KEYNES'S RELEVANCE TODAY

Edited by

Fausto Vicarelli
Professor of Economics
University of Rome

MACMILLAN

© Gius. Laterza & Figli, Rome, 1983, 1985

First published as *Attualità di Keynes*
by Laterza 1983
First published in English by
THE MACMILLAN PRESS LTD 1985
London and Basingstoke
Companies and representatives
throughout the world

Filmsetting by Vantage Photosetting Co. Ltd
Eastleigh and London

British Library Cataloguing in Publication Data
Keynes's relevance today.
1. Keynes, John Maynard   2. Keynesian economics
I. Vicarelli, Fausto   II. Attualità di Keynes.
English
330.15'6   HB99.7
ISBN 0–333–36345–0
ISBN 0–333–36346–8 Pbk

Printed and bound in Great Britain by
Anchor Brendon Ltd, Tiptree, Essex

Contents

Preface

Is Keynes relevant today? Can his message help us to understand the economic problems now facing the world? Confronted with the contradictory problems of unemployment and inflation do 'Keynesian' policies still merit our consideration?

These are questions of more than merely academic interest and it is not only economists who ask them or who have the duty to provide an answer. The crisis affects everyone; everyone must contribute to the search for a solution. Inevitably, however, the economics 'profession' is in the front line. The centenary of Keynes's birth provides an excellent opportunity to ask the profession awkward questions. Today it is capitalism itself, that same capitalist reality which Keynes placed at the centre of his concerns, which is raising these questions.

The economists who have agreed to give an answer in the studies contained in this book come from differing theoretical and ideological backgrounds and do not all share the same faith in the possibility of applying the wealth of experience accumulated by Keynes to the solution of our present problems. They do however share one common conviction, namely that there exists no law of nature governing the workings of the capitalist system, in other words, that it is senseless to abandon the role of economic policy, trusting exclusively in the 'invisible hand' of competition. The most recent deleterious fruits of all-out free enterprise serve to strengthen this conviction.

The original Italian edition of these studies was dedicated to Federico Caffè, not only in homage to one of the economists who has made the greatest contributions to making Keynes's thought known in Italy, but also as an example of that spirit which distinguished Keynes's own works, and which he himself summed up so admirably: 'We have to invent new wisdom for a new age. And in the meantime we must, if we are to do any good, appear unorthodox, troublesome, dangerous, disobedient to them that begat us.'

University of Rome   FAUSTO VICARELLI

List of Contributors

Frank Hahn, University of Cambridge, UK.

Sir John Hicks, All Souls College, Oxford, UK.

J. A. Kregel, University of Groningen, The Netherlands.

Giorgio Lunghini, University of Pavia, Italy.

Joan Robinson, University of Cambridge, UK.

Josef Steindl, Austrian Institute for Economic Research, Vienna, Austria.

Paolo Sylos Labini, University of Rome, Italy.

Fausto Vicarelli, University of Rome, Italy.

Sidney Weintraub, University of Pennsylvania, USA.

Frank Wilkinson, University of Cambridge, UK.

1 Some Keynesian Reflections on Monetarism[1]

FRANK HAHN

I take monetarism to be the doctrine that the perfectly competitive economy in Walrasian equilibrium is adequately descriptive of the world we live in and that the model itself can be treated roughly enough to survive the coarse-grained hands of econometricians. This characterisation may be found surprising since it makes no mention of money. But almost everything monetarists have said about money is trivial, not to say banal, once one has jumped through the Walrasian hoop. My characterisation may also be found to be surprising since it seems to embrace upright economists who do not regard themselves as monetarist. That really cannot be helped when one is using any kind of simple categorisation. The important aspect for me is that monetarism can have no truck with Keynes and indeed must regard him as some sort of crank. For Keynes not only considered it possible that people could be involuntarily unemployed but even talked of an equilibrium with such unemployment. He thought that these unsatisfactory states could be rendered more agreeable by rather simple actions on the part of the Government. None of this is wrong – in the Walrasian equilibrium context – it simply does not make sense. It is, if you like, so ungrammatical as to be incomprehensible. This really is the centre of my concern. Is it the case that if we accept a world of self-seeking rational agents we will by simple logic be driven to renounce Keynes and all his works as mumbo-jumbo?

But first I want to concentrate on the way in which monetarists reach their conclusions. Surprisingly very few monetarists have either a grasp or an understanding of the fundamentals of the theory they believe they are using. It is, as Macaulay used to say, known to every school boy, that an agent's best choice of action will remain unaffected if all

1

money prices (including of course money wages and expected prices), are different in the same proportions as his money wealth is different. From this we conclude that, taking any Walrasian equilibrium, if every agent's money wealth were different in the same proportion and if prices including expected prices were all different in the same proportion from their previous value the economy would still be in equilibrium. This elementary result is then translated by monetarists into 'a k-fold change in the money stock of an economy will bring about a k-fold change in all money prices'. It is hard to live in a world in which such sloppiness goes not only unpunished but also seems to be rewarded. In any case the correct *homogeneity* property of agent's choices will have to be just as much a part of a Keynesian theory based on rational actions as of any other such theory. The difference for Keynesian theory amongst other differences will be the recognition of multiple equilibria. To this I return at length later.

But let me start at the beginning. As far as I am concerned that is the beautiful theory which we call the Arrow–Debreu model. It showed that it is logically possible to describe a world where greedy and rational people responding only to price signals take actions which are mutually compatible. The theory does not describe the invisible hand in motion but displays it with its task accomplished. The importance of this intellectual achievement is that it provides a benchmark. By this I mean that it serves a function similar to that which an ideal and perfectly healthy body might serve a clinical diagnostician when he looks at an actual body.

Now one of the mysteries which future historians of thought will surely wish to unravel is how it came about that the Arrow–Debreu model came to be taken descriptively; that is as sufficient in itself for the study and perhaps control of actual economies. Having spent most of my life as an economist on this theory I confess that such an interpretation never occurred to me. Indeed it was clear from the beginning that we only had half a theory anyway since there was (and is), no rigorous account, derived from first principles, of how the Arrow–Debreu equilibrium comes to be established. But even the half which we had was quickly seen to have serious gaps: it could not account for money or a stock-exchange, there were, more importantly, no increasing returns possible, there was no theory of actual exchange, the number of firms was taken as exogenous and one would require set up costs to make sense of firms anyway, information was symmetric and complete, labour was sold like peanuts are sold, unborn generations implausibly made themselves felt on current markets and there

were far too many markets anyway. If ever a theory was straightfor-
wardly falsified it is the theory of a capitalist economy in Arrow–
Debreu equilibrium. But it was never meant to be so obviously
falsified; it was designed as both a reference point and a starting
point.

However it will now be argued that these remarks are beside the
point for my present concern since few monetarists have any knowledge or understanding of Arrow–Debreu theory and those that have
do not care to use it. The models which for the most part *are* in use are
founded on simple microeconomic textbooks and use very special
functional forms and are in any case 'macroeconomic'. It is true that in
these models prices and wages are at all times clearing the Walrasian
markets which the construction contains but the models themselves
have been given a sequential structure which is not the case in the
Arrow–Debreu world.

All of this is indeed correct. But it is my contention that it is precisely
this having one foot in the tranquil Arrow–Debreu waters and the
other in seemingly plausible *ad hoc* models that makes the work of
these economists so unsatisfactory. For instance they often claim that
they can apply the Fundamental Theorem of Welfare Economics
which is firmly based on Arrow–Debreu theory to their world of
implicitly missing markets and transaction costs. Recently a book
published by one of them for instance claimed that rational expectations equilibria were Pareto-efficient.[2] The history of the 'Optimum
Quantity of Money' shows that it was only when it was examined by
General Equilibrium theorists that sense could be made of it. Similarly
monetarists either construct miniature models in which equilibrium is
unique or when the multiplicity stares them in the face they arbitrarily
pick one of them.

It is at this point that I must, with some reluctance, face a number of
methodological questions. I must do so because they keep coming up
in discussions even with the wise and good and because if I do not get
them out of the way now it may detract from the substantive points to
come. To be as brief as possible I shall be schematic.

(a) 'Simple models are what we should aim for'. This always strikes
me like the Parson's urging that virtue is better than vice. It is also
without content or as no doubt Americans would prefer to say: it is not
operational. Like virtue, simplicity has its own reward if it works. It
works, if it provides robust insights. For instance amalgamating investment and consumption into something called total expenditure instead
of treating them separately, no doubt reduces equation numbers and

allows monetarists to ignore variables like productive capacity. But it
also gives not only wrong insights but the model is not robust when the
distinction between the two kinds of expenditures is re-introduced.
This really gives the clue: successful simplification is so by virtue of the
robustness of its qualitative message to complication. If one is a true
simplifier and not just sloppy and lazy then one must be able to claim to
arrive at essentials which are also to be found in what one regards as
complicated. Current monetarist writing does not survive this test.

(b) 'Economics is not a game of chess and our theories must be of a
kind where they can be used'. Keynes after all urged us to be like
dentists. The message here is that General Equilibrium theory which is
not specialised and simplified is so general that 'anything could happen'. To this my first answer is that while this is too sweeping it is true
that many things could happen and that this may not only by a
reflection of our ignorance but also of the world. Here is one example:
President Reagan announces that he has seen the error of his ways and
that he will now proceed to some old fashioned pump-priming. One
possible outcome is purely monetarist: prices and interest rates will
rise to nullify the effects otherwise to be expected. That is because
many people have come to believe Chicago. Another outcome is that
observing all the slack in the economy and seeing a converted President, people will expect higher demand and output, prices will not
change much and the Keynesian results ensue. All of this is really an
aspect of multiple equilibria. But if I do not know which of these two
and of the many intermediate outcomes will occur what is the point of
enshrining a guess in some highly special model in which one or the
other is bound to occur? It is true that I can then say something but it
seems to me better to have kept quiet. The circumstances that we must
always make public choices does not seem to me to lead to the
conclusion that we must always cook the books. On the contrary. The
economist's main contribution at present is precisely to urge that many
things can happen. This might stop politicians putting all their eggs into
one basket.

(c) 'Macro-economics is different from Micro-economics'. If it is
then I for one do not know what it is. It can hardly be the case that
models which look on the world as if there were a single firm, a single
household, and a single good thereby create some new kind of
economic theory. Of course, like in physics and perhaps in Marxian
economics it could be otherwise. There could be theories – holistic
theories – in which aggregates do not behave as simply added micro-
entities. Indeed General Equilibrium theory itself shows that the

interaction of many individuals needs a special theory. In our present state of knowledge macroeconomics is simply the project of deducing something about the behaviour of such aggregates as income and employment from the micro-theory which we have. The whole enterprise of giving microeconomic foundations to macroeconomics is therefore mis-named. If macroeconomics before this enterprise was innocent of microeconomics it is not easy to see that it was anything at all. But of course Keynes never went on such a hair-brained path and he can claim to have founded the subject. Almost two-thirds of *The General Theory* is in fact devoted to microeconomics.

If one looks more closely one finds, as usual, that this corrupt use of language, this sloppiness in making sentences, is sinister in intent. For what many people who set out to look for foundations meant was that the Walrasian equilibrium economy cannot accommodate the Keynesian insights. They then drew the conclusion that there were no such insights. It did not seem necessary to enquire whether the Walrasian equilibrium model was itself adequate or logically robust. The true question then is whether there are rigorous models of the economy whose premises are no less acceptable at least than those of the Walrasian model, which can in fact support Keynesian contentions? That question cannot be answered if we start *by fiat* as the Lucasians[3] do, with a world in which Walrasian markets always clear. (I ought here to add in parenthesis that Keynes himself is much to blame for the muddle. He had a poets' intuition and a practical man's grasp but he did not begin to know how to theorise rigorously.)

(d) The last methodological point which I wish to make is this: The answer which one receives over and over again to one's criticisms is that the model 'works' and that the theorist's concerns are therefore of no relevance. Just so might an ancient Roman have spoken about the oracles or the method of finding a propitious time for battle by consulting the entrails of animals. This certainly worked as well as does most econometrics. The view I am here considering can be traced back to Friedman and to old fashioned and discredited positivism. But a fact not confirmed by theory is a fact we do not understand. It cannot be brought into proper relation with what we know or think we know. That does not mean that we should reject the fact if such it is. It means that all our work still remains to be done. If a monetarist model is logically flawed then I for one do not give a fig for its predictive power. I chose to be an economist – not a witch doctor.

Here is an example. Everyone knows by now that Walrasian sequence economies have many – mostly a continuum of rational expectations equilibria.[4] Amongst these there may be just one which seeks the steady state or there may also be a continuum of these. Some others may become infeasible in a thousand years time. Monetarist econometricians have chosen to work with models in which there is only one path that converges to the steady state. They then declare that this is the path which an actual economy follows. Since there is nothing in the theory which suggests that this is so or how it could be so they add that their latest three-stage econometric estimate based on this sort of assumption 'works'. If they are also trying to placate you they will mumble something about transversality conditions. This however gives the game away. For these conditions are only relevant in an optimising context. Thus their 'explanation' is implicitly that the economy must behave as if someone performed an infinite optimisation exercise on it. But *that* is precisely the issue at hand – indeed it is at the heart of Keynes. His description of an actual capitalist economy makes it very clear that it would not be Pareto-efficient, leave alone Ramsey-optimal. From an epistemological point of view the whole sequence of arguments is illiterate. It may be that tomorrow someone will turn up who forecasts the economy by scanning tea-leaves and who has great success in this as econometricians understand success. He might be a very useful person to President Reagan or to someone playing the stock exchange. But it is hard to see how anything he does has any bearing on the enterprise which is economics. Let us recall that Ptolemy can be made to 'work' even now but that we reject it because there is no way of understanding his construction.

I now leave methodology behind me and come to the centre of my argument. This I fear will be a little more technical. It will be in two parts. The first will repeat at a rather more general level what I have already touched on before, namely that monetarists' doctrines are not logically entailed by their theory. The second will argue that there are very strong grounds for looking for another theory anyway.

If we are going to have theories which can encompass some of the important world phenomena which I have enumerated as being beyond Arrow–Debreu theory we shall, it is I think universally agreed, have to modify this theory to give it a sequential structure. By this I mean that there will have to be trading at every date. This, for a careful theorist then entails the necessity of forging an endogenous theory of markets. But this I shall not now discuss and I shall take 'missing' markets as given.[5] Even so an agent's plans and current action will now depend on expectations. We know next to nothing about expectations and that is why we take the step of demanding that they be rational. In the present Walrasian context a rational expectations equilibrium occurs when each agent knows the prices which will clear markets in each date-event pair when all agents are equally clever.

So let us stop right here. The theory as such says nothing about the underlying stochastic process and so the definition which I have just given is not the same as that used by macroeconomists of the R.E. type when they ask expected prices to be unbiased estimators of actual price. Much less do they say that agent's activities depend only on their actuarial expectations. Every school boy – to go back to Macaulay – knows that this is a very special and not very plausible case. But there are also several logical problems of which I wish to pick only one. There is nothing in the world as God and Mammon have created it that guarantees, or indeed makes it likely in any precise sense, that for each date-event pair market clearing prices are unique. When that is so neither I nor anyone else has the slightest idea how to formulate a rational expectations equilibrium. But as I have already stressed non-uniqueness of equilibria is what Keynesian policy prescriptions must be about. The problem does not arise for those macroeconomists who are filling the journals with three or four log-linear equations. Not only are there no relative prices, (in fact many do not distinguish between wages and prices), but in the nature of such models multiple solutions cannot arise.

This is worth a moment's pause. When these equations are written down they almost always include an error term with zero mean and with no serial correlation. If one thinks about this one comes to realise that the underlying economy of many agents and goods is assumed to be exposed to lots of uncorrelated shocks which are idiosyncratic to different agents and that as it were, steps are taken instantaneously to 'cancel' these shocks. Lucas has recently realised that these are tall assumptions and by abandoning them has got himself a trade cycle model with always clearing markets.[6]

But let us now accept a unique Walrasian rational expectations equilibrium as describing an economy as it would be if it were not continuously surprised by the quite inexplicable actions of Government or the Central Bank. I want you on the way to notice one quite startling implication. In such an economy although there would be trading at every date there would, like in the Arrow–Debreu economy, be decisions only at one date – the first. The economy unfolds as dates and states unfold. But 'all things and all manner of things' have already been provided for. In this world firms need a high powered executive only once to make all the plans for all contingencies and dates. Thereafter it is all routine. At least this is the way the world would look in the absence of a random government. Such a government would be the only occasion for decision-making. This seems to me pretty close to nonsense for someone engaged in fashioning a theory to his econometric purposes. It also is an extraordinarily difficult way to analyse the Schumpeterian circumstance of the world.

But let us close our eyes and proceed. The economy in the equilibrium which I have described is by no means at rest. As states unfold the allocation of labour will change, some firms contract and others expand. Indeed total employment will vary from state to state as the appropriate real wage varies. So what exactly is the 'natural rate hypothesis' in this world? The latter is supposed to have something to do with search, a phenomenon I have not seen formally incorporated since Phelps studied it[7] and Diamond's splendid recent paper[8] which is not in this mould anyway. Is the amount of search independent of state and independent of the number of people seeking work? If there is a wage distribution why is it not given and what are the conditions under which it is invariant under the unfolding state?

However, let us shut our eyes to this difficulty; also no doubt some stochastic definition of the natural rate can be cooked up. The problem which I do not think we can shut our eyes to is the central confusion between the sentence starting 'there exists' and one starting with 'it is the case'. It is a confusion which I regret to say is much in evidence amongst students, which must be their teacher's fault. In suitable conditions a Rational Expectations equilibrium of the type here discussed, exists. But no one has shown that it is the case that an economy always seeks that equilibrium. I do not mean that no one has shown 'empirically' I mean that no one has shown it theoretically and by that in turn I mean that no one has done this at the level of serious theory. So the answer one gets is 'that it works' and that, as I have already argued, is not an answer at all. Half the story is simply missing – the invisible hand is super-invisible.

Now I have already remarked that Lucas, by far and away the most accomplished in this group, has noticed the difficulty and has in fact shown that even though markets clear at every date mistakes rationally made may never wash out. But he has not considered what this discovery entails for his rather famous monetarist ineffectiveness proposition. For it is by no means the case that on these errant cyclical paths monetary policy fully anticipated must be ineffective. To show that, he would need to show that the errors people make must have the homogeneity property. But that must be wrong, at least in general if for no other reason than that there is no precise account of how the errors are formed. Thus if I cannot disentangle a monetary from a real shock the manner in which I resolve the ambiguity is quite open to the extent that it depends on my priors and who is to say that they are independent of monetary policy.

Let us consider an example. Firms, wrongly for whatever reason, expect that investment in fixed capital goods has become more profitable, when the monetary policy is a constant stock of money. The economy will now follow a certain path in which the initial error will not quickly go away because it is embodied in the extra fixed capital which firms have installed. Indeed one can readily see how cycles may arise. Now let the monetary policy be one in which the money stock rises in proportion to the difference between the actual and some target income. If we accept monetarist doctrine then this will leave the path unaffected in real terms but the price level will behave differently. But firms who invest, borrow money or do not pay out money and the holding of money depends on the nominal and not on the real interest rate. So here at once is a source of real effectiveness and non-homogeneity of the error. But there is a much more serious argument: if all firms were to believe that under the second monetary policy the future would be different than under the first then it would be different and there is nothing to gainsay that, since we are *not* in rational expectations equilibrium. That is, agents may know a model of the economy but there is no 'the' model since there is no way in which they can model each other's mistakes. Keynesian agents will make different mistakes from monetarist agents.

So even in this rarefied and fundamentally silly model there does not seem much joy for monetarists. But perhaps this is too rarefied. I was recently taken to task by a high ranking economist at the Bank of England for just this failing.[9] He argues that sensible people were monetarist in a 'pragmatic and Friedmanite way' which I take to mean that sensible people had no good reason to believe what they do believe. But let me try to be sensible.

Now to (a). We know that except for 'shoe-leather' effects the monetary aggregates are, on any monetarist theory, irrelevant if they are foreseen. That is, they have no 'real' consequences. If however in our simple, sensible and pragmatic mood we believe that they do have real effects then we have to be persuaded that some particular formula dreamed up by a central banker by which the money supply is to be governed yields the best real effects. Since no such argument has been offered I conclude that after all nothing more is at stake than the provision of a simple formula – any formula – which will permit agents to forecast prices. So it must after all be the case that monetarists believe monetary policy which is not random to have no real effects. But that is so plainly false that we had better extend a helping hand and consider the proposition that monetary policy properly forseen can have no lasting real effects.

Indeed there is a pragmatic monetarist view that a change in monetary policy, in particular a change to a more restrictive policy is bound to be 'painful' in the short run. In puritanical Britain this promised joy through pain is much admired. Suppose then that it is true that we must first be punished before we can enjoy the benefits of what Mrs Thatcher calls 'honest' money. Then for less masochistically inclined economists a simple cost-benefit question arises. How many billions of pounds of GNP is 'honest' money worth? In fact: what precisely is the benefit of such money and how long will it be delayed? I cannot myself answer this question since for monetarists, as I have already argued, 'honest' money should have no benefits – long run or short run. If you think that you can control the rate of change in money prices by controlling the money supply then you can set it at zero or 12 per cent and it should make very little difference – certainly not several percentage points of GNP. But of course the model may be wrong. It is simply that on their own grounds, pragmatic or otherwise – these witch doctors have no leg to stand on. The arguments do not cohere at the crudest level and that really is an end on it.

So now I turn to the view that there are the strongest grounds for breaking out of the Walrasian straight jacket and indeed that some of the breaking out which has already been achieved is impressive and rather favourable to a roughly Keynesian view. Before I do this I reiterate once more my warning: the circumstance that I consider it crucial that we look beyond the Walrasian horizons does *not* mean that I believe this to be possible without a thorough knowledge of where these horizons are. Progress in a subject is rarely made by throwing out hook line and sinker, what went before. Mostly it comes as a natural and inevitable development.

I shall concentrate on the single proposition that the Walrasian model seriously understates the scope of externalities and as a consequence is too sanguine in its belief that capitalist outcomes cannot be improved by explicit cooperation. To put it somewhat more theoretically it seems to be the case that rather slight departures from the economy's description lead to rather large changes in our judgement of its performance and the role of policy. There are very many ways in which this can be argued but I shall concentrate on only one.

Of course even in orthodox economics there may be externalities: smoke and laundries and beekeepers and apple farmers are familiar to the undergraduate. It can be argued that such externalities can be eliminated by appropriate allocations of property rights. For the externalities which concern me that is not the case. They arise from the nature of the economic game and from the manner in which the players in such a game can communicate. Some of the most prominent monetarists – the name of Barro comes to mind – are quite unaware of these and consequently have become advocates of a Panglossian view of the world which in its silliness has not often been surpassed in our subject. They have decided that no state of the economy can be an equilibrium unless it is Pareto-efficient. Since the economy is in equilibrium more or less all of the time, a syllogism has been completed. We are asked to share their naïve glee at this confusion.

Let me start then with what appears an old fashioned Keynesian argument. Assume, provisionally of course, that there are people who at the going real wage would prefer to work but cannot find anyone to employ them. However in the market for goods tranquillity reigns: firms employ just as many as they regard most profitable and manage to sell what at the going prices they wish to sell. Households on the markets for goods buy at the going prices what they consider best. Keynes's proposition then went as follows. At the going wage no firm would wish to have more labour given the output and hiring decisions of all other firms. However if all firms together cooperatively hired more labour the demand of the newly employed would shift the demand curves facing firms to the right. If they are producing under diminishing-returns the real wage would be somewhat lower but under our provisional postulate that would not lower the supply of labour. There would then be a new state of the economy in which again, except possibly still on the labour supply side, all agents were in equilibrium. This new state would have more employment and under mild assumptions would Pareto-dominate the old state. All of this can be made precise and ship-shape. The Nash-like externalities here are clear to the naked eye.

Since this story as such is perfectly correct everything turns on what I have called the provisional hypothesis that there are states in which there are people willing to work at the going wage who cannot find jobs. In the first instance that may be taken to mean that the price mechanism does not work infinitely fast to clear Walrasian markets and only a madman would deny that. This then leads to the next stage in the Keynesian argument which has been much neglected. This is that if in the situation which I have outlined we leave it all to the game in which agents can only communicate by price signals the outcome is slow and the process will involve changes in relative prices and relative wages and so in allocations. Expectations enter the story in an important but uncertain way. As the price level falls people with debt committments in terms of money are made worse off or even bankrupt. The nominal interest rate will also take time to adjust and may not do so monotonically. A prevailing expectation of falling prices may, for a time, discourage investment. In short, there is a complex and not well understood dynamic process to be examined. But suppose that it succeeds after trials and tribulations and with considerable real cost, in guiding us into the Walrasian haven. It will do so largely by the twin forces of lower real wages and higher real cash balances. But then Keynes very reasonably thought it not sensible to reach the good cooperative outcome in this absurdly costly uncertain and roundabout way. For exactly the same outcome can be achieved by a direct route. Let the government give everyone a gift of money. Agree with the monetarists that prices will rise, but do not agree that money wages will rise since labour is 'off its supply curve'. Employment will increase on impeccable monetarist grounds. Since output will be higher once again on impeccable monetarist grounds, real cash balances will be higher. There will be no bankruptcies and we do not have to rely on the slow and uncertain process of money wage declines. Of course here too there is an appeal to a dynamic which none of us can vouch for. But it seems no worse, indeed a great deal more persuasive, than that of the monetarists.

It has not escaped my attention that if under the government policy all money wages had risen as well, the state of the economy would have been unchanged except for distribution effects through debt. I often think that monetarists are bewitched by such homogeneity theorems. Of course they are correct but they are also irrelevant here. Since by hypothesis there are more people willing to work than there are jobs at the going wage the monetarists' own arguments predict a declining real wage. So let us not be held up by such observations.

In any case in the first instance Keynes's argument is not that markets cannot deliver (much less that money wages are rigid downwards) but quite simply that the route the economy must take when workers must signal their willingness to work by lower money wages is more costly and more uncertain than is the alternative which he proposed. It will be clear that such arguments do not apply to uncorrelated price adjustments which take place when, say, there is a change in preferences between bananas and fish.

But matters are really more Keynesian than Keynes proposed because he rather unwisely retained a Marshallian foundation. What needs to be recognised is that price signals in themselves are sufficient for coordinating agents' actions only in perfectly competitive, that is in general, in 'large' economies. Even then constant returns cause a problem since at competitive prices producers do not know how much to produce until they know how much is demanded. I think that there is in any case no good ground for doubting a commonplace observation that firms in investing and producing not only attempt to calculate the price at which they will be able to sell but consider how much can be sold. No car manufacturer, no steel producer, no shop owner, no gas station manager believes that he can sell any quantity at the going price. So at the root of a good deal of Keynesian analysis there is that other upheaval of the 1930s, the imperfect competition revolution. But imperfect competition is intrinsically a situation with externalities because what Ostroy has called the 'no surplus condition' is in general not satisfied.[10] That is for instance removing one firm and redistributing its inputs amongst remaining firms may lead to a reduction in output less than is represented by the profits of the departing firm.

When firms have to consider demand functions rather than prices in making their decisions it is elementary to see that these functions will depend on employment, (or income) as long as the labour market is not in perfectly competitive equilibrium. This is just another way of making the familiar Clower point. At this stage of the argument Keynes considered another source of externality. He argued that workers cared not only about their real wage but also about their position in the wage distribution. In particular he maintained that if all real wages were lowered together an unemployed worker would be willing to work even though, given all other wages he had been unwilling to reduce his own because of the worsening of his relative position such a lowering would imply. Hence there may be many equilibria with different levels of employment and different real wages. Again Keynes seems to me to be here appealing to a phenomenon we both observe in others and in ourselves. You will notice that it does not entail any assumptions that real wages are downwardly rigid. What it does do is to pay some attention to the otherwise totally mysterious manner in which real wages might be changed.

There are of course many other features of the labour market which merit attention. Unions and training and selection and contracts to name a few. But the most important one is simply that this market is not at all like a fish market. This is so because the relation between employer and worker is of some duration and because workers are capable of calculating and following strategies. The axiom that wages must change as long as the Walrasian excess demand for labour differs from zero lacks merit on these grounds alone.

But my argument started with involuntary unemployment and has finished with some partial arguments that this could be consistent with equilibrium if we do not ask for a Walrasian auctioneer but allow agents to set prices. Let me now be as Lucasian as I can be and simply deny the possibility of involuntary unemployment not just in equilibrium but ever. Does that, admittedly slightly bizarre, resolve deliver me into the hands of the monetarists?

I am glad to report that even this putting of my head into the devil's mouth keeps me perfectly safe.

It will be agreed that production in a firm is rarely the outcome of labour alone. Let us say that it also requires capital. So the marginal product of labour will depend on both the amount of labour and capital employed. Now either the economy is in a steady state or it is not. Suppose the latter. Then its future is of interest. Since we are now Lucasians let us consider only Rational Expectations futures. Let us further suppose that all paths of the economy will eventually get arbitrarily close to a unique steady state. Then as I have noted before it will still be the case that there is not a unique path of this kind. Indeed in many cases there is a continuum. Which one (if any) the economy will choose depends on the expectations of agents. There is no reason to suppose that all these paths are equally desirable. But more importantly until the steady state is reached there are many different evolutions of what has been so tendentiously called the natural employment level and there is, as far as I can see, no way at all of deciding which path the economy will take or of telling a story of how it comes to take anyone of them at all.

I must break off here to return to a technical point which I have already mentioned once and which is of practical relevance simply because it is so poorly understood by many who conceive themselves engaged in providing econometric evidence for monetarism. If one could think of an economy as behaving through time as if it were guided by a Ramsey maximiser then indeed it would often be the case that there is a unique path of an infinitely lived economy would follow from any given initial condition. But there is not the slightest reason to suppose that the economy behaves in this way or indeed could behave in this way. Certainly expectations may be rational for a thousand years and yet the economy could then have many possible futures. To require rational expectations over infinite time is just nonsense. But even when there are such expectations, provided there is no social maximand which guides the economy, there can be a whole manifold of rational expectations paths. This is a logical canker at the heart of rational expectations theory and until someone resolves this indeterminacy we had better remain quiet. In particular it is something of a scandal that so much macroeconometrics appeals to transversality conditions to resolve this fundamental indeterminacy. It is a scandal because such conditions belong to optimisation theory and only foolishness can turn it into a descriptive theory.

The outcome of all this is that there seems to be no such thing as *the* natural level of employment and output. But there is worse to come.

Let us once again be as forthcoming as possible and drop the objection I have just raised. However let us not insist that the world is uncertain so that we are now thinking of a stochastic equilibrium through time. Then as the economy unfolds the appropriate level and distribution of employment will differ from one moment to the next. It is true that we can under our self-denying ordinance say exactly what values these variables as well as all prices should have in an equilibrium. But what makes them so? Just think of an example. In equilibrium at date two and state two, wages for equilibrium must again be the same in both industries but half the labour force which worked in (a) must now work in (b). What brings this about if relative wages never differ? It cannot be part of rational expectation as formulated that you have to forecast which industry you will work in in any state. The invisible hand has here become a metaphysical hand. In fact of course the required inducements to reallocation as well as the process itself will be a potent cause of disturbances. But to the theorists there is an even more troubling matter. Agents will have to forecast adjustment processes and I cannot see how that is to be done.

I have recently argued elsewhere[11] that considerations such as these may lead to the view that there is something which one might call the *natural rate of inflation.* It is a commonplace enough idea: essentially it says that the reallocations required for different states will be accomplished at lower utility cost if we bring it about by letting some prices and wages rise while none fall than would be the case if some prices and wages also had to fall. I cannot claim that this conclusion has the status of a general theorem although it is true in plausible enough examples. However it shows how much work the monetarists have to do before they begin to deserve serious attention.

So even on purely Walrasian grounds one can see that we are being invited to board a leaking ship. But it is also a ship of folly. For instance to take just one example a passenger is asked to believe that three and a half million unemployed give or take half a million searchers are to be explained by their desire to substitute present for future leisure.

My conclusion then is this. If one takes Walrasian theory seriously then one cannot take seriously the use monetarists make of it. Moreover, and far more important, if one takes Walrasian theory seriously then one understands the many lacunae which it has and the need for quite large scale modifications and amplifications. I have argued that from the point of view of macro-theory the Walrasian model greatly underestimates what may be important externalities and indeed cannot even discuss the existence of a certain kind of these. In this view I have been anticipated by Diamond and Weitzman. Weitzman makes the simple but much neglected point that without set up costs there would be no firms and indeed there would be no meaning to unemployment. There are thus increasing returns and one can show benefits of cooperation over non-cooperation in finite economies. Diamond's work is very close to my own thinking. He has presented several models but essentially what is happening is that there are externalities working through demand. Thus for instance in a search situation my decision to search more for an exchange partner will increase the probabilities of someone else finding a partner.

In my own work[12] I have taken as one case the situation which arises with implicit labour contracts. I have modified the usual model by including an incentive problem which has the consequences that workers cannot get full insurance. Hence lay-offs are accompanied by utility losses to the laid off. Putting this in a general equilibrium context it will be the case that the demand for goods will depend not just on prices but also on lay-offs. One can then show in certain economies that there are multiple rational expectations equilibria which can be Pareto-ranked. Understanding comes from making that lay-offs in one industry adversely affect profitability in other industries and lead to higher lay-offs in these.

But of course we were all anticipated by Keynes. Macroeconomic writings in the last ten years have highlighted his claim to the title of great economist. His theoretical sloppiness is rendered trivial by his remarkable insight and by his directness. He saw the unemployed of the Great Depression. He saw them marching, protesting, and queuing up at labour exchanges. He concluded that they would prefer to work. It is hard to see how any scientifically minded investigator could have reached any other conclusion. He then realised that there was something to be explained which contemporary theory claimed to be impossible. There were Lucasians before Lucas. He hit on a most interesting answer which the vulgarisation of subsequent text books has rendered as rigid money wages. The answer turned as I have argued on the kind of game a labour market is. There were under its rules grave difficulties in any one worker changing his wage or any one player doing so and there was no way in which they could do it all together. However the Government could act in such a way as if all workers had changed their wage simultaneously. He did not, to repeat myself, argue that money wages would never fall. If anything he argued that if they did the consequences might be undesirable since unlike modern monetarists he did not ignore the long run of the past represented by debts denominated in money. It did not occur to his sane mind that everyone would accurately forecast the price level of each date when contracting a debt. He gave an account of expectation with due attention to contagions and the difficulty of disentangling the 'real' from the spurious occasioned by other agent's expectations. It is difficult to believe that future historians of thought will not come to recognise his analysis here as vastly superior as a guide to understanding than current practice.

Once the possibility of involuntary unemployment is recognised ordinary theory requires us to put quantities like income as well as prices as argument of the excess of demand functions and as variables subject to expectations. It is this move which conspicuously allows for cooperation to dominate competition.

If there are involuntary unemployment states, transitory or not, there is a possible role for government policies fully anticipated or not. It is at this point that the monetarists have done most harm and strong argument can be made on the grounds of welfare economics that monetarist writings should be taxed and Keynesian ones subsidised. For once one admits that involuntary unemployment states are possible government pump-priming can have one of two effects. To reiterate what I have already argued before. If citizens have been reared on the current mumbo-jumbo, especially if bankers and businessmen, who are amongst the most credulous of people, have been thus indoctrinated then all that may result is a rise in prices. On the other hand if those citizens had been raised on Keynes they would come to expect that people will buy more cars and washing machines and even hamburgers. Since there is absolutely no evidence of diminishing returns when there is excess capacity and labour, the economy could deliver these goods at more or less constant prices. More importantly no one could have any inducement to raise prices if others do not. Wages would on good orthodox lines not rise because we have involuntary unemployment. A beneficent scenario is possible. Moreover if sane people like that expected such policy whenever such bad states occur the carrying out of it may not even be necessary. We have here a classic instance of a proposition first made, I believe, by Max Weber: what social scientists say and write affects the material which they study. That does not mean that they can never be right – there is, as it were, at least one fixed point, in this mapping. In the present case there are at least two: a monetarist and a Keynesian. It just so happens that the latter is vastly to be preferred on grounds of welfare to the former.

One should now ask how the present mess came into being. For macroeconomics today is in the state in which astronomy would be if Ptolemaic theory once again came to dominate the field. There can in fact be few instances in other disciplines of such a determined turning back of the clock. A great deal of what is written today as well as the policy recommendations which have been made would be thoroughly at home in the twenties. So something needs explaining and I hope that some good intellectual historian will attempt to do this soon.

You may recall that when Miss Prism commanded Cecily in *The Importance of Being Earnest* to study her chapter on political economy she urged her to omit the section on the Indian repuee 'since it was altogether too sensational'. I am more liberal than Miss Prism but I urge you to recognise that Monetarism or what passes for modern macroeconomics is also 'altogether too sensational'. It represents the triumph of artifact over plain and direct thinking. It is sensational in its conclusion that the market always yields the best of all possible worlds. It is sensational in its contention that there are no social phenomena relevant to economic life which are not captured by prices. It is sensational in the sheer bravado of reducing the beautiful structure of General Equilibrium theory to one or two log linear equations and in its neglect of every subtlety. It is sensational in its ignorance of both the scope and limit of economic theory. Above all it is sensational in its confidence in conclusions which are neither proven nor plausible. For all these reasons I am not a monetarist.

But I now want to sum up. I make two main claims: first that serious Walrasian analysis does not support monetarist doctrines which are supposed to be based on the Walrasian model. Second that in any case the Walrasian model itself is not robust when it appears in its sequential form. I also argued that it is a peculiar intellectual strategy to counter the Keynesian claim that (labour) markets may not clear in the Walrasian sense by adopting an *axiom* that they always clear. Indeed this is an occasion for justified rudeness. The further strategy of referring to all economies not in perfect competition equilibrium as being in disequilibrium must, I think, be explained on non-scientific grounds such as obtuseness or ideological commitment. The misuse of the fundamental homogeneity proposition of rational choice is glaring and probably due to a lack of skill in theorising. The influence of the elementary textbook economics in recent years is surprising, but on a rationalist hope, transistory.

But while Monetarists are an easy target it does not entail the conclusions that Keynesians are safe. They have shared one of the main faults of the Monetarists which is a careless and cavalier attitude to theory by which I mean that they were too uninterested in intellectual coherence and too eager for the policy fray. Keynes himself never seems to have noticed that Marshallian value theory was ill-matched to his main contentions. Indeed the Monetarists are in some sense a punishment for the intellectual carelessness of the whole school. Nonetheless I have maintained that there are Keynesian insights which should make economists itch to explore (and possibly discuss) but which monetarists show no sign of understanding. These largely concern a possibly fundamental externality associated with the manner in which agents in a (not 'large') economy can communicate. I have briefly reported on some preliminary work here. Much remains to be done and much is still in doubt. But it is already clear that those of us engaged on this task will do better than play that old scratchy record that is Monetarism.

NOTE

1. This is based on a political economy lecture given at Harvard in December 1982 under the title: 'Why I am not a Monetarist'.
2. M. Beenstock; *A Neoclassical Analysis of Macroeconomic Policy* (Cambridge University Press, 1980).
3. By the 'Lucasians' I mean Lucas and his many followers.
4. See for instance: N. Wallace, 'The Overlapping Generations Model of Fiat Money', in *Models of Monetary Economics*, ed. J. H. Kareken and N. Wallace. (Federal Reserve Bank of Minneapolis, 1980); J. A. Scheinkman, 'Discussion of N. Wallace, "The Overlapping Generations Model of Fiat Money",' in *Models of Monetary Economics* ed. J. H. Kareken and N. Wallace (Federal Reserve Bank of Minneapolis, 1980); F. H. Hahn, *Money and Inflation* (Oxford: Basil Blackwell, 1982).

5. F. H. Hahn, 'Equilibrium with Transactions Costs', *Econometrica*, vol. 39, 1971; R. Radner, 'Competitive Equilibrium under Uncertainty', *Econometrica*, vol. 36, 1968.
6. R. Lucas, 'An Equilibrium Model of the Trade Cycle', *Journal of Political Economy*, vol. 83, 1975.
7. E. H. Phelps, ed., *Micro-economic Foundations of Employment and Inflation* (NY, 1970).
8. M. L. Weitzman, 'Increasing Returns and the Foundation of Unemployment Theory', *Economic Journal*, vol. 92, 1982; P. A. Diamond, 'Aggregate Demand Management in Search Equilibrium', *Journal of Political Economy*, vol. 90, Oct. 1982.
9. Review of F. H. Hahn: *Money and Inflation*, by C. Goodhart, *Economic Journal*, 1983.
10. J. Ostroy, *No-Surplus Condition as a Characterization of Perfectly Competitive Equilibrium*, *J.E.T.*, 22 (2), April 1980; L. Makowski, *No Surplus in Large Economies*, *J.E.T.* (1980).
11. F. H. Hahn, op. cit.
12. F. H. Hahn, 'Implicit Contracts and Involuntary Unemployment' (forthcoming as Cambridge Discussion Paper).

2 Keynes and the World Economy

SIR JOHN HICKS

After what has happened in the last ten years, it is becoming easier to see the work of Keynes in historical perspective. He was essentially a monetary economist; his writings are an intellectual counterpart to the monetary revolution of our time.

That has been a drama in (so far) five Acts. The first was the breakdown of the Old Gold Standard in the First World War. In the second (say 1924–33) there was an attempted restoration of that standard, which failed. In the third, the later thirties and, in some respects, the Second World War years themselves, there was a search for a New Standard. In the fourth, which may be reckoned to have begun at some date soon after 1945 and to have lasted until 1971, there was a Dollar Standard. In the fifth, since 1971, there has been no standard.

The work of Keynes, as is evident from these dates, belongs to the second and third of these Acts. In the second, where it leads up to his *Treatise on Money* (1930) he was critical of the Restored Gold Standard, but he was not attacking it as such. He saw that it could not work, just as it had been instituted, or re-instituted; but he was seeking to modify it, or reform it, so as to make it workable. In the third, as we know from his work in the creation of the IMF, towards the end of his life, he was still looking for a Reformed Standard, which could be workable.

But where, in relation to that Search, stands his most famous work, the *General Theory* of 1936? There is nothing, or appears to be nothing, in that book about the Standard. He seems to have put it from him, and that is of course the way the book has been widely read. But we know that after all he was to come back to it; so it can have been only temporarily that he put it from him. Why?

21

When we look at the book from that angle, there is another characteristic of it which stands out. There is practically nothing in it – nothing, certainly, in its formal structure – about international trade. What was the economy to which his model, constructed as it was with such skill and insight, was intended to apply?

It may well be said, and there is much force in this, that the book was written for economists. It was intended to be used as a basis for economic teaching, as indeed it has. It is common practice, in teaching, to begin with the case of a closed economy; then to go on to imports and exports, and balances of payments, afterwards. Keynes was just giving what corresponded to the first part of the course; he was leaving it to others to fill in the remainder.

That is certainly how he has been widely taken; but it is very doubtful if it is right. For though the book was written for economists, it has a close relation with the doctrines that he was preaching to a much wider circle. One can hardly believe that he would have taken so much trouble with his closed economy model unless he had thought it to be much more directly applicable.

To what could it have been applicable? If it was to be applied to the economy of a single nation, it could only have been to one where external trade was minimal, or to one (like Russia or the Germany of the date when he was writing) where it was tightly controlled. It is impossible to believe that such were the main applications that he had in mind. The only alternative is to suppose that it was meant to apply to the 'world economy'.

That would not make bad sense, at the time in question. The years when the book was being written were the years of the monetary crisis – the strictly monetary crisis – of 1931–3, and those of the recovery, the disappointing recovery, which followed. It was very possible to maintain – Keynes would not have been the only economist to maintain – that the monetary crisis was due to an inadequacy in the supply of base money – the base money of the international system consisting (at that time) of its *total* gold reserves – when confronted with what Keynes was to call a rise in liquidity preference. There was not enough base money for the banking system to be able to come to the rescue. That constraint was removed by the devaluations of sterling in 1931 and of the dollar in 1933; so that after that there was no monetary reason why there should not be a re-expansion. But how far would it be safe to allow that expansion to go?

It seems to me that this was the point where the revolution, in Keynes's own thinking, occurred. It was here that he had to pass from consideration of the monetary system (of the understanding of which he was a master) to consideration of the *real* economy, which, I fear it must be recognised, he understood less well. It is true that long before he wrote the *General Theory*, he had been turning that way. His *Treatise* (of 1930) had been narrowly monetary; it was concerned with price-levels and with their variations, not with output and employment. But even before he published the *Treatise*, he was claiming that he knew how to 'conquer unemployment'. That the prescription he was offering in his 1928 pamphlets would have involved a devaluation of sterling is, one may be sure, a consequence he would not have refused.

Between 1928 and 1935, the need to 'conquer unemployment' had become far more intense; so it is not surprising that with this background, he chose full employment as his target. He did not altogether forget that it can be a dangerous target. He defined full employment, in effect, as the maximum that could be reached by expansionary measures; he did not deny that there was some residue of unemployment which would still be out of reach. (I have myself found that it makes for clarity if one calls the unemployment which is curable by the measures that he was recommending 'Keynesian unemployment', thus keeping the distinction, while avoiding his 'involuntary' and 'voluntary', which, as generally recognised, do not give a fair impression. It does no harm to leave open the possibility that, even since 1970, we may, for most of the time, have been in a state of 'Keynesian full employment'.)

Keynes was greatly assisted, in working out the consequences of the point of view which he had thus adopted, by his belief that the level of money wages is in practice rather rigid. (Here again he qualified his statements, but that some belief in wage-rigidity is deeply rooted in his work can hardly be denied.) It was not thought up when writing the *General Theory*; it goes back, in his thinking, to a much earlier stage. It was because of his belief in wage-rigidity that he made his famous attack in 1925 on the British return to the gold standard *at the old parity*; it was in relation to the then existing level of money wages that he was claiming that sterling, after April 1925, was over-valued. It is doubtless true that during the 1920s and 1930s the wage-level, in Britain, was becoming more 'sticky' in money terms. But when one considers the great variations, both upward and downard, that had occurred in 1918–21, to have laid such stress upon rigidity, when the rigidity had set in so very recently, does seem a bit peculiar. After all, as his critics so often, and surely correctly, insisted, it is real wages in which trade unions are interested, not money wages.

Yet if we do allow ourselves to assume that wages are rigid, how much easier does economics, and economic planning, become! One can then think, as Keynes has taught us to think, in terms of the 'macro' magnitudes (income, consumption, investment and so on), for they then have *real* meanings as well as the money meanings which are so readily calculated. It is not hard to allow the assumption that the wage-level is constant (or approximately constant) within the period to which the 'macro' statistics refer; and if it varies from period to period, we can rely upon the statisticians to make corrections. But that is not enough. It has to be supposed that (in conditions of Keynesian unemployment) the wage-level is *rigid*; so that it would have been unaffected if there had been changes in other variables; that it would, for instance, be approximately the same if expansionary measures were taken as if they were not. The wage-level must not just be constant; it must also be rigid, or firm.

So when we ask – where, in the *General Theory*, is the Standard – there is nowhere to find it but here. The Keynes model is not just formally expressed in wage-units; it is on a Labour Standard.

A Labour Standard expresses the value of money in terms of labour, just as the Gold Standard expressed it in terms of gold. But the old Gold Standard did not just express it; it fixed it, for it had a mechanism for fixing it. Central banks stood ready to exchange money for gold, so long as their gold reserves lasted. When the reserves gave out, of course it would break down; but in normal times, so long as suitable measures were taken, one could be confident that this would not happen. The weakness of a Labour Standard is that it has no reserves. There is no bank, no authority, which is able to guarantee, at all, the convertibility of money into labour. So it is no more than a pseudo-standard.

If one takes it (as I think one must) that the apparent reliability of a Labour Standard in Keynes's own time was a historical accident, how does one explain what happened in what I have called Act IV, the happy years of the present century, 1950 to 1970, or thereabouts? I have called them the years of the Dollar Standard – the years, that is, when the US dollar was most definitely at the centre of the international monetary system. For the US the dollar was their national currency; for other countries it was the international currency. So the working of the Dollar Standard, inside the US is one thing; outside it is a different matter.

Let us look first at the outside countries (which include, at that stage, the West European countries). It was open to them to pursue rather

Keynesian policies – Keynesian indeed more in the sense of his earlier and of his later writings than of the *General Theory*. They could aim at a full employment target, so long as that was consistent with the maintenance of convertibility of their currency into dollars, at a recognised rate. If there was inconsistency, but it looked like being no more than temporary, they could get assistance; but if it was more serious, they would have to devalue. It was recognised that devaluation would be necessary, if there was a 'Fundamental Disequilibrium'; but this was accepted to be a mark of failure, which should thus if possible be avoided. It was further noticed that after a devaluation, restrictive measures would have to be maintained for a time, in order to defend the new parity; so that 'disequilibrium', once it had occurred, could not be set right without some temporary retreat from the full employment target. That could be more readily achieved, and continue to be achieved, by a readiness to use measures which would avoid the devaluation way out.

Such measures, it was thought, and often found, could be prescribed by adherence, in budgetary policy, to canons which had emerged from Keynes's work and from that of his followers; not just budget-balancing, a criterion which with the growth of the public sector became increasingly difficult to interpret, but something more subtle. On the whole, during my Act IV, that was usually enough, when it could be carried through. But it was later to appear that it had been lucky that it had been for so long very nearly enough.

For the major weakness of the Keynes theory, and of the policies that had been based on it, remained its Labour Standard. Why should the level of money wages be dependable? It was only by accident that in Act II it had seemed to be dependable. In Act IV it was less dependable, but did not seem to do so badly. Was that also any more than an accident?

There are many things which affect the level of money wages, some economic, some (we may say) 'social'. If the monetary system adjusts itself to the level of money wages, as on the principles of the *General Theory* it might be expected to do, the social forces gain in power, relatively to the economic. There are many social forces; the degree of development of trade-union power is only one of them. Another, since it is real wages in which trade unions, and their members, are essentially interested, is the behaviour of the prices of the goods on which wages are spent. That, of course, leads in principle to a vicious circle; as we have now so much experience to know. But if it so happens that economic forces are favourable to a rise in real wages, at an unchanged level of employment, a modest rise in money wages is consistent with a rise in real wages, at stable prices. It seems to me that the main reason for the lack of serious wage-inflation, during my Act IV, was the real economic growth, that was experienced in so many nations; there was a minimum of external shocks to disturb, even temporarily, the rise in real wages. Of course that smooth growth was itself greatly helped by the moderation of wage-behaviour. There were a number of favourable factors which worked together, each making it easier for the others.

I turn to the case of the dollar country – the US – where, as I have said, things must have been different. I can say less about it, since I know less about it. Only towards the end of the period did Americans have to begin to bother about their balance of payments; how far, even then, they needed to bother about it, is an open question. For most of the time (in Act IV) Americans could behave as if their country was a closed economy; so that principles which were derived from the work of Keynes, in the *General Theory*, could have seemed to apply. I suppose that the same factors as moderated wage-inflation in Europe would have moderated it in America – perhaps even more in America, for the greater fluidity of the labour market in America should have made the social forces making for rising money wages distinctly weaker. One would also guess that there was at this stage a fair consilience, in effect, between the canons of budgetary behaviour which would have been derived from Keynesian principles and those which came from pre-Keynesian tradition. So, for a while, it was possible to maintain a condition of fairly high employment, fairly stable prices, and fairly steady growth.

It seems usually to be held, by American economists, that what brought this to an end was the Vietnam war, which imposed a political obstacle to the maintenance of financial orthodoxy – of either type. It is arguable whether this need have led to the abandonment of the dollar standard; one still wonders whether it was inconceivable that some other way out could have been found. Something, one fears, played a part in the decision to float which came from the adulation of the free market, which had become so fashionable; though this was a case to which, on classical liberal principles, the rule of freedom did not apply.

So to Act V, where nothing is left except the Labour Standard, the pseudo-standard, with its inherent fragility. And with the Oil Shock of 1973 the extent of that fragility was fully revealed. This must have led, whatever methods had been taken to deal with it, to a check to the steady growth which had characterised Act IV. The attempt to keep real wages on a course which could not be maintained must have led to pressure on money wages; so long as the monetary system adjusted itself to the movement of money wages (all that was left of what had been Keynesian principles) there was bound to be a wage-explosion. If that was to be contained, at any finite rate of inflation, there was bound to be depression, and unemployment. The Keynesian ship had been driven quite off course.

How much, in these days of its defeat, has he still to teach us? To look at his work in historical perspective, as I have been trying to do, may give us some help, though not as much as one would like. He had himself had to make recommendations in similar confusions, at the ends of the two wars; and in each case it was towards the restoration of a monetary constitution that he directed his efforts. What he had then to emphasise was the need to avoid, in its design, excessive rigidity; it must not be so rigid as to be unworkable. That is a lesson that has indeed been learned from him; as it has turned out, only too well. If we are to get anything useful from him now, we must dig down deeper.

It is generally accepted, by economic theorists, that his main contribution was to abolish the so-called 'classical dichotomy', the notion that real factors and monetary factors, in the working of an economy, can be studied separately. The counterpart of that teaching, in terms of practice, is the contention that monetary policy, and fiscal policy, and labour market arrangements, belong together. They are a team, each of them having its own function, which the others need to respect. Things are bound to go wrong if any of the three pushes aside the others.

3 Budget Deficits, Stabilisation Policy and Liquidity Preference: Keynes's Post-War Policy Proposals

J. A. KREGEL

I DEFICIT SPENDING AND ECONOMIC POLICY

Economists are often accused of being out of touch not only with the real world but with common opinion. The early 1960s are today regarded with nostalgia by many economists as the period in which 'Keynesian' policies 'worked'. In the United States these were the Kennedy–Johnson Years of the New Frontier and the Great Society based on the sustained growth in GNP generated by Walter Heller's tax cut.[1]

I can still remember attending a seminar by Paul Samuelson who during this period was at least informally associated with the formulation of government policy.[2] Samuelson started his talk by challenging his audience to name the economic problem most discussed in local bars and beauty parlours across the land. Being economics students eager to impress we tried all manner of bright responses. The right answer was the national debt! According to Samuelson, the fact that the government did not balance its budget was the greatest cause of unease for the man in the street – and this in the Golden Age of 'Keynesian' growth based on functional finance. It seems paradoxical that in a period when growth and employment conditions resemble the 1930s more than the 1960s the national debt should again be the centre of attention. But today it is not the man in the street, but finance and treasury ministers who appear to be most concerned.

From Germany, Belgium, Holland and the United States to Italy and Japan the financial pages of newspapers are filled with lurid descriptions of government deficits running 'out of control' and governments of all political complexions are introducing policies to cut back government spending as unemployment rates reach and surpass those of the 1930s. Even those who continue to profess faith in 'Keynesianism' (e.g. France and Spain) have abandoned 'functional finance' as inappropriate given the size of existing deficits. The wheel has turned, and the success of restrictive monetary policies in reducing inflation in the late 1970s by producing a collapse in economic activity has caused budget deficits to increase to the point that the reduction of government expenditure dominates policy discussions for the 1980s.[3]

Traditional 'Keynesian' policy leads to self-contradiction. Much like the dilemma for 'Keynesian' policy of demand management produced by the coexistence of inflation (requiring a *reduction* in deficit spending) and rising unemployment (requiring an *increase* in deficit spending); the co-existence of rising budget deficits and rising unemployment has led to the belief that deficit financing no longer works to decrease unemployment. The problem is thus different from that noted by Samuelson. As can be seen from Table 3.1, it is not the size of the government debt that is out of proportion. In most countries its proportion of GNP is below the level of the 1960s when deficit spending was widely accepted. Rather the problem is the current deficit as a proportion of GNP. Thus, irrespective of whether 'Keynesian policy' may have been effective in the past, it is widely believed that it is either inappropriate or ineffective given present

TABLE 3.1   *Ratio of outstanding debt to GNP: central government*

	1960	1965	1970	1975	1980[a]
USA	46.6	37.6	29.3	28.1	28.0
Japan	6.0	4.3	6.6	10.4	24.6
Austria	–	–	9.1	10.5	19.1
France	28.4	17.4	12.6	8.9	10.1
Germany	7.4	7.2	7.0	10.5	15.6
Italy	37.0	32.3	35.9	53.7	60.8
Netherlands	44.0	31.9	28.6	22.3	31.5
UK	–	–	52.9	42.9	40.1

NOTE   [a]latest available.

SOURCE   IMF Financial Statistics.

ratios of deficits to national income. In response to those who continue to recommend the 'Keynesian' prescription of higher deficits it is pointed out that there is a limit to the ratio of the deficit to national income: some form of state socialism.

At this point, Keynes himself would have objected that although he had no particular love of capitalism, he had an even lower opinion of socialism. The object of Keynes' original policy proposals was to create conditions in which capitalism might exhibit its full growth potential. His policy concern was motivated by the fear that 'It might turn out to be true that anything at all closely resembling free enterprise is incapable of dealing with the problem of structual unemployment. If so, I feel sure that free enterprise will go by the board. ... I have not abandoned the view that something like free enterprise can be made to work' (Keynes, 1980, XXVII, p. 354 and 1972, XI, p. 294).

II   THE PLACE OF TRANSFER EXPENDITURES

There is a widely adopted explanation for the failure of government expenditure policies. It was never envisaged that transfer payments should take such a large proportion of government expenditures. This objection does not seem valid, for Keynes had argued, at least for the short-period, that expenditure was expenditure – it made no difference whether it was 'productive' or not. Indeed, the study of Keynesian growth models of the Harrod–Domar type suggested that expenditure that was too efficient in increasing productive capacity might produce a tendency to chronic excess capacity. Thus the rising trend of current relative to capital expenditures should decrease the risk of excess capacity and make full employment easier to achieve.

There is, however, a legitimate point to be made as regards transfer payments. Initially transfers such as unemployment benefit and other social security payments were viewed as 'automatic stabilisers' in that they moved counter-cyclically (cf. for example Keynes's discussions of Meade's proposals for implementation of the Beveridge Report on Social Insurance in Keynes, 1980, XXVII, pp. 203ff and 1983, XI, pp. 439–44).

Recent experience, however, has been contrary to Keynes's expectation that 'it is not intended in future to ... put the benefits and the contributions on a cost of living sliding scale' (ibid., p. 204). Rather, the real value of income transfers has tended to increase in good times and to remain fixed in real terms in bad. Tables 3.2 and 3.3 show that continued growth has produced a continual rise in the proportion of transfers in national income, leading to overall increases in government expenditure in excess of the rate of growth of output. It is this tendency which has associated 'Keynesian' policy proposals with state socialism as a limit.

TABLE 3.2   *Ratio of income maintenance expenditures to GNP: central government*

	1960–61	1970–71	1979–80
USA	5.46	6.68	8.57
Japan	1.89	2.84	6.88
Austria	13.33	14.93	17.78
France	11.48	13.15	17.38
Germany	11.51	12.09	15.21
Italy	–	9.6	14.30
Netherlands	9.05	15.12	19.87
UK	5.6	7.14	9.23

SOURCE   OECD National Accounts.

TABLE 3.3   *Rate of increase of public expenditure relative to GDP*

	Good times 1965–69	1969–73	Bad times 1973–79
Canada	1.49	1.19	1.16
USA	1.40	1.06	1.11
Japan	0.92	1.42	1.88
France	1.10	0.93	1.33
Germany	1.15	1.22	1.41
Italy	1.00	1.29	1.22
UK	1.34	1.12	1.15

SOURCE   OECD *National Accounts of OECD Countries*, vol. 2, detailed tables, 1962–79 (Paris, July 1981).

The figures of Table 3.3 show that in precisely those periods when the role of government should have been declining, expenditures were increasing, and vice versa. The performance of the UK and the USA was clearly pro-cyclical while only that of Japan is clearly anti-cylical.

III   KEYNES'S LONG-TERM POLICY PROPOSALS

Keynes himself did *not* ever directly recommend government deficits
as a tool of stabilisation policy – this came rather in Lerner's concept of
functional finance – and when he did consider them as temporary
measures he showed a net preference for investment over consumption spending (cf. also Kregel, 1975, Appendix). It is interesting to
note that the main policy recommendation that Keynes made in the
General Theory was on his own admission 'conservative':

> The State will have to exercise a guiding influence on the propensity
> to consume partly through its scheme of taxation, partly by fixing the
> rate of interest ... it seems unlikely that the influence of banking
> policy on the rate of interest will be sufficient by itself to determine
> an optimum rate of investment. I conceive, therefore, that a some-
> what comprehensive socialisation of investment will prove the only
> means of securing an approximation to full employment.... But
> beyond this no obvious case is made out for a system of State
> Socialism which would embrace most of the economic life of the
> community. (Keynes, 1973, VII, pp. 377–8)

Keynes also outlined optimal policy as one in which 'State action
enters in as a balancing factor to provide that the growth of capital
equipment shall be such as to approach saturation-point at a rate which
does not put a disproportionate burden on the standard of life of the
present generation' (ibid., p. 220).[4] The *General Theory*, is, indeed,
sparing in its formal policy proposals.

Keynes's position was amplified considerably in efforts to trace out
British post-war employment policy. Keynes's clearly enunciated lack
of enthusiasm for budget deficits was motivated by a clear preference
for policy to make sure deficits should not occur. Keynes viewed
budget deficits as the direct result of *failure to achieve stable full
employment* national income growth rather than as an efficient remedy
for unemployment. This, of course, only implied that budget balancing
measures in a slump could not make either employment conditions or
the deficit improve.

It did not imply that deficits were the ideal method of maintaining
national income or of recovering from a slump. For Keynes 'the main
task should be to *prevent* large fluctuations by a stable long-term
programme. If this is successful it should not be too difficult to offset
small fluctuations by expediting or retarding some items in this long-

term programme' (Keynes, 1980, XXVII, p. 322). This follows directly from the analysis of the *General Theory* which identifies fluctuations in investment as the *causa causans* of the level of activity.[5] *The stabilisation of investment was Keynes's primary policy goal.*

This stability could be achieved:

> If two-thirds or three-quarters of total investment is carried out or can be influenced by public or semi-public bodies, a long-term programme of a stable character should be capable of reducing the potential range of fluctuations to much narrower limits than formerly, when a smaller volume of investment was under public control and when even this part tended to follow, rather than correct, fluctuations of investment in the strictly private sector'. This policy, says Keynes, 'has nothing whatever to do with deficit financing' which 'would be a last resort' only to be contemplated if 'the volume of planned investment fails to produce equilibrium. (ibid., p. 352)

Thus the long-term investment programme, which Keynes estimated 'unlikely to be less than $7\frac{1}{2}$ per cent or more than 20 per cent of the net national income' could be expressed by means of a 'capital budget', which would be balanced in the long-term, separate from the current budget. The capital budget was conceived as producing the long-term level of investment associated with stable income and full employment: 'the capital budgeting is a means of attempting to cure disequilibrium if and when it arises' (ibid., p. 353).

> It is important to emphasise that it is no part of the purpose of the Exchequer or the Public Capital Budget to facilitate deficit financing, as I understand the term. On the contrary, the purpose is to present a sharp distinction between the policy of collecting in taxes less than the current non-capital expenditure of the State as a means of stimulating *consumption* and the policy of the Treasury's influencing public capital expenditure as a means of stimulating *investment*. There are times and occasions for each of these policies: but they are essentially different and each, to the extent that it is applied, operates as an alternative to the other. (ibid., p. 406)

Keynes warned against 'confusing the fundamental idea of the capital budget with the particular, rather desperate expedient of deficit financing' (ibid., pp. 353–4) and expressed 'doubt if it is wise to put too much stress on devices for causing the volume of consumption to fluctuate in preference to devices for varying the volume of investment' (ibid., p. 319).

Keynes justified this emphasis on preventive measures to stabilise income through the control of investment on political as well as theoretical grounds:

> it is not nearly so easy politically and to the common man to put across the encouragement of consumption in bad times as it is to induce the encouragement of capital expenditure. The former is a much more violent version of deficit budgeting. Capital expenditure would at least partially, if not wholly, pay for itself. . . . Moreover, the very reason that capital expenditure is capable of paying for itself makes it much better budgetwise and does not involve the progressive increase of budgetary difficulties, which deficit budgeting for the sake of consumption may bring about or, at any rate, would be accused of bringing about. (ibid., pp. 319–20)

Thus, far from the fearless deficit financer Keynes's position might better be summed up: 'Emphasis should be placed primarily on measures to maintain a steady level of employment and thus to prevent fluctuations. If a large fluctuation is allowed to occur, it will be difficult to find adequate offsetting measures of sufficiently quick action' (ibid., p. 323).

From Keynes's (and the Kennedy–Heller position of the 1960s) point of view the rising budget deficits and rising share of transfer payments in government expenditure in the face of stagnant output and rising unemployment in the 1970s represent *not* the failure of Keynesian policy but rather a failure to apply that policy. Equally, R. C. O. Matthews' classic (1968) paper's conclusion that the existence of surpluses over the period eliminate Keynesian policy as the cause of the stability of full employment may prove just the opposite result, with Britain's performance in the mid-late 1960s demonstrating the effects of not introducing a tax policy to offset fiscal drag as was done in the US. Indeed, his findings concerning the higher share of investment in output provide partial confirmation of the position Keynes argued in the development of the long-period employment policy in the Treasury in the early 1940s. Matthews, however, lumps government expenditure with private consumption and eliminates the effect of nationalisation, thus precluding a test of whether or not Keynes's suggestions were in fact followed. Matthews's analysis thus cannot be considered a satisfactory test because it mistakes demand management via fiscal deficits for Keynes's more positive policy recommendation. Keynes clearly was sceptical of any attempt to make the kind of short period budget adjustments that Matthews classes as 'Keynesian': 'I doubt if much is to be hoped from proposals to offset unforeseen short-period fluctuations in investment by stimulating short-period changes in consumption' (Keynes, ibid., p. 323). 'It is quite true that a fluctuating volume of public works at short notice is a clumsy form of cure and not likely to be completely successful' (ibid., p. 326). Keynes would certainly not have been surprised by the failure of such measures in the 1970s, nor by Matthews discovery of their absence in the UK in the post-war period. On the other hand, he would have considered the current rapid increase in deficits a straight-forward result of the operation of the multiplier: 'much less effort is required to prevent the ball rolling than would be required to stop it rolling once it has started. ... After the slump has fully developed, the relevant figures get dreadfully large' (ibid., p. 316).[6]

It must be concluded that there is no foundation for considering budget deficits as a positive part of employment policy. In assessing Keynes's rejection of deficit financing and preference for a long term investment programme it should be noted that it was given in the light of post-war reconstruction. In a letter to Josiah Wedgwood he explains why he considered the scale of investment expenditure of primary importance with the rate of interest adapted to achieve that end.

> The question then arises why I should prefer rather a heavy scale of investment to increasing consumption. The main reason for this is that I do not think we have yet reached anything like the point of capital saturation. It would be in the interests of the standards of life in the long run if we increased our capital quite materially. After twenty years of large scale investment I should expect to have to change my mind. ... But certainly for the first ten years after the war – and I should expect for another ten years after that – it would not be in the interest of the community to encourage more expenditure on food and drink at the expanse of expenditure on housing. ... There is also a subsidiary point that at the present stage of things, it is very much easier socially and politically to influence the rate of investment than to influence the rate of consumption. (Keynes, 1980, XXVII, p. 350)

In 1930 in his *Economic Possibilities of Our Grandchildren* Keynes had warned that the resolution of the economic problem in the sense of 'absolute needs' (i.e. those independent of the situation of others) were in sight of solution 'within a hundred years' (Keynes, 1972, IX, p. 326). Clearly Keynes did not fear the decline in the propensity to consume except in particular national cases.

It is, indeed, interesting to note that one of the few policy recommendations of the *General Theory* concerns not the level of aggregate spending but the propensity to consume:

> Income taxes, especially when they discriminate against 'unearned' income, taxes on capital profits, death duties and the like are as relevant as the rate of interest; whilst the range of possible changes in fiscal policy may be greater in expectation at least, than for the rate of interest itself. If fiscal policy is used as a deliberate instrument for the more equal distribution of incomes, its effect in increasing the propensity to consume is, of course all the greater. (Keynes, 1973, VII, pp. 94–5)

It is entirely consistent with his later position that Keynes should omit mention of the effect of government deficit on the aggregate propensity to save and instead emphasise the effect of fiscal changes on the propensity to consume via changes in the distribution of income between high and low savers.

Two points concerning the implementation of Keynes's government investment programme should be amplified. As noted above Keynes was not eager to introduce socialism to Britain, yet the proportion of total investment that would come under State control would have severely curtailed the private sector. Having seen both the British Civil Service and Stalin's Russia from the inside there is no question of his scepticism concerning the desirability of State control (cf. Keynes, 1972, IX, pp. 295ff).

In 'The End of *Laissez-Faire*' (Keynes, 1972, IX, pp. 272–94), referring to Bentham's distinction between the *Agenda* and *Non-Agenda* of desirable government activity, Keynes notes two changes in the 'forms of government' that would be required to support his policies:

> I believe that in many cases the ideal size for the unit of control and organisation lies somewhere between the individual and the modern State. I suggest, therefore, that progress lies in the growth and the recognition of semi-autonomous bodies within the State-bodies whose criterion of action within their own field is solely the public

good.... I propose a return... towards medieval conceptions of separate autonomies. ... It is easy to give examples ... the universities, the Bank of England, the Port of London Authority ... the trend of joint stock institutions ... to approximate to the status of public corporations rather than that of individualistic private enterprise. (ibid., pp. 288–9, cf. also the reference to 'semi-public' bodies in Keynes, 1980, XXVII, p. 322)

The second point is to distinguish services which are '*technically individual*' from those which are '*technically social*', i.e. 'to those decisions which are made by *no one* if the State does not make them. The important thing for government is not to do things which individuals are doing already ... but to do those things which are not done at all' (ibid., p. 291). Keynes lists three areas: (a) risk, uncertainty and ignorance, (b) the level of saving and (c) the size of population.

It is thus clear that although Keynes recommendations for the share of state-controlled investment (7–20 per cent of NNP) were high, this did not mean direct state operation; rather a combination of state, semi-autonomous and socialised joint stock forms. It clearly did not imply wholesale expropriation of the expropriators, although it may have seemed so to the captains of private industry.

While Keynes recommended that these semi-autonomous bodies should behave as if 'motives of private advantage are excluded' (ibid., p. 288) this did not mean that they should operate without reference to traditional economic principles. In commenting on the financing of the social security system proposed in the Beveridge Report Keynes comments:

We need to extend, rather than curtail, the theory and practice of extra-budgetary funds for state operated or supported functions. Whether it is the transport system, the Electricity Board, War Damage or Social Security. The more socialised we become, the more important it is *to associate as closely as possible the cost of particular services with the sources out of which they are provided* even when a grant-in-aid is also required from general taxes. This is the only way by which to preserve sound accounting, to measure efficiency, to maintain economy and *to keep the public properly aware of what things cost.* (Keynes, 1980, XXVII, pp. 224–5, italics added)

Thus, Keynes clearly believed that the socialisation process involved only the elimination of the 'motives of private advantage' in the interest of public benefit, not the elimination of economic efficiency. Indeed in his desired budgetary position in full employment equilibrium:

> 'I should aim at having a surplus on the ordinary Budget, which would be transferred to the capital Budget, thus gradually replacing dead-weight debt by productive or semi-productive debt.' In difference from the under-employment situation, in full employment conditions 'I should not aim at attempting to compensate cyclical fluctuations by means of the ordinary Budget. I should leave this duty to the capital budget.' (ibid., pp. 277–8)

Keynes's statements all arise from particular situations, yet it is possible to assemble a summary of his policy recommendations for post war employment policy:

1. Preservation of full employment in the long-term will require 'socialisation' of investment.
2. The 'socialisation' of investment should occur primarily through 'semi-autonomous' public corporations and 'socialised' private joint stock corporations.
3. Government influenced spending should be from $\frac{1}{3}$ to $\frac{3}{4}$ of total investment spending and be in the range of $7\frac{1}{2}$ per cent to 20 per cent of net national income.
4. It should be more stable than pre-war government investment spending which tended to be pro-cyclical.
5. It should not vary positively with private investment expenditures.
6. The budget should be divided into a 'capital' and current budget: The 'capital budget' should be balanced in the long-term but may be adjusted to offset exogenous cyclical changes, the current budget may as a last resort show surpluses or deficits to offset short-term failure of the capital budget but also be balanced over the long-term.[7]
7. If full employment (from 3 per cent to 5 per cent unemployed) is maintained the budget should be balanced and public debt should eventually become a declining portion of net national income.
8. Services provided by the State should be primarily those considered as 'technically social'.
9. All State provided services should be furnished efficiently, i.e. to cover costs and capital charges, no direct permanent net subsidies financed by budget deficits were contemplated.[8]

IV KEYNES'S PROPOSALS AND POST-WAR ECONOMIC PERFORMANCE

It is not the primary purpose of this paper to speculate on how the traditional 'Keynesian' wisdom concerning the generalised benefits of deficit spending developed despite Keynes's own very clear warnings on the dangers of their continuous existence. More important is an assessment of the feasibility of Keynes's proposals and to discover whether the UK or any other economy in fact carried them out.

Although Keynes considered his proposals for the socialisation of

TABLE 3.4 *Ratio of Gross Domestic Investment to GNP (average)*

	1900–13	1914–49	1950–60
USA	20.6	14.7	19.1
Germany	–	14.3[a]	24.0
Italy	15.4	13.5	20.8
UK	7.7	7.6	15.4

NOTE [a] 1915–37

SOURCE adapted from Cornwall (1977), table 2.11.

TABLE 3.5 *Ratio of United Kingdom gross capital formation to GNP (decade averages)*

	Gross domestic fixed capital formation	net foreign investment
1860–69	7.2	3.0
1870–79	8.1	3.9
1880–89	6.1	4.9
1890–99	6.9	3.2
1900–09	7.8	3.9
1910–14	6.0	6.9
1920–29	8.7	2.4
1930–39	9.5	–1.0
1950–59	14.8	.8

SOURCE adapted from Deane and Cole (1967), table 82, p. 308.

investment as 'conservative' they called for government control of investment ranging from $7\frac{1}{2}$ per cent to $20\frac{1}{2}$ per cent of *net* national income. Keynes suggested that this would represent between $\frac{2}{3}$ and $\frac{3}{4}$ of total investment in the economy. This would make the figures for investment as a proportion of national income between 10 per cent and 28 per cent. Tables 3.4 and 3.5 give evidence on the ratio of *gross* investment to gross product for the economy as a whole. They suggest that Keynes's lower estimates were not excessively optimistic from a historical point of view when it is recalled that Keynes was presuming near full employment to result and given his experience of the war period. The figures for the UK, e.g. 9.5 per cent for the 1930–39 period of depressed conditions and the pre-first war figures for the USA and Italy support the feasibility of Keynes's proposals.

Table 3.6(d) gives similar evidence for the post-war period. A number of countries are seen to be near the upper range (Austria, Germany, The Netherlands) and Japan exceeds it by some margin.

The rest of Table 6 gives evidence on government investment, presenting figures for the central government (Table 3.6(a)), general government (Table 3.6(b)) and government plus public corporations (Table 3.6(c)). It is presumably the latter which Keynes had in mind when he formulated his range of $7\frac{1}{2}$ per cent to 20 per cent. Figures are not immediately available for all countries, but Japan, the Netherlands and the UK are near the lower range for the 1960s. The US is the exception at less than half, suggesting that the US is well characterised as representative of free enterprise (although note that defence spending (5–8 per cent) is not included).

Keynes also attached importance to the stability of government investment expenditure. This is more difficult to judge due to the lack of pre-war figures. Table 3.5 suggests that in the UK both government and total investment were more stable post-war.

A more recent test of the stability of governments' investment policy is provided by the reactions to the Yom Kippur war and the change in the price of energy. Since it is central government expenditure most directly influenced by policy, reference may be made to Table 3.6(a). Here the USA shows behaviour contradictory to Keynes's recommendations, central government investment falling by over one half. France and the Netherlands show similar behaviour. Keynesian behaviour is shown for Austria and Italy and for the UK until 1977 when the IMF letter of intent accepted by the Labour government in 1976 led to sharp cuts which were continued by the Tories (cf. Table 3.8). Japan follows Keynes's recommendation that capital spending should move to offset exogenous shocks, increasing investment after 1973.

TABLE 3.6 MEASURES OF GOVERNMENT AND TOTAL GROSS FIXED CAPITAL FORMATION AS A RATIO OF GROSS DOMESTIC PRODUCT

TABLE 3.6(a) *Ratio of central government gross fixed capital formation to gross domestic product (averages)*

	1955–64	*1962–72*	*1973–79*	*1977–79*
USA	0.41	0.41	0.18	–
Austria	1.93	1.46	1.44	–
France	0.86	1.59	0.82	–
Germany	0.66	–	–	–
Italy	0.70	1.50	1.45	1.42
Netherlands	1.35	1.76	1.02	0.86
UK	0.61	1.01	1.01	0.84

TABLE 3.6(b) *Ratio of general government gross fixed capital formation to gross domestic product (averages)*

USA	3.25	2.75	1.98	–
Japan	9.78	4.62	5.63	6.03
Austria	5.45	4.84	5.11	–
France	2.75	3.91	3.28	3.06
Germany	3.80	4.07	3.50	3.31
Italy	2.53	2.88	3.14	3.17
Netherlands	4.63	4.76	3.65	3.32
UK	2.07	4.47	4.08	2.99

TABLE 3.6(c) *Ratio of general government gross fixed capital formation + public enterprises to gross domestic product*

USA		3.50	2.81	–
Japan		8.78	9.46	9.85
Netherlands		8.77	6.61	6.06
UK		7.94	7.46	6.08

TABLE 3.6(d) *Ratio of gross fixed capital formation to gross domestic product (averages)*

USA	18.8	18.0	17.5	17.8
Japan	31.24	32.75	32.60	31.06
Austria	26.30	26.84	26.33	25.36
France	22.53	23.15	22.83	21.70
Germany	27.48	25.13	21.83	21.60
Italy	24.75	21.03	20.14	19.06
Netherlands	26.57	24.74	21.30	21.40
UK	18.08	18.18	18.94	18.00

NOTE Period averages, current values.

SOURCES OECD (1966) and (1981).

TABLE 3.7(a)   *Ratio of unemployment to total labour force (averages)*

	1962–72	1973–79	1977–79
USA	4.65	5.66	6.30
Japan	1.22	1.45	2.00
Austria	1.67	1.50	1.66
France	1.86	4.24	5.26
Germany	0.80	3.21	3.70
Italy	4.62	6.00	6.70
Netherlands	1.82	5.61	6.30
UK	3.08	4.61	5.60

SOURCE   adapted from A. Maddison (1982) pp. 207–8.

TABLE 3.7(b)   *Variability of GNP and unemployment: USA*

Period	Standard deviation of GNP GAP [a]	unemployment rate: mean	unemployment rate: standard deviation
1920–41	12.99	11.52	7.59
1900–45	13.58	7.77	6.51
1946–76	3.56	4.95	1.34
1962–73	2.46	4.74	0.88
1966–76	2.26	5.25	1.66

NOTE   [a] GNP – trend GNP/trend GNP.

SOURCE   Bailey (1978).

Tables 3.7(a) and (b) show that those countries that generally followed stable government investment programmes also had more stable levels of unemployment and output. Indeed Japan and Austria had rates below that which Keynes thought possible or desirable, while the US experience from 1962–73 now appears remarkable.

Finally, Table 3.8 gives more recent evidence on government policies concerning investment commitments in real terms, suggesting that even those countries that initially carried out Keynesian policies have not continued to do so. The combination of rising internal deficits and falling international trade possibilities leading to policy to reduce government spending. Table 3.9 suggests that these cuts have pre-served transfer payments at the expense of capital expenditure. In combination with rising government deficits such results have been

TABLE 3.8 *Changes in public gross fixed investment (annual % changes in 'volume')*

	1978	1979	1980	1981	1981 IV
USA	7.3	−5.6	1.3	−6.8	−8.6
Japan	16.1	3.1	−3.5	4.8	0.0
France	−3.0	1.5	1.4	−0.7	−
Germany	6.4	9.1	5.1	−6.9	−
Italy	−2.1	3.0	14.9	6.4	−
UK	−8.8	−3.9	−5.0	−17.9	−18.8

SOURCE adapted from Bank for International Settlements, Fifty-second Annual Report, 1981, p. 11.

used to demonstrate that 'Keynesian' policies no longer work. From the argument given above, however, Table 3.10 simply reflects the failure of governments to pursue Keynes's recommendations concerning public investment policy, the deficits being the objective evidence, not of the failure of Keynes's policy, *but of a failure to carry it out.* Economists could well recall Kennedy's belief that 'The true causes of deficits were not "wild-eyes spenders" but "slow economic growth and periodic recessions. . . . Any new recession would break all deficit records"' (Lekachman, 1966, p. 274 quoting Kennedy's December 1962 speech to the Economic Club of New York).

TABLE 3.9 *Ratio of government income transfers to GDP*

	1973	1979	1980
USA	12.1	11.6	12.7
Japan	6.7	14.3	14.7
Austria	−	−	−
France	21.6	27.4	27.9
Germany	17.0	20.8	20.7
Italy	20.5	25.5	25.6
Netherlands	27.4	36.2	37.0
UK	16.0	19.1	19.6

SOURCE adapted from Bank for International Settlements, Fifty-first Annual Report, p. 24, 1980.

TABLE 3.10   *Ratio of public sector deficit to GDP*

	1973	1979	1980
USA	0.3	(0.5)	1.2
Japan	3.0	4.7	4.0
Austria	–	–	–
France	(0.1)	0.6	(0.3)
Germany	(0.7)	2.9	(3.5)
Italy	8.7	9.4	7.9
Netherlands	(1.1)	3.0	3.3
UK	4.6	3.3	3.7

NOTE   (   ) = surplus.

SOURCE   adapted from Bank for International Settlements, Fifty-first Annual Report, p. 24.

V   POSTSCRIPT: SUPPLY SIDE ECONOMICS

Kennedy had argued (in an act of anticipatory plagiarism of the 'supply-side' school of 'incentive' economists?) 'An economy hampered by restrictive tax rates will never produce enough revenues to balance our budget, just as it will never produce enough jobs or enough profits' (ibid). Indeed, many supply-siders supported the Economic Recovery Act tax cuts on the basis of the Kennedy–Johnson tax cut.

As seen above, Keynes recommended the use of fiscal policy in order to reduce the rise in the propensity to save due to the effect of rising incomes and the effects of an unequal distribution of income on the average propensity to save. In the conditions of expansion of the early 1960s the tax bill simply prevented the emergence of an excessive surplus in the full employment budget. Its net effect on the distribution of income is unclear (the proportionate reductions in personal tax rates were generally equal). It should, however, be noted that the tax cut was not proposed in slump conditions nor in conditions of a full employment budget deficit. The supply-side tax cut of 1981, however, was made in conditions of stagnant growth, rising unemployment, and budget deficits. Further, it presumed a positive relation between work effort and economic incentives as represented by after–tax incomes, whereas the Kennedy tax reduction relied upon the aggregate effects of Keynes's psychological propensity to consume; the former relies on individual decisions to adjust productive effort to real income, a decision over which individuals have very little control, while the latter aimed at preventing the creation of a budget surplus by relying on the aggregate relation between income and expenditure, the degree of effort assumed constant.

This difference between the supply-siders and Keynes's justifications for tax reduction suggests why Keynes was so hesitant to propose increased budget deficits as a policy in the slump. The supply-side analysis requires not only the stability in the parameters of individuals' labour supply and labour market demand curves but also that individuals can control their supply of labour. Keynes, on the other hand, believed that labour demand curves were dominated by the behaviour of aggregate variables beyond the control of any individual action, i.e. he rejected the second neoclassical postulate (cf. Kregel, 1980). Further he stressed that in depressed conditions, such aggregate relations would be highly unstable. Thus any changes in prices, whether due to higher wages per unit of work effort due to tax reduction or income transfers or higher expected returns on investment due to investment tax credits or investment subsidies, would in general be more than offset by shifts in the aggregate expenditure curves caused by changes in expectations. It is indeed not surprising that the current US Administration complains that 'the speed with which the economy adjusts to the Administration's policies will be largely determined by the extent to which individuals ... believe the Administration' policies will work (*CEA*, 1982, p. 21). Keynes expressed these expectational factors in terms of 'liquidity preference' representing the 'degree of our distrust in our own calculations and conventions concerning the future' (Keynes, 1973, XIV, p. 116). Changes in the rate of interest or the rate of wages could always be offset by opposite changes in expectations, government manipulation of tax and interest rates could only increase the state of uncertainty and the instability of behavioural relations.

Keynes's proposed high and stable level of investment was meant to decrease our degree of distrust in our calculation of future conditions. By thus creating more stable, more certain conditions (cf. the reference to reduction of the 'evils' of 'risk uncertainty and ignorance' (Keynes, 1972, IX, p. 291) as within the proper scope for government action because they are beyond the control of individuals) the degree of liquidity preference would be reduced. A reduction in liquidity preference would bring both reduction in interest rates and increased expectation of future return by raising the efficiency of capital. In an uncertain world, economic policy can only attempt to shift the curves in the desired direction. The ultimate results of movement along them can never be certain. Thus Keynes rejected intervention via the price mechanism which relied for their success on the stability of aggregate expenditure and the state of expectations.[9] At the same time, Keynes had sufficient experience in financial matters during slump conditions to recognise that recommending an increase in deficit spending in conditions in which the deficit was rising because of falling revenues and increasing unemployment compensation could make it impossible to finance the required increase in debt and avoid breakdown of the currency (cf. Keynes, 1971, IV (*Tract on Monetary Reform*), ch. 2, 'Public Finance and Changes in the Value of Money', pp. 37ff). Keynes returned to this theme when he stressed, in the *General Theory*, the crucial importance of stability in the purchasing power of money (Keynes, 1973, VII, p. 236–42).

It is interesting that supply-siders have now come to embrace the false 'Keynesian' position on the advantages of deficits, but that stability of the value of money has required a monetary policy with real interest rates in excess of expected returns to new investment projects. This has produced declining rather than expanding levels of output. Keynes would have argued that interest rates could be reduced *and* the value of money stabilised with a stable programme of government investment and stable money wages which would reduce liquidity preference and increase the efficiency of capital, producing the desired expansion in output.

One final question remains. Keynes's employment programme implied a sharp curtailment of the place of private investment in the economy. Kalečki (1943) had very early recognised the existence of political barriers to a policy of permanent full employment independent of the 'euthanasia' of the 'rentiers' and the 'crowding out' of private capitalism which Keynes's post-war programme seemed to imply. At the same time Keynes was clearly in favour of full financing of government services and of keeping 'the public properly aware of what things cost'. Such a policy clearly left very little scope for purely 'political' expenditures. Indeed, Keynes's programme benefited no particular group or ideology directly. Yet, Keynes felt that unless structural unemployment could be eliminated the civilised world as he knew it was doomed.

The post-war period has demonstrated that instead of providing economic stability by means of Keynes's suggested programme for government investment with all its implications for the role of the private sector, governments have responded to their constituents clear requests for greater economic stability with particular, individual guarantees of real income and employment. At the same time trade unions supported similar guarantees in their employment contracts. Satisfying these demands has created permanent commitments which have led on the one hand to the increasing share of transfer payments at the expense of capital expenditures as governments have been led to guarantee income levels rather than the level of employment, and to a higher share of wages at the expense of investment on the other as private enterprise has been led to guarantee individual's jobs rather than increasingly productive employment. This response to the demands for economic security was doomed to failure at the first downturn in economic activity, just as it was bound to produce massive deficits in such conditions. Instead of acting to ensure aggregate stability, the policy of guaranteeing individual or group incomes has failed for precisely the same reasons that perfectly competitive free enterprise based on individual initiative fails to produce full employment, because it is incapable of recognising the 'technically social' problems of the economy. As long as governments depend upon and respond to individual interest the changes concerning the role of government in economic policy that Keynes's programme required cannot occur. As Professor Caffè (1975) has noted, 'Keynes's work is not restricted to the identification of insoluble contradiction or the prediction of imminent catastrophe; rather it seeks out those actions most likely to lead to improvement of society. This "world vision" predominates the many reconsiderations and re-examinations of Keynes's work and remains of vital importance even today.'

Keynes's vision and programme have not yet been applied because governments, even the most progressive, have not been able to overcome the weight of private interests. Careful to weigh their effects on the ability of perfect competition to produce full employment, Keynes appears to have underestimated their influence on the performance of governments. Thus, Keynes's theory and policy recommendations represent today the challenge to resolve the problems of the political economy of the relation of free enterprise and government control of investment. The purely economic aspects of Keynes's proposals are as valid today as they were 50 years ago. It is the resolution of the political and social changes that will be required to make them possible that represents the challenge that Keynes's theory poses to economists today. The failure to recognise the distinction between the economic correctness of the argument and its possibility of implementation has led to a rejection of the former because of a failure to resolve the latter and thus to the political expedient of returning to the same policies that produced the Great Slump simply because they are politically feasible given the existing social and political organisation. Keynes's 'vision', as Professor Caffè reminds us, looked forward to solution, not backward to impossibility.

NOTES

1. A good brief description of Heller's use of the idea of fiscal drag to convince President Kennedy of the need for a tax cut is given in Lekachman (1966) pp. 266ff.
2. Lekachman, op. cit. pp. 194ff notes that Samuelson headed president-elect Kennedy's policy committee (which did not recommend tax or expenditure change).
3. Given the recommendations of 'supply-side' economists' concerning tax cuts it is interesting to recall the argument used by President Kennedy: 'Our true choice is not between tax reduction... and the avoidance of large federal deficits' for 'An economy hampered by restrictive tax rates will never produce enough revenues to balance our budget, just as it will never produce enough jobs or enough profits.' If deficits existed they were caused by 'slow economic growth and periodic recession'. 'Any new recession would break all deficit records' (quoted in Lekachman op. cit., p. 274).
4. Compare Kalecki's (1944, p. 49) statements: 'The government spending programme must be on such a scale that it will establish full employment in combination with investment adequate to expand productive capacity *pari passu* with the increase in population and productivity of labour' and 'The difficulties encountered in achieving full employment by stimulating private investment reflect the fundamental error of this conception. The proper role of private investment is to provide tools for the production of consumption goods, and not to provide enough work to employ all available labour' (p. 52).
5. 'The theory can be summed up by saying that, given the psychology of the public, the level of output and employment as a whole depends on the amount of investment. I put it in this way, not because it is the only factor on which aggregate output depends, but because it is usual in a complex system to regard as the *causa causans* that factor which is most prone to sudden and wide fluctuation' (Keynes, 1973, XIV, p. 121).
6. Earlier he had warned against reaction to correct such deficits as follows: 'Yet if we carry "economy" of every kind to its logical conclusion we shall find that we have balanced the budget at nought on both sides with all of us flat on our backs starving to death' (Keynes, 1972, IX, p. 239).
7. Thus exogenous cyclical changes at a high level of employment are to be met by changes in the capital budget while if 'the volume of planned investment fails to produce equilibrium, the lack of balance would be met by unbalancing one way or the other the current Budget. Admittedly this would be a last resort...' (Keynes, 1980, XXVII, p. 354).

8. It should not be necessary to point out that these factors only concern domestic employment policy. Keynes clearly recognised that Britain's post-war recovery programme 'must be properly proportional to the resources which are left *after* we have met our daily needs and have produced enough exports to pay for what we require to import from overseas.... The export industries must have the first claim on our attention. I cannot emphasise that too much' (Keynes, 1980, XXVII, p. 267). To this end Keynes worked towards reorganisation of the International Financial System in a form that was complementary to domestic full employment policy and attempted to organise trade in primary commodities for the same ends. On the latter cf. M. Tonveronachi (1981).

9. Ohlin (1950) notes that although 'it is generally accepted that stability in employment to a very large extent depends on stability in investment and that therefore the sum of private and public investment at home and net foreign investment is the "strategic" quantity'. ... 'This is not an idea that was brought to the fore by Keynes's General Theory, as writers of the "Keynesian school" have asserted' (p. 28). Ohlin rather associates the proposition with 'ordinary business cycle theory' and part of 'the theory worked out in the early thirties as part of an analysis of remedies for unemployment in Sweden' (p. 140).

REFERENCES

Baily, M. N. (1978), 'Stabilization Policy and Private Economic Behaviour'. *Brookings Papers on Economic Activity*, no. 1.

Bank for International Settlements, Annual Reports (1980, 1981), Basle, June 1981, 1982.

Caffè, F. (1975), 'L'Economia Keynesiana e la Politica Economica', *Rassegna Economica*, vol. XXXIX, July–Aug.

CEA (Council of Economic Advisors), (1982), *Economic Report of the President*, Washington, Feb.

Cornwall, J. (1977), *Modern Capitalism* (London: Martin Robertson).

Deane, P. and Cole, W. A. (1967), *British Economic Growth, 1688–1959*, 2nd edn (Cambridge University Press).

International Monetary Fund, International Financial Statistics, various issues.

Kalecki, M. (1944), 'Three Ways to Full Employment', in *The Economics of Full Employment* (Oxford: Basil Blackwell).

Kalecki, M. (1943), 'Political Aspects of Full Employment', in *Selected Essays on the Dynamics of the Capitalist Economy* (Cambridge University Press, 1971).

Keynes, J. M. (1971), *A Tract on Monetary Reform, The Collected Writings of J. M. Keynes*, vol. IV (London: Macmillan).

Keynes, J. M. (1972), *Essays in Persuasion, The Collected Writings of J. M. Keynes*, vol. IX (London: Macmillan).

Keynes, J. M. (1973), *The General Theory of Employment, Interest and Money*, vol. VII (London: Macmillan).

Keynes, J. M. (1973), *The General Theory and After Part II. Defence and Development*, vol. XIV.

Keynes, J. M. (1980), *Activities 1940–1946 shaping the Post-War World: Employment and Commodities*, vol. XXVII.

Keynes, J. M. (1983), *Economic Articles and Correspondence: Academic*, vol. XI.

Kregel, J. A. (1973), *The Reconstruction of Political Economy*, 2nd edn (London: Macmillan, 1975).

Kregel, J. A. (1980), 'I Fondamenti Marshalliani del Principio della Domanda Effettiva di Keynes', *Giornale degli Economisti e Annali di Economia*, March–April.

Lekachman, R. (1966), *The Age of Keynes* (New York: Random House).

Maddison, A. (1982), *Phases of Capitalist Development* (Oxford University Press).

Matthews, R. C. O. (1968) 'Why has Britain had Full Employment Since the War'. *Economic Journal*, vol. LXVIII, Sept.

OECD (1966), *National Accounts Statistics*, 1955–64, Paris, Mar.

OECD (1981), *National Accounts of O.E.C.D. Countries*, 1962–79, vol. II, detailed tables, Paris, June.

Ohlin, B. (1950), *The Problem of Employment Stabilization* (London: Oxford University Press).

Tonveronachi, M. (1981), 'Review of *The Collected Writings of J. M. Keynes (1980) Vol. XXVII*', *Moneta e Credito*, vol. XXXIV, no. 136, Dec.

4 Capitalist Equilibrium: from Soho to Bloomsbury

GIORGIO LUNGHINI

A lecturer in political economy in a German university writes me that I have completely convinced him, but . . . his position forces him "as other colleagues" *not to express* his convictions.

(K. Marx to L. Kugelman, 1869)

This book is chiefly addressed to my fellow economists. I hope that it will be intelligible to others. But its main purpose is to deal with difficult questions of theory, and only in the second place with the applications of this theory in practice.

(J. M. Keynes, 1936)

. . . back again in our old headquarters in Dean Street. . . . Everyone tried to create a bourgeois existence, to adapt to the circumstances. We could not be the only ones to remain *bohemians* when all the others were becoming philistines. But we found this *somersault* extremely difficult to accomplish.

(J. Marx, née von Westphalen, 1855–57)

One could live in the middle of Bloomsbury and yet say that one was very anti-Bloomsbury.

(R. F. Harrod, 1951)

Someone looking through Whiteley's general catalogue would find only things and prices; another would find what we believed we had found, a profoundly moving human drama.

(E. V. L. and G. M., *What a Life!*, 1911)

I

So many things have happened since those days of 1883, so many Marxisms, so many Keynesisms, that *Kapital* and the *General Theory*

51

could have been taken from the shelves of the British Museum and read as they should be, as pure and simple classics.

We are still living in the same world in which Marx died and Keynes was born; we are more aware that we are 'driven along the adventurous road of speculation, credit frauds, stock swindles and crises'[1], and that 'the capital development of a country becomes a by-product of the activities of a casino'; yet, the paradox of poverty in the midst of plenty still resists the confutations of academic logic. Marx and Keynes consider the causality and injustice associated with capitalist equilibrium from different viewpoints, and explain its capacity for survival in different ways as simulating a natural law. But their works show and seek to demonstrate that this equilibrium only occurs by chance and is not a norm that must be respected at any cost; other conditions were conceivable and therefore possible. The conditions of capitalist equilibrium do not arise spontaneously, neither are they reproduced mechanically. There are binding constraints, but they can be cut or loosened. Why should history never be allowed to change them?

II

Keynes conceded that we owe to Marx one pregnant observation (even if a highly illogical use was subsequently made of it): in the real world which is not a 'co-operative economy' the nature of production cannot, as economists often seem to suppose, be represented as a case of the type C–M–C – 'Commodity–Money–Commodity', that is, to exchange a commodity against money which is to be used to acquire another commodity. This may represent the position of the individual consumer, but it certainly is not that of the business world where one parts with money only if it can be exchanged for a commodity which can ultimately be sold for *more* money according to a process of the type M–C–M'. Ricardo's inability (as well as that of so many other economists) to conceive of the economic system in anything but equilibrium can be traced, in Marx's view, to this representation of capitalist production as a mode of production in which there is no difference between purchase and sale, as if the business of exchange were immediate; or, as a process of *social* production in which society followed a predetermined plan to divide its means of subsistence and its productive inputs in a manner and in the proportions required for the satisfaction of the various individuals' needs and the various sectors' requirements for social capital to allow it to produce the outputs required. This does not imply that theories based on these hypotheses exclude the possibility of crises, only that when they actually occur they must be considered as *accidental*, caused simply by *chance*. Marx inverted this point of view, denying the error upon which it rested: *it is equilibrium, not crisis that occurs by chance*, because it is not true that goods are exchanged against goods. Such a position must be rejected, above all, because of the role played by money in a process in which constant capital is present: 'it is a pretty conception that – in order to reason away the contradictions of capitalist production – abstracts from its very basis and depicts it as a production aiming at the direct satisfaction of the consumption of the producers'.

Why is the 'metaphysical equilibrium of sellers and buyers' false? Because it is an equilibrium which recognises only unity in the process of purchase and sale, not separation; and because money is not only a *medium* which allows exchange to take place, but is at the same time the *medium* which dissolves the exchange of good against good into two independent acts, separated by both time and space. The immediate objective of the capitalist is to reconvert his commodities, or better his capital-commodities, into capital-money and in this way procure his gain. The principal motive in this process is then not consumption, or income, as it indeed is for those who sell commodities with the sole intention of converting them into means of subsistence. But, this is not capitalist production, in which income appears as a result, not as the determinant aim: everyone sells in order to sell, i.e. to transform commodities into money. It is precisely this simple observation which allowed Marx (and which was to allow Keynes) to formulate not only a criticism of the theory of equilibrium founded on the relation between demand and supply, but also an analysis of the conditions of capitalism as it actually exists, as an analysis of the necessary and possible – 'not natural', nor certain or probable – conditions for the reproduction of capital and the capitalist relations of production.

III

It is in the crises on world markets that the contradictions of bourgeoise production show themselves. Now, instead of trying to discover the contradictory elements which explode in these catastrophes, the apologists content themselves with the very negation of the catastrophes and, faced with their periodic regularity stubbornly repeat that if production were only carried out according to the textbooks, crises would never occur. If contradictions eliminated with such fantasy do not really exist crises would not occur; but the crises are a reality because the contradictions do exist. In some 'crude and primitive' state of society in which production is only for use and not for exchange, equilibrium should indeed occur when supply is equal to demand. This would be the normal state of affairs because there would be no reason for tensions or other factors to disturb the coincidence between supply and demand. If the capitalist mode of production, rather than being a specifically developed, particular form of social production were instead a mode of production which had remained unchanged since the stage of its early rude beginnings, then its particular antitheses and contradictions would not exist, nor would crises exist. The real difficulty that one encounters in trying to give general definition to the concept of demand and supply on the other hand, consists in the fact that it seems to dissolve into tautology when one encounters the immediate identity of the theory of prices and the theory of value (in the manner of J. S. Mill, for example: 'Value, at any moment, is the result of demand and supply').

Marx points out that from the point of view of the supply of products found on, or brought to, the market nothing assures that the quantity of social labour embodied in the production of a particular commodity corresponds to the range of social needs to be satisfied, so that – demand remaining unchanged – the commodity is sold at its market value. It is only when the society efficiently controls production, regulating it in advance, that there is a link between the measure of the socially necessary labour time embodied in the production of a particular product and the range of social needs that the article has to satisfy (and it is for this reason, according to Marx, that the exchange or sale of commodities at their values constitutes a rational, natural law of equilibrium: it is on this basis that one must start an explanation of the exceptions, not with the exceptions to explain the laws themselves). From the side of demand it is necessary to note that commodities are acquired as means of production or as means of subsistence, that is, to enter as either productive consumption or individual consumption. Demand thus comes from both the capitalists and from the consumers. The two forms of demand at first sight seem to presuppose a determined quantity of social needs matched on the supply side by given quantities of social production in the various lines of production. It would thus appear as if demand represents a determined social need of a particular magnitude which requires, in order to be satisfied, the presence on the market of a given quantity of a particular article. But, the quantitative determination of this need is absolutely elastic and flexible. Its fixed character is only apparent.

What is then meant by equilibrium between demand and supply? According to Marx, when demand and supply are equal to each other they cannot explain anything because they exert no influence on market value and shed no light on the reasons why the market value is expressed by precisely one sum of money rather than another. The true intrinsic laws of capitalist production cannot be explained on the basis of the reciprocal action of demand and supply because these laws show themselves in their pure form only when demand and supply cease to act because they are in equilibrium. In reality, demand and supply never equilibrate each other, or if they do it only occurs by chance. As long as one is only concerned with purchase and sale it is sufficient to consider directly the producers of the commodities as such, dealing face to face. But, proceeding with such an analysis one discovers that demand and supply presuppose the existence of diverse classes and categories who divide the total income of society amongst themselves; the expenditure of their income on consumption thus gives rise to the demand corresponding to that income. On the other hand, in order to understand the demand and supply which has its origin in the relations between producers as such requires a complete knowledge of the structure of the capitalist process of production.

IV

Whatever the form of the process of production in a society, it must be a continuous process, must continue to go periodically through the same phases. A society can no more cease to produce than it can cease to consume. When viewed, therefore, as a connected whole, and as flowing on with incessant renewal, every social process of production is, at the same time, a process of reproduction.... If production be capitalistic in form, so too, will be reproduction.

But, it is in the circulation process (which in and of itself is at the same time a process of reproduction) that the crisis becomes manifest, or that the capitalist equilibrium manifests itself.

In the capitalist system, however, the transformation of the annual product takes place by means of a unilateral process. There is on one side a mass of simple purchases, and on the other a mass of simple sales such that equilibrium may result only on the assumption that the value of the unilateral sales coincides with the value of unilateral purchases. The fact that the production of commodities is the general form of capitalistic production already implies the role that money plays in it, not only as a means of circulation but as money capital. Money produces particular conditions for the normal transformation, and thus for the normal process of reproduction, on both a simple and expanded scale which are peculiar to this mode of production. They may develop into an equal number of conditions of abnormal reproduction, i.e. into the possibility of crises, since equilibrium itself – given the primitive character of this reproduction – occurs by chance. The so-called 'schemes of reproduction' (and in particular the scheme of expanded reproduction) represent the simplest and most powerful instrument for the clarification of the sense and the force of the Marxian thesis that equilibrium in the cyclical process of capital is possible, but that its realisation is only a random occurrence.

V

According to Engels, the section of *Capital* dedicated to 'The Reproduction and Circulation of the Aggregate Social Capital' (BookII, Part III) gave Marx particular difficulties. One can understand why once it is recognised that these schemes were meant to describe a *process*. For Marx, capital is a 'movement', a cyclical process which goes through different stages, and which itself exhibits three different forms of cyclical process. It is for this reason that it can only be understood by movement and not as something in a state of rest which must inevitably be the case when it is presented by means of algebraic formulae.

In order to understand the exact form taken on by capital in each of its various stages it is further necessary to assume that the commodities are sold at their values and that this occurs in unchanging conditions (ignoring as well any changes in value that may occur during the cyclical process) and above all that the system is one of pure capitalism in which there are only two classes: capitalists and workers.

Marx subdivided the aggregate product into two departments: means of production and means of consumption. In each department the separate branches of production which are operating in it were considered to form one single branch. In each capital was divided into its two constituent parts: variable capital which considered according to its value is equal to the sum of the wages paid for the labour power employed in that department, and constant capital, or the value of all the means of production employed in the department. The value of the annual aggregate product is thus also subdivided into a part of value which represents the constant capital, c, consumed during production and a part of value added by the annual aggregate labour. This latter part is divided in its turn into the substitution of the anticipated variable capital, v, and the surplus that remains which makes up the surplus value, s. Just as the value of any single commodity, the value of the annual aggregate product of each department is divided into $c + v + s$. For Smith and for Ricardo, on the other hand, the value of a commodity could be expressed in terms of the equivalent of the labour power used and the surplus value so created; however, the consideration of constant capital is indispensable to understanding the essential role of money and monetary circulation in the process of reproduction, and in particular the role of money – of hoarding – in the reproduction of the value of fixed capital in a framework of the production of commodities.

It is for this reason, above all, that the case of simple reproduction takes on such importance in the Marxian 'dynamic', even though it appears to be its negation inasmuch as it assumes that consumption is the sole aim of the production process. In the capitalistic process of production, in fact, money capital 'constitutes the form in which every individual capital appears upon the scene and opens its process as capital. It therefore appears as the *primus motor*, lending impetus to the entire process', acting with constant repetition at short intervals as the motor of the process. In the scheme of simple reproduction of productive capital, in addition to the assumptions of unchanged conditions and the purchase-sale of commodities at their values, it is assumed that the entire surplus value is expended by capitalists on personal consumption rather than being reserved in whole or in part for accumulation. Naturally, this is an unreal assumption since the capitalistic process is treated as if it produced only use values for consumption rather than surplus value and profit for accumulation. It is just as if the capitalist produced commodities solely in order to substitute, or to exchange, them for commodities with different use values. In such conditions the process of production could never expand. On the other hand, the proportions which place a limit on the expansion of the production process are not arbitrarily prescribed, but rather technically determined in such a way that the realised surplus value, even if destined for accumulation, often can expand only by means of the repetition of several cycles until a sufficient volume is achieved to allow it to really operate as additional capital (it must thus be hoarded up to that time). The surplus value is thus accumulated in hoards and in this form constitutes latent money capital, latent because as long as it stays in the form of money it cannot operate as capital. Whether it is simple or expanded reproduction depends on the way the capitalist decides to spend the realised surplus value: hoarding it, spending it as income on luxury goods, or buying new means of reproduction (as a true capitalist). The scale of reproduction thus depends entirely on the capitalists' spending decisions, with the only limit given at any moment in time by the technical conditions (i.e. by the past decisions of the capitalists concerning the techniques of production).

VI

The scheme that Marx uses as the basis for his investigation of simple reproduction is the following (the numbers may represent any monetary unit – millions of marks or francs or pounds sterling):

I   *Production of Means of Production*

Capital	$4000c + 1000v$	$= 5000$
Commodity–Product	$4000c + 1000v + 1000s$	$= 6000$

II. *Production of Articles of Consumption*

Capital	$2000c + 500v$	$= 2500$
Commodity–Product	$2000c + 500v + 500s$	$= 3000$

Determining the conditions of reproduction signifies determining the conditions in which the supply of each department – the value of its production – is equal to the demand for its output. In the case of simple reproduction the demand for means of production should be equal to the value of the means of production that must be replaced in each department because they are used up in production. The demand for articles of consumption, on the other hand, should be equal to the value of the articles of consumption upon which the workers have spent their wages and the capitalists the surplus value which they have appropriated (and which under the assumption of simple reproduction they do not invest to expand the scale of production). In this equalisation of the demand for the products of each department to its supply, those exchanges that occur within each department disappear from view, and not only for reasons of algebraic manipulation. The necessary condition for simple reproduction may thus be reduced to $I(v + s) = IIc$. If we were now to examine the transformation necessary for the process of simple reproduction, and leave aside for the present the money circulation which brings them about, three basic points emerge:

(a) The $500v$, representing wages of the labourers, and $500s$, representing surplus value of the capitalists, in department II, must be spent for articles of consumption. But their value exists in articles of consumption worth 1000, held by the capitalists in department II, which replace the advanced $500v$ and represent the $500s$. Consequently the wages and surplus-value of department II are exchanged within this department for products of this same department. Thereby articles of consumption to the amount of $(500v + 500s)$ II $= 1000$ drop out of the total product.

(b) The $1000v$ plus $1000s$ of department I must likewise be spent for articles of consumption; in other words, for products of department II. Hence they must be exchanged for the remainder of this product equal to the constant capital part, $2000c$. Department II receives in return an equal quantity of means of production, the product of I, in which the value of $1000v + 1000s$ of I is incorporated. Thereby $2000IIc$ and $(1000v + 1000s)I$ drop out of the calculation.

(c) There still remains $4000Ic$. These consist of means of production which can be used only in department I to replace its consumed constant capital, and are therefore disposed of by mutual exchange between the individual capitalists of I, just as the $(500v + 500s)II$, by an exchange between the labourers and capitalists, or between the individual capitalists of II.

All the transformations required in order to meet the conditions of reproduction are accomplished by means of a circulation of money which promotes reproduction just as much as it renders its understanding more difficult, but which is of decisive importance because the variable portion of capital must ever resume the form of money, as money-capital converting itself from the form of money into labour-power. The presence of money and of credit, each in the appropriate form, is thus also a necessary condition for reproduction. And that is not all, the fact that capitalist production is production of commodities means that money plays a crucial role in the process of substitution of fixed capital and makes a crisis (of hoarding or of realisation) possible even with simple reproduction on a constant scale:

> A disproportion of the production of fixed and circulating capital is one of the favourite arguments of the economists in explaining crises. That such a disproportion can and must arise even when the fixed capital is merely *preserved*, that it can and must do so on the assumption of ideal normal production of the basis of simple reproduction of the already functioning social capital is something new to them.

VII

It has already been pointed out that, for Marx, simple reproduction, reproduction on a constant scale, appears as an abstraction, inasmuch as on the one hand the absence of accumulation or reproduction on an extended scale is a strange assumption in capitalist conditions, and on the other hand conditions of production do not remain exactly the same in different years although this is the assumption of simple reproduction. However, to the extent that accumulation does take place, simple reproduction is always a part of it, and can therefore be studied by itself, and is an actual factor of accumulation since the material substratum of extended reproduction is produced within simple reproduction.

In normal conditions part of the surplus-value will be spent as revenue and the other converted into capital. Any average movement will exhibit both aspects but, in order 'not to complicate the formulae' it is preferable to suppose that all surplus-value is converted into capital. It must further be supposed that in the given technical conditions there is sufficient money to expand the functioning constant capital and to establish new industrial concerns; and that production on an expanded scale has already taken place for in order that the money (surplus-value hoarded in money form) may be converted into elements of productive capital one must be able to buy these elements on the market as commodities. The essential difference, with respect to the case of simple reproduction is in that case the entire surplus value of department I is spent as revenue, that is on commodities produced in department II, while in the case of expanded reproduction it is spent on means of production for means of production.

In order to make the passage from simple to expanded reproduction it is thus necessary that department I be able to produce a smaller amount of the elements required for constant capital in department II and a larger quantity for department I. 'This transition', however, 'does not always take place without difficulties'. Expanded reproduction requires not only additions to constant capital, but also additions to variable capital; it is thus necessary that the portion of newly created money capital capable of being converted into variable capital should always find labour power into which it can be transformed. Thus, since department I has to furnish from its surplus product the additional constant capital for department II, department II will furnish in this sense the additional variable capital for department I. Department II accumulates for department I, and for itself, the necessary variable capital, reproducing a greater part of its total production, and thus also of its surplus product, in the form of necessary articles of consumption.

The complexity of the conditions necessary for expanded reproduction and the crucial and autonomous role of the decisions and the means of expenditure of the capitalists is more than evident even without consideration of the problems related to monetary circulation. Write $c_1 + v_1 + s_1$ as the value of the commodity-product of department I and $c_2 + v_2 + s_2$ as the value of the commodity-product of department II.
Then write

$$s_1 = \Delta c_1 + \Delta v_1 + s_{l1}$$
$$s_2 = \Delta c_2 + \Delta v_2 + s_{l2}$$

where Δc is the part of the surplus-value of each sector committed to the creation of additional constant capital, Δv the part set aside for additional variable capital and s_l the part which may be expended on capitalists consumption. Equating supply and demand in the two departments yields

$$c_1 + v_1 + s_1 = c_1 + c_2 + \Delta c_1 + \Delta c_2$$
$$c_2 + v_2 + s_2 = v_1 + v_2 + \Delta v_1 + \Delta v_2 + s_{l1} + s_{l2}$$

Eliminating the terms that disappear from the aggregate product and thus drop out of the calculation and recalling the definition $s = \Delta c + \Delta v + s_l$, it follows from the two equalities that the conditions for expanded reproduction are $v_1 + \Delta v_1 + s_{l1} = c_2 + \Delta c_2$. It is obvious that if the capitalists consumed the entire surplus-value in luxuries the necessary conditions for expanded reproduction would coincide with those of simple reproduction. In both cases the contradictions of capitalist production are apparent:

> The labourers as buyers of commodities are important for the market. But as sellers of their own commodity – labour–power – capitalist society tends to keep them down to the minimum price. Further contradiction: the periods in which capitalist production exerts all its forces regularly turn out to be periods of over-production, because production potentials can never be utilised to such an extent that more value may not only be produced but also realised; but the sale of commodities, the realisation of commodity-capital and thus surplus-value, is limited, not by the consumer requirements of society in general, but by the consumer require-ments of a society in which the vast majority are always poor and must always remain poor.

This is, in fact, the principal secret in making the worker into a rational consumer:

> Mr Drummond visits the cutlery works of Turner's Falls (Connec-ticut River), and Mr Oakman, the treasurer of the concern, after telling him that especially American table cutlery beat the English in quality continues: 'The time is coming that we will beat England as to prices also, we are ahead in quality now, that is acknowledged, but we must have lower prices, and shall have it the moment we get our steel at lower prices and have our own labour down.'

VIII

According to Keynes it is one of the curiosities of the history of economic theory that the heretics of 100 years earlier, who had challenged the validity of the Classical formula of Commodity–Money–Commodity with the formula M–C–M', should have been inclined to believe *either* that M' should always necessarily be greater than M or that M should always necessarily be greater than M', depending on whether they lived in a period in which one or the other of the two cases dominated actual conditions. Marx, and those who believed the capitalist system to be based on exploitation, maintained the inevitable excess of M', while Hobson or Foster and Catchings or Major Douglas maintained the inevitable excess of M since they believed in the inherent tendency of the capitalist system toward deflation and unemployment. Marx was close to the truth, which lay in between, when he added that a continual excess of M' would inevitably be interrupted by a series of crises of gradually increasing intensity, bankruptcies and unemployment, during which M must be presumed greater. Given the intentions of Keynes's argument it should have, at the very least, served to reconcile Marx's followers with those of Major Douglas, leaving the Classical economists isolated in their belief that M and M' are always equal.

> Now I range myself with the heretics. I believe their flair and their instinct move them towards the right conclusion. But I was brought up in the citadel and I recognise its power and might. A large part of the established body of economic doctrine I cannot but accept as broadly correct. I do not doubt it. For me, therefore, it is impossible to rest satisfied until I can put my finger on the flaw in that part of the orthodox reasoning which leads to the conclusions which for various reasons seem to me to be inacceptable. I believe that I am on my way to do so. There is, I am convinced, a fatal flaw in that part of the orthodox reasoning which deals with the theory of what determines the level of effective demand and the volume of aggregate employment; the flaw being largely due to the failure of classical doctrine to develop a satisfactory theory of the rate of interest.

IX

According to Keynes, traditional analysis of capitalist equilibrium is defective because it does not succeed in correctly identifying the independent variables in the system: saving and investment are not the determinants of the system, but rather the twin results of the systems' determinants which are the propensity to consume, the schedule of the marginal efficiency of capital and the rate of interest. These determinants are in themselves complex and each one is susceptible to being influenced by prospective changes in the others. However, they remain independent in the sense that their values cannot be determined one from the others. Traditional analysis recognised the fact that saving depends on income, but ignored the fact that income depends on investment in such a way that when investment changes income must necessarily adjust in an amount sufficient to cause a change in saving equal to the change in investment. It is precisely for this reason that equilibrium not only is possible, but also normal in the sense that there must always be some position of equilibrium; but it is not necessarily optimal. It is perfectly possible that (effective) demand should equal income, while at the same time the equality between demand and supply on the money market and on the labour market is accompanied by an excess supply of labour. The existence of involuntarily unemployed labour is not a sufficient condition to ensure that an eventual reduction in the wage rate, however achieved, should modify the decisions which determine the volume of employment.

For Keynes, as for Marx, the classical equilibrium (and for Keynes this included neoclassical) which applies to all markets and carries with it connotations of stability and optimality is not in fact a natural, necessary nor general case. The scope of the *General Theory*, indeed all of Keynes's work, is to demonstrate and elucidate how the postulates of classical theory are only applicable to a special case and not to the general case, to the situation that can only be considered as the limiting point of all possible situations of equilibrium. In addition, the characteristics of the special case presupposed in the classical theory (in Keynes's sense) turn out not to be applicable to the economic society in which we actually live, with the consequence that its divulgation is not only beside the point, but disastrous when applied to the facts of actual experience.

X

Keynes' *General Theory* is one of the most instructive examples in the entire history of modern economic analysis of the difficulty of the art of thinking in terms of models, and of the limits – when the pseudo-analogies with the physical sciences are overcome – of treating as parameters, as unexplained magnitudes, precisely those factors which are thought to be the most important, so important that they cannot be given explanation. The true unknowns are the parameters and at most it is possible to postulate or impose mechanisms or rules of stability: 'economics', for Keynes, was 'a moral science ... it deals with introspection and with values. I might have added that it deals with motives, expectations, psychological uncertainties. One has to be constantly on guard against treating the material as constant and homogenous. It is as though the fall of the apple to the ground depended on the apple's motives, on whether it is worth while falling to the ground, and whether the ground wanted the apple to fall, and on mistaken calculations on the part of the apple as to how far it was from the centre of the earth'. Keynes distinguished precisely, but not definitely, between dependent and independent variables. The distinction is completely arbitrary from an absolute point of view; it must be based on experience alone concerning the variability of the influence of the different factors on the equilibrium position whose determination forms the object of the *General Theory*: the national income in a given economic system at a point in time, and thus the amount of employment. For Keynes this implied the identification of the prevalent factors in the determination of equilibrium. To this end Keynes treated nearly everything as given: the quality and quantity of the available labour force, the quality and quantity of the available productive capacity, the existing techniques, the degree of competition, the tastes and habits of consumers, the disutility of the different intensities of labour and of supervisory and organisational activity, and even the social structure, including the forces, different from those treated as variable, which determine the distribution of the national income. This did not imply that Keynes considered these factors as constant, but only that within the argument of the *General Theory* and its particular objectives, the effects and consequences of changes in these factors were left out of account. Independent variables, on the other hand, were the propensity to consume, the schedule of the marginal efficiency of capital and the rate of interest: precisely the three principal lacunae in economic knowledge. Finally, the dependent variables were the level of employment and national income (measured in wage units). Relative prices played no important role in the determination of equilibrium.

XI

The factors considered as given in the *General Theory* influence the independent variables, but do not completely determine them. For example, the schedule of the marginal efficiency of capital depends in part on the existing productive capacity, which is a given factor, but it also depends on the state of long-period expectations which cannot be determined from the given factors. In the last analysis the following may be considered as independent variables: (a) the three fundamental psychological factors (i.e. the psychological propensity to consume, the psychological attitude to liquidity and the psychological expectation of future yields), (b) the wage unit as determined by bargaining between workers and employers, and (c) the quantity of money as determined by the actions of the Central Bank. Taking as given the factors cited above, these variables determine national income and employment; but even these variables are susceptible to further analysis. They are not the basic and independent building blocks of the system. Indeed, for Keynes, 'Our final task might be to select those variables which can be deliberately controlled or managed by central authority in the kind of system in which we actually live'.

The *General Theory* is a theory of capitalist equilibrium in a pure capitalist system in which the State plays no active or constituent part. It is precisely because the capitalist system in its pure state is not capable of self-regulation leading to and maintaining an equilibrium position with full employment of all human resources that the external intervention of the State is necessary. A State that in Keynes's social philosophy has exactly the same structural position, and is no more precisely defined, as the marginal efficiency of capital has in the *General Theory*: a potential *causa causans*, but certainly something completely different from some bourgeois Chamber of Commerce, indeed rather the opposite. The theoretical basis of Keynes's social philosophy is, in fact, the certainty concerning the end of *laissez-faire*:

> Let us clear from the ground the metaphysical or general principles upon which, from time to time, *laissez-faire* has been founded. It is *not* true that individuals possess a prescriptive 'natural liberty' in their economic activities. There is *no* 'compact' conferring perpetual rights on those who Have or on those who Acquire. The world is *not* so governed from above that private and social interest always coincide. It is *not* so managed here below that in practice they coincide. It is *not* a correct deduction from the principles of economics that enlightened self-interest always operates in the public interest. Nor is it true that self-interest generally *is* enlightened; more often individuals acting separately to promote their own ends are too ignorant or too weak to attain even these.
>
> Experience does *not* show that individuals, when they make up a social unit, are always less clear-sighted than when they act separately.

XII

The capacity of a text to render useless or to contradict all the interpretations that have been drawn from it is impressive. Here is the first summary scheme, that Keynes gives, in Chapter 3 of the *General Theory*, which sets out the essential characteristics of his vision of capitalist equilibrium:

When employment increases, aggregate real income is increased. The psychology of the community is such that when aggregate real income is increased aggregate consumption is increased, but not by so much as income. Hence employers would make a loss if the whole of the increased employment were to be devoted to satisfying the increased demand for immediate consumption. Thus, to justify any given amount of employment there must be an amount of current investment sufficient to absorb the excess of total output over what the community chooses to consume when employment is at the given level. For unless there is this amount of investment, the receipts of the entrepreneurs will be less than is required to induce them to offer the given amount of employment. It follows, therefore, that, given what we shall call the community's propensity to consume, the equilibrium level of employment, i.e. the level at which there is no inducement to employers as a whole either to expand or to contract employment, will depend on the amount of current investment. The amount of current investment will depend, in turn, on what we shall call the inducement to invest; and the inducement to invest will be found to depend on the relation between the schedule of the marginal efficiency of capital and the complex of rates of interest on loans of various maturities and risks.

Thus, given the propensity to consume and the rate of new investment, there will be only one level of employment consistent with equilibrium; since any other level will lead to inequality between the aggregate supply price of output as a whole and its aggregate demand price. This level cannot be *greater* than full employment, i.e. the real wage cannot be less than the marginal disutility of labour. But there is no reason in general for expecting it to be *equal* to full employment. The effective demand associated with full employment is a special case, only realised when the propensity to consume and the inducement to invest stand in a particular relationship to one another. This particular relationship, which corresponds to the assumptions of the classical theory, is in a sense an optimum relationship. But it can only exist when, by accident or design, current investment provides an amount of demand just equal to the excess of the aggregate supply price of the output resulting from full employment over what the community will choose to spend on consumption when it is fully employed.

In classical theory, both ancient and modern, on the other hand, it is supposed that effective demand assumes, or can always assume, a value equal to the aggregate supply price of output, whatever the level of employment. This is the equivalent of saying that effective demand, rather than having a unique equilibrium value, is an infinite series of equally admissible values such that the level of employment is in neutral equilibrium for every level of employment except for its maximum value. Competition among entrepreneurs will drive the level of employment towards such a maximum which is the unique position of stable equilibrium. For Keynes on the other hand, in any given situation there is a unique level of employment compatible with equilibrium. Such an equilibrium is stable even if employment is not a maximum. It is sufficient that aggregate demand equal aggregate supply and that variations in investment produce variations in income according to the multiplier theory. According to Keynes this analysis furnishes an explanation of the paradox of poverty in the midst of plenty. But it is an incomplete analysis (and probably cannot be complete) because we do not possess a satisfying analysis of the propensity to consume, or a definition of the marginal efficiency of capital, or a theory of the rate of interest, the three unknowns which determine the level and the stability of capitalist equilibrium.

XIII

For Keynes the level at which capitalistic equilibrium was established, and thus the level of employment, is determined, via the schedule of the marginal efficiency of capital by the 'uncontrollable and disobedient psychology of the business world' (beside the 'cumulative oppressive power of the capitalist to exploit the scarcity- value of capital' without which such psychology would only be of interest to psychoanalysts). In as much as the marginal efficiency of capital is subject to unforeseen collapse and violent change, the 'schematic' part of the *General Theory* should lead to the conclusion that the system should be violently unstable. The actual course of events in fact contradicts this logical conclusion because 'it is an outstanding characteristic of the economic system in which we live that, whilst it is subject to severe fluctuations in respect of output and employment, it is not violently unstable. Indeed it seems capable of remaining in a chronic condition of sub-normal activity for a considerable period without any marked tendency either towards recovery or towards complete collapse ... an intermediate situation which is neither desperate nor satisfactory is our normal lot'.

Now, Keynes argues, since these facts of experience do not follow by logical necessity, it is necessary to suppose that the atmosphere and the psychological propensities of the modern world must be of such a character as to produce these results. It is thus necessary to consider what hypothetical values of the psychological propensities would lead to a stable system.

The conditions of stability that Keynes considers capable of explaining the observed results are the following:

(a) The marginal propensity to consume is such that the multiplier is greater than one, but not very large.
(b) Moderate changes in the prospective yield of capital or in the rate of interest will not be associated with very large changes in the rate of investment;
(c) moderate changes in employment are not associated with very large changes in money wages.

It is important to note that these conditions help to explain a characteristic feature of the capitalistic system which it would be impossible to explain in general terms: the fact that the system oscillates around an intermediate position appreciably below full employment and above that minimum level beyond which the system itself is threatened. Keynes himself alerts us to the fact that this is not a reason to 'conclude that the mean position thus determined by "natural" tendencies, namely, by those tendencies which are likely to persist, failing measures expressly designed to correct them, is, therefore, established by laws of necessity. The unimpeded rule of the above conditions is a fact of observation concerning the world as it is or has been, and not a necessary principle which cannot be changed'.

XIV

For one hundred years neoclassical theory has held hegemony over economics in its general equilibrium or the partial equilibrium version. From the time it was first constituted as an academic discipline economic analysis has been recognised as scientific only through the canon of the nucleus of the classical and neoclassical notions of equilibrium with its associated postulates concerning the natural or necessary order of an economic system composed completely of rational agents in a stable structure. As a consequence *the* economic problem was viewed as a problem of the calculation of the appropriate system of prices, social relations are reduced to simple relations of exchange. How powerful and attractive this vision of society was can be seen by the practical inefficiency of internal criticism (such as that given by Sraffa in 1960 which appeared to many as being definitive) and in the willingness on the part of the dominant theory to accept and incorporate the infinite points of criticism (starting with those of Sraffa himself in 1925 and 1926) concerning the existence of imperfections in capital markets which might be such as to produce disequilibrium situations. It would only be necessary to remove them from reality via reforms, or to encompass them within the theory by means of mathematics, in order to allow equilibrium to re-emerge and persist. In this respect, precisely because they cannot be reduced to equations on a chalkboard, the criticisms of Marx and Keynes are equivalent despite the well discussed fact that the political implications of the two are in general opposed: both criticise the normal notion of equilibrium, not only on the two fronts of method and realism, but above all on the more important ground of relevance. There is at least one thing that Marx and Keynes have in common (it has also been noted by Schumpeter): Keynes's theory of collapse, for all its differences, has one important characteristic in common with Marx's: collapse is engendered by causes which are intrinsic to the functioning of the economic mechanism and not by factors external to it. The fixed point in the two otherwise incompatible theories is that for both Keynes's human logic as well as for Marx's dialectic, the capitalist system is one whose equilibrium, and thus existence, is due either to curious chance or active planning. Thus, not only may an equilibrium exist for any set of conditions and level of activity of the system, but it can be maintained given the apposite stability conditions. It is not so much that imperfections impede the perfect equilibrium, but that they allow undesirable equilibria. But this implies that even though undesirable equilibria normally occur, they are intrinsically precarious and could be changed if only one had the desire to change the conditions that determine them. The political and philosophical differences that separate Marx and Keynes are more profound than the similarities that unite them. These similarities are not, however, limited to the plane of simple national accounting schemes, but extend to a number of analytical problems. The sub-division of the economy into two sectors of consumption goods and investment goods is indeed a consequence of a similar vision of the fundamental asymmetry of the capitalist structure which manifests itself, above all, in the automony of invest-ment decisions and the crucial role of money in the process of reproduction. This vision concerns the fact that capitalistic production finds its measure, its unique limit, in capital itself: production does not take place with reference to the existing limit of consumption demand, but is only limited by capital itself. The existence and stability of equilibrium, the level of activity and unemployment that they deter-mine, its consequences on the employment of labour power and of past labour power which also determines the distribution of social product, all these characteristics of capitalist equilibrium are made to depend, simply but tautologically, on the aims and objectives which control the process of production and reproduction of capital.

At the very moment in which the crisis takes form within the theory, and since a theory cannot explain such changes in its own structure except by producing its own self-destruction, the problem of equilib-rium and of structural change is shifted elsewhere, to the world of action, to a social class or to an undefined State.

Neither for Marx nor for Keynes is there in capitalist equilibrium, nor in any other equilibrium for that matter, anything that can in any sense be described as natural. It is not a logically necessary condition because it contradicts good sense; neither is it necessarily eternal since institutions, conventions and habits – as well as the fears – that assure it have not always been present in the past and will be, or can be, presumed to change in the future. The actual configuration of capitalist equilibrium is not given by nature as a sort of 'centre of gravitation', neither is it a logical truth, a sort of theorem of economic science. Both Marx and Keynes used reason up to their, and its, ultimate capacity and to the point of demonstrating the precariousness of actual condi-tions, reasoning out all of that part of their argument with calm (Calculemus!); practically all of the rest – all of the future – is left open. No policy can be founded or formulated completely, on the basis of theory. Not only is it true that the actual course of events is extremely complex and cannot be depicted by schematics or general principles (as *Akademia* and its *vested interests* would have it), but above all it is not true that all political problems can be reduced to problems of good administration, and as such to solution on the basis of simple calcula-tion.

Institutions are, by their nature, taken to constitute and impose themselves as parameters on civil society. Individual behaviour must conform to them and thus seeks to authorise and conserve adaptation, calculation, and conformity as political canon. The fallacies, the controversies, the conflicts and the contradictions are thus reduced to, and punished as, errors of calculation. Of necessity, and by construction, they must thus become manifest elsewhere, considered furtively and treated as heretical in order that they can be repressed by so-called moral reason, rather than linked to vested interests.

In fact, the rhetoric of institutions is convincing. It has to convince, at all costs, if institutions and existing norms are to be considered as given by nature and thus one of the many, among the principal, laws to which human nature must adapt itself at whatever cost. Marx and Keynes, and the other minor heretics (armed with even lesser capacity to be heard), were not convinced that the economic problem exists *per se*, as a simple and eternal question of adapting given means to given ends.

This is certainly a problem that everyone must resolve daily, but this does not make it a theoretically relevant problem. If things were so a best-selling economics textbook would make not only its author, but all of humanity, rich and happy. All things considered, the differences between Marx and Keynes are innumerable, but the point of departure is the same: you have to go to the British Museum, but you also have to come out. Soho and Bloomsbury are very close, parameters are not constants.

NOTE

1. These two descriptions of the world are found in the third section of the third book of Marx's *Capital* and in ch. 12 of J. M. Keynes's *The General Theory of Employment, Interest and Money*. Keynes's comments on Marx (referred to in sections 2 and 8) are to be found in vol XXIX of Keynes's *Collected Writings*; the apple metaphor is found in vol. XIV, the declaration of heresy in vol. XIII, and the verification of the end of *laissez-faire* (which dates from 1926) in vol. IX. Marx's assessments of Ricardo, and others, referred to in sections 2 and 3 appear in ch. 17 of *The Theories of Surplus Value*. Sections 3, 5, 6, and 7, quote from vol. II (especially the third section) and section 4 from vol. I of *Capital*. The citations for sections 9 to 13 are found in *The General Theory*, in particular (in order) in ch. 14, 18, 22, 24, and 18.

5 Ideology and Logic

JOAN ROBINSON with FRANK WILKINSON

I have always felt that it was a serious misfortune that religion came to the West in the form of an implausible piece of history for this created a clash between the requirements for the development of spiritual life and the requirements of intellectual honesty. At a lower level – the sphere of economic theory – there is a similar conflict between ideology and logic.

The main strands in current economic thought are neoclassical, Marxist and post-Keynesian. Keynes was brought up in the Marshallian tradition of neoclassical theory to which he remained broadly committed until the 1930s when the main problem was mass unemployment. Marxism was rejected by Keynes, who made no attempt to go into the logic of its theoretical framework, but when Kalecki arrived soon after the publication of the *General Theory* we found he had reached our theoretical position from an essentially Marxian starting point.

I MARXISM

When I first read *Das Kapital* I pointed out the logical error in the theory of the falling rate of profit but it is only recently that Marxists have begun seriously to discuss this point.[1] The tendency for the rate of profit on capital to fall as capitalism develops is evidently necessary for Marxist ideology, which represents capitalism as a system of exploitation that ends by destroying itself. The appeal of revolution is to hastening the decay of capitalism and preparing the workers to take over. The system is still unfair and oppressive but if real wages could rise under capitalism the appeal to revolution is much weakened.

73

*It was a generally accepted tenet in the orthodox economics of Marx's day that there is a long-run tendency for the rate of profit on capital to fall. Marx accepted this view and set himself to account for the phenomenon of falling profits. His explanation does not turn upon the difficulty of realising surplus value – that is, the phenomenon of a deficiency of effective demand – but is intended to be valid even when that problem does not arise.

He based his explanation upon the rising organic composition of capital. Capital accumulation and technical progress do not necessarily involve an increase in the value of capital per man employed. Inventions may, on balance, reduce capital cost per unit of output as much as labour cost, for they may improve the efficiency of labour in making machines as much as in working machines. This possibility Marx allows for. He shows how 'cheapening the elements of constant capital' offsets the tendency of the organic composition of capital to rise.[2] Technical progress may also reduce the period of turnover of capital goods. Chemical processes are speeded up and the development of transport economises the stocks which it is necessary to hold at each stage of production and of marketing. This tends to reduce capital per man employed. Nevertheless, Marx takes the view that there is on balance a strong tendency for capital per man to increase as time goes by, and this assumption is a natural one to make.

Marx's law of the falling tendency of profits, s, then consists simply in the tautology: when the rate of exploitation is constant, the rate of profit falls as capital per man increases. Assuming constant periods of turnover, so that physical capital plus real wages, $c + v$, measures the stock of capital: when s/v is constant and c/v is rising, $s/c + v$ is falling.

This proposition stands out in startling contradiction to the rest of Marx's argument. For if the rate of exploitation tends to be constant, real wages tend to rise as productivity increases. Labour receives a constant proportion of an increasing total. Marx can only demonstrate a falling tendency of profits by abandoning his argument that real wages tend to be constant. This drastic inconsistency he seems to have overlooked, for when he is discussing the falling tendency of profits he makes no reference to the rising tendency of real wages which it entails.

What happens to the rate of profit if real wages remain constant?

* This and some other passages in sections 1 and 2 are taken from my published works. As these points have never been answered there seemed no advantage in repeating them in other words.

With constant real wages, the rate of profit rises or falls, as capital per man increases, according as the ratio of the proportionate increase in product to the proportionate increase in the stock of capital exceeds or falls short of the ratio of profits to product. Suppose that the net product is 100 and that net profits and wages in the first instance are each equal to 50 so that the ratio of profit to product is $\frac{1}{2}$. Suppose that an increase of capital per man from 100 to 110 leads to an increase in net product from 100 to 108. Then wages remain equal to 50 and profits rise to 58. Thus a 10 per cent increase in the stock of capital leads to a 16 per cent increase in the total of profits, and the rate of profit on capital rises. If the product rose to only 105, when capital per man increased to 100, the rate of profit on capital would be constant. With any lower ratio of increment of additional product to increment of capital the rate of profit would fall.

An attempt might be made, on this basis, to rescue Marx from his inconsistency by arguing that, in a given state of knowledge, the marginal productivity of capital must be assumed to fall very sharply beyond a certain point. On that assumption, accumulation will lead sooner or later to a falling rate of profit, even when real wages are constant. But it is very unnatural to assume given knowledge in a dynamic system, and, certainly, that assumption is alien to Marx's method, for, in his scheme, an increase in the ratio of capital to labour can only occur as a result of what, in the academic scheme, would be regarded as a change in technical knowledge. If technology develops as capital accumulates, there need be no tendency to diminishing returns, and with constant returns there can be no tendency for the rate of profit to fall (always assuming that the problem of effective demand is ruled out). The most that we can say is that periods of falling profits may occur when capital per man increases very rapidly relatively to the rate of advance in technical knowledge. In Marx's view, however, technical knowledge is not an independent factor, and when accumulation is rapid a strong stimulus is applied to labour-saving invention.

Moreover, the whole apparatus of the theory of *value* is designed to exclude the notion of attributing productivity to capital, and allows no room for the neoclassical concept of the marginal productivity of a particular factor. A theory of falling profits based on the falling marginal productivity of capital would be something quite different from Marx's theory.

Marx's theory, as we have seen, rests on the assumption of a constant rate of exploitation. Certain causes which may lead to a rise in the rate of exploitation he treats as offsetting tendencies. Hours of work may be lengthened (with a constant daily wage) and the intensity of work may be increased, for instance by speeding up machines. Real wages may be reduced or an increasing amount of labour may be employed in direct services, where both capital per man and real wages are abnormally low. To these tendencies, which all help to raise the rate of exploitation, there are obvious limits, and Marx argues that they cannot be sufficiently strong to offset the falling tendency of the rate of profit. This may be readily admitted. But the rise in the rate of exploitation which comes about through a rise in productivity, with constant hours and intensity of work, and constant real wages, is not limited in the same way. Productivity may rise without limit, and, if real wages are constant, the rate of exploitation rises with it. Marx appears to have been in some confusion upon this point, for when he begins to discuss the effect of a rise in productivity on the rate of exploitation, he switches over in the middle of the argument to discussing the effect of changing the length of the working day.

> To the extent that the development of the productive power reduces the paid portion of the employed labour, it raises the surplus-value by raising its rate; but to the extent that it reduces the total mass of labour employed by a certain capital, it reduces the factor of numbers with which the rate of surplus-value is multiplied in order to calculate its mass. Two labourers, each working 12 hours daily, cannot produce the same mass of surplus-value as 24 labourers each working only 2 hours, even if they could live on air and did not have to work for themselves at all. In this respect, then the compensation of the reduction in the number of labourers by means of an intensification of exploitation has certain impassable limits. It may, for this reason, check the fall of the rate of profit, but cannot prevent it entirely. (*Das Kapital*, vol. III, p. 290 (85))

The trouble probably arose, like most of the obscurities in Marx's argument, from his method of reckoning in terms of *value*. With given labour-time, of given intensity, the rate of *value* created is constant. Thus $v + s$ is constant. It might seem, at the first glance, that s/v can rise only if wages fall. But this is an illusion. An increase in productivity reduces the *value* of commodities, and the *value* of labour-power, with constant real wages. Thus v falls towards zero, and s/v rises towards infinity, and all the time real wages are constant. Alternatively, it might be argued that Marx was unconsciously assuming that increasing productivity does not affect the wage-good industries, so that constant real wages are compatible with a constant rate of exploitation. But, however we interpret it, Marx's argument fails to establish a presumption that the rate of profit tends to fall, when the problem of effective demand is left out of account.

It may seem idle to object to Marx's argument, based on a constant rate of exploitation, while at the same time maintaining that the assumption of constant real wages is unrealistic. If the rate of exploitation were in fact constant, and if Marx was right in supposing that technical progress tends to require an increase in capital per man, it might appear that his formula – when s/v is constant and c/v rising, $s/c + v$ is falling – would after all embody an important truth. But the appearance is deceptive. For c/v does not depend solely upon technical conditions, but also upon employment per unit of capital equipment. It may be true that capital per unit of capacity is highly variable. And it varies, not only between boom and slump, but also over the long run. There are always booms and slumps, but in some periods slumps are deeper and longer than in others, so that the average utilisation of capital, good years and bad, tends to be less in some periods than in others. And, with given equipment, the lower is utilisation, the greater is c/v. Thus Marx's formula merely shows that, given s/v, profits tend to rise or fall with the state of trade. There needs no ghost come from the grave to tell us this.

In short it seems that Marx started off on a false scent when he supposed that it was possible to find a theory of profits without taking account of the problem of effective demand, and that his explanation of the falling tendency of profits explains nothing at all.

Unfortunately, the behaviour of the rate of profit in reality is strongly influenced by the state of effective demand so that it is impossible to frame an hypothesis of how it would behave in the absence of such influence, so as to submit the theory to historical tests.

II THE NEO-CLASSICALS

Ricardo maintained that 'The principal problem of Political Economy' was to determine the laws that regulate distribution.

> The produce of the earth – all that is derived from its surface by the united application of labour, machinery, and capital, is divided among three classes of the community; namely, the proprietor of the land, the owner of the stock or capital necessary for its cultivation, and the labourer by whose industry it is cultivated.[3]

Ricardo was particularly concerned with distribution between profits and rent, but he also provided a theory of the relation of profits to wages. Capitalists are necessary to organise production. They are able to do so because there are men available to work who have no property and cannot live unless a capitalist is willing to advance them wages ahead of selling the product of their work.

Profit, in Ricardo's scheme, is the difference between the value of the product of a team of men, net of rent and of replacement of physical inputs, and the value of the wage that they receive.

Marx turned Ricardo's theory of profits into the theory of exploitation. Labour produces *value* and the capitalist takes a large part of it.

The neoclassical theory that came into fashion after about 1870 was, consciously or unconsciously, a reaction against Marx.

It consisted mainly of dodging the question of distribution and concentrating on the analysis of the relative prices of commodities. In this sphere, the academics were able to score some points and perhaps it was foolish of the Marxists to allow themselves to be drawn into an argument about this relatively trivial question instead of taking the position that prices of particular commodities are not important – what matters is the overall rate of exploitation in the economy as a whole.

Now that we have the benefit of Piero Sraffa's interpretation of Ricardo, we can state the whole analysis quite simply.

As a first approximation, assume both that there is a uniform rate of profit on capital throughout the economy and that the value of capital per man is the same in all lines of production. Then prices are proportional to the labour time required to produce the various commodities. We can read Volume I of Marx taking this approximation to have been made. (For Marx it may have had some deeper meaning, but there is no point at this time of day stopping to argue about it.)

The second approximation is a uniform rate of profit with different capital to labour ratios in different industries. 'Prices of production' then obtain. This is the point that Piero Sraffa has cleared up.

A third approximation would be to allow for a hierarchy of different rates of profit connected with the different levels of monopoly power amongst large and small firms. Even this, of course, is far too simple for the actual hurly-burly in which actual prices are formed but it provides a starting point for the study of reality.

All this, however, is a development from Ricardo's theory of the prices of goods produced with the aid of produced means of production – equipment and stocks produced by labour with the aid of equipment and stocks.

The neoclassical theory had a completely different basis. It purports to derive a system of prices from the relative scarcity of commodities in relation to the demand for them.

The Walrasian conception of equilibrium arrived at by higgling and haggling in a market illuminates the account of prisoners of war swapping the contents of their Red Cross parcels.

It makes sense also, with some modification, in an economy of artisans and small traders. This was the kind of world that Adam Smith evidently had in mind when he said that we do not depend on the benevolence of the butcher, the baker, and the brewer to get us a dinner. (He did not mention this in connection with his pin factory.)

Two essential characteristics of industrial capitalism are absent in these economic systems – the distinction between income from work and income from property and the nature of investments made in the light of uncertain expectations about a long future.

The textbook system attempts to get rid of time by supposing that all decisions about the whole future can be made today. This rules out any realistic discussion of capitalist behaviour. Moreover it fails to deal with the distinction between wages and profits. Everyone is to receive 'rentals' for the 'factors of production' with which they are endowed and 'factors', as for Walras, consist of such things as particular types of machines and labour trained in particular skills.

Now, an owner on day one of a machine, say for making buttons, can envisage himself retaining funds from its gross rental to invest in a machine for making sausages, if that is going to offer a higher yield. A capitalist is not interested in buttons or sausages *per se* but in the profit he can get from them. He is interested in the return he can get on the value of his investment; there must be a tendency to equalise the rate of profit on the value of means of production in different lines. The value of investment is influenced by the wages paid to workers operating machines for buttons or sausages. Thus the level of the rate of profit is related to the level of wages.

This system operates only in terms of a rate of interest derived from subjective discount of the future in the minds of consumers. This is just a *jeu d'esprit*, but in real life the principle of prices influenced by scarcity relatively to demand is of great importance, particularly for commodities of which supply depends mainly on natural resources. The neoclassicals had a right to point out that it was not given sufficient weight by Ricardo or Marx.

Marshall tried to combine neoclassical supply and demand theory for the short run with a classical theory of the rate of profit for the long run. There are many valuable ideas in Marshall but it must be admitted that they are in a terrible muddle. The modern textbook theory is mainly derived from Walras. It concentrates on the analysis of equilibrium and does not have any coherent theory of the distribution of the product of industry between wages and profits.

However, it is impossible to set up a theory that entirely neglects the question of distribution. The modern theory mixes two other strands of neoclassical thought with Walras.

One of these was concerned to provide an explanation of rentier income from interest and dividends. The rentier was said to provide the service of abstinence which provided capital to industry. (Income from property in land was put under a different heading.) Marshall thought it more tactful to call owning property *waiting* rather than abstinence, but in the first account of the matter that he gave he was sufficiently candid to say that it means nothing more than owning wealth.

> ... That surplus benefit which a person gets in the long run by postponing enjoyment, and which is measured by the rate of interest (subject as we have seen to certain conditions) is the reward of waiting. He may have obtained the *de facto* possession of property by inheritance or by any other means, moral or immoral, legal or illegal. But if, having the power to consume that property in immediate gratifications, he chooses to put it in such a form as to afford him deferred gratifications, then any superiority there may be in deferred gratifications over those immediate ones is the reward of his waiting. When he lends out the wealth on a secure loan the net payment which he receives for the use of the wealth may be regarded as affording a numerical measure of that reward ...[4]

Later, Marshall evidently realised that he was giving too much away. In later editions of the *Principles* a passage similar to the above is linked to the justification of interest because 'few people would save much without reward'.

Now, to treat interest as the reward of saving is a confusion. The dimensions are wrong. The wealth on which a rentier receives interest (if he chooses to lend it) is a stock in existence today; saving is a rate per unit of time at which he is adding to the stock. Is he supposed to get interest on the saving he is doing this week, or this year or this minute?

Obviously, the reward of saving is owning some more wealth. One of the advantages, though by no means the only one, of owning wealth is the possibility of getting interest on it.

But why is it possible to get interest? Because businesses make profits and are willing to borrow.

The confusion between profits and interest ought to have been cleared up once and for all when Keynes pointed out that profit is what a businessman hopes to get on an investment and interest is what he has to promise to pay for finance. But the confusion is still to be found in the modern textbooks.

The most prevalent textbook theory in the pre-Keynesian era was based on the vulgarised American version of neo-classical thought that was put out by J. B. Clark. On this view: 'What a social class gets is, under natural law, what it contributes to the general output of industry.' The owners of wealth provide a factor of production called 'capital' which is embodied in 'capital goods' – equipment and stocks. A single quantity of 'capital' can be extracted from one set of machines and embodied in another, receiving as its reward the profit determined by the 'marginal productivity' 'of capital' to the economy as a whole.

Thorstein Veblen, reviewing a book by J. B. Clark, immediately pointed out the fallacy:

... Here, as elsewhere in Mr. Clark's writings, much is made of the doctrine that the two facts of 'capital' and 'capital goods' are conceptually distinct, though substantially identical. The two terms cover virtually the same facts as would be covered by the terms 'pecuniary capital' and 'industrial equipment' ...

... This conception of capital, as a physically 'abiding entity' constituted by the succession of productive goods that make up the industrial equipment, breaks down in Mr. Clark's own use of it when he comes to speak of the mobility of capital; that is to say, so soon as he makes use of it ...

... The continuum in which the 'abiding entity' of capital resides is a continuity of ownership, not a physical fact. The continuity, in fact, is of an immaterial nature, a matter of legal rights, of contract, of purchase and sale. Just why this patent state of the case is overlooked, as it somewhat elaborately is, is not easily seen. But it is ... plain that, if the concept of capital were elaborated from observation of current business practice, it would be found that 'capital' is a pecuniary fact, not a mechanical one; that it is an outcome of a valuation, depending immediately on the state of mind of the valuers; and that the specific marks of capital, by which it is distinguishable from other facts, are of an immaterial character ...

After the Keynesian revolution, Professor Samuelson (ignoring Veblen) took up J. B. Clark's interpretation of capital and this became the orthodox neo-neoclassical view.

In 1953 I tried to find out what it meant. I was reinforced by the publication of Piero Sraffa's *Production of Commodities by Means of Commodities* in 1960. Does a quantity of capital mean a number of dollars or a list of machine tools, railway lines and other hard objects? And which is it that has a 'marginal product'?

The only answer we got was: let us pretend that it does not make any difference.

However, the theory of profits based on the productivity of capital is still taught all over the world. What does 'the productivity of capital' mean? No one could deny that modern industry, for better or worse, causes output to grow as never before. Capitalist accumulation, as Marx said, ripens the productive power of social labour as though in a hot house.

Joseph Schumpeter took over his analysis from Marx and put it into a different ideological setting.[5] Instead of explaining profits by exploitation, Schumpeter gives the credit to the heroic entrepreneur who takes the risks of investment in the 'gale of creative destruction' that competitive technical progress brings about. But entrepreneurs, that is, businessmen, do not make technical progress. They use what comes to them from the general development of science and engineering. They, in turn, foster development, so that investment generates knowledge and knowledge generates investment in an ever-widening spiral.

J. B. Clark pictures an isolated primitive man, who 'makes by his own labour all the goods that he uses' and maintains that 'the inherent productive power of labour and capital is of vital concern to him'.

Veblen points out that the productive power of the primitive hunter does not reside in his bow and arrows.

... The loss of these objects – tangible assets – would entail a transient inconvenience. But the accumulated, habitual knowledge of the ways and means involved in the production and use of these appliances is the outcome of long experience and experimentation, and given this body of commonplace technological information, the acquisition and employment of the suitable apparatus is easily arranged . . .

As technology develops, the means of production which it requires grow more and more elaborate.

. . . Through 'difficulty of attainment' in adequate quantities, the apparatus and its ownership become a matter of consequence; increasingly so, until presently the equipment required for an effective pursuit of industry comes to be greater than the common man can hope to acquire in a lifetime. The commonplace knowledge of ways and means, the accumulated experience of mankind, is still transmitted in and by the body of the community at large; but, for practical purposes, the advanced 'state of the industrial arts' has enabled the owners of goods to corner the wisdom of the ancients and the accumulated experience of the race . . .

Capitalism fostered the application of science to technology and grew into the all-embracing system we know today.

Schumpeter remarked that in the great bureaucratic organisation of a modern corporation, with its own laboratories, 'innovation itself has become a matter of routine'. There is no longer any need for the heroic entrepreneur. But still the corporations are cornering accumulated experience, as Veblen says, for their own ends.

They can still do so partly through 'ownership of goods', that is the power to command great sums of finance that can be embodied in large units of productive equipment. But much more important is their power to command the educational system. The engineers, accountants, designers and salesmen – all the numerous highly specialised experts that man what Galbraith calls the technostructure of large-scale business, are provided for the corporations by the educational system. They are paid salaries above the level of operative workers; they are taught to feel themselves superior and they attach their loyalty to their employers rather than to their class fellows.

The educational system in a modern economy (even in the USSR) is devoted to providing the required numbers both of experts for the technostructure and of operatives who are taught to think of themselves as too stupid to master technology, though they are allowed the necessary training required for productive work.

Today, the native workers in Europe are getting to feel superior in their turn, and 'guests' are called in from the underdeveloped world to do the low-class jobs. In all this the analysis is vague and unreasonable but the ideology is clear – it is the defence of *laissez-faire*.

III   THE QUANTITY THEORY OF MONEY

Before the Keynesian revolution there was no theory of the prices in terms of money of particular commodities, only a discussion of relative prices of commodities in terms of each other governed by supply and demand. Money prices were introduced by means of the quantity formula, $MV = PT$. This was perhaps the most vapid element in traditional teaching.[6] If we had a register of PT, the money value of all the transactions in a certain market area over a certain period, then if we knew what medium of exchange, M, was used we could discover V, the average number of times each item of M was used in a transaction in the period. There is not a sharp distinction between tokens that are used in transactions and reserves that are held in a liquid form for contingencies, for instance in bank accounts. It is being used in a transaction in the period in question which causes a particular token (a note, a coin, or a bank cheque) to become part of M. A higher MV is a symptom, not cause of a higher level of PT and it in no way helps to distinguish a rise in PT due to greater real activity from one due to a rise of prices. When inflation has set in, with prices of commodities and rates of pay rising from month to month, the amount of money used in transactions is rising correspondingly.

IV   KEYNES

In his heart Keynes was just as committed to 'freedom' as any neoclassic. When it came to drafting the last chapter of the *General Theory* he produced a version that was all on that side of the question. He sent it to me saying: 'I know this won't do. It is just how it welled up' (or words to that effect). He was too clear headed and too honest to allow ideological conviction to make a barrier to argument. The last chapter was redrafted to bring the theoretical analysis to bear on 'the outstanding faults of the economic society in which we live' which are 'its failure to provide for full employment and its arbitrary and inequitable distribution of wealth and incomes'. But in the published version, and indeed, in the *General Theory* as a whole, there remains an ambiguity about the operation of the system which, as we shall see turned out to be a serious weakness – it is often not clear whether the argument is to be applied to a 'closed system' – the capitalist world as a whole or to a single country trading with others.

Keynes worked at two levels – on high theory and comments on current affairs. When the *Treatise on Money* was being finally prepared for the press he produced (with Hubert Henderson) the pamphlet *Can Lloyd George Do it?* in support of Lloyd George's election manifesto – proposals to abolish unemployment by a programme of public works.

The argument is put forward in the form of estimates of the effects upon employment to be expected from various schemes of public expenditure.

Generally speaking, the indirect employment which schemes of capital expenditure would entail is far larger than the direct employment. This fact is one of the strongest arguments for pressing forward with such schemes; for it means that the greater part of the employment they would provide would be spread far and wide over the industries of the country. But the fact that the indirect employment would be spread far and wide does not mean that it is in the least doubtful or illusory . . .

. . . In addition to the indirect employment with which we have been dealing, a policy of development would promote employment in other ways. The fact that many workpeople who are now unemployed would be receiving wages instead of unemployment pay would mean an increase in effective purchasing power which would give a general stimulus to trade. Moreover, the greater trade activity would make for further trade activity; for the forces of prosperity, like those of trade depression, work with a cumulative effect. When trade is slack there is a tendency to postpone placing orders, a reluctance to lay in stocks, a general hesitation to go forward or take risks. When, on the other hand, the wheels of trade begin to move briskly the opposite set of forces comes into play, a mood favourable to enterprise and capital extensions spreads through the business community, and the expansion of trade gains accordingly a gathering momentum.

It is not possible to measure effects of this character with any sort of precision. . . . But, in our opinion, these effects are of immense importance. For this reason we believe that the effects on employment of a given capital expenditure would be far larger than the Liberal pamphlet assumes. These considerations have a bearing, it

should be observed on the time factor in Mr Lloyd George's pledge.
It is a mistake to suppose that a long interval would elapse after, let
us say, the work of road construction had been commenced before
the full effect on employment would be produced. In the economic
world, 'coming events cast their shadows before', and the knowledge
that large schemes of work were being undertaken would give an
immediate fillip to the whole trade and industry of the country.[7]

R. F. Kahn went off for his summer holiday with this in his rucksack
and took up the challenge to measure this effect. He came back with his
analysis of what became known as the *multiplier* – the argument that an
increase in expenditure on investment will, within a short time, push up
employment and income to the level where saving is increased to an
equal extent. One of the main 'leakages' which limits the extent of this
'secondary employment' is the increased expenditure on imports due
to the increase in home activity and income. This was accepted by
Keynes and has held firm ever since as the essential point of the
short-period theory of effective demand.

In the argument that followed, the emphasis was laid on the possibility of achieving and maintaining a 'high and stable level of employment' and not much attention was given to the deterioration in the
balance of payments which would result from one country pursuing the
policy in isolation.

In June 1944, when the end of the war was in sight, Keynes's
ambivalence about the possible contradictions between planning and
'freedom' was expressed in a letter concerning Hayek's book *The
Road to Serfdom*.

My dear Hayek,
  The voyage has given me the chance to read your book properly.
In my opinion it is a grand book. We all have the greatest reason to
be grateful to you for saying so well what needs so much to be said.
You will not expect me to accept quite all the economic dicta in it.
But morally and philosophically I find myself in agreement with
virtually the whole of it; and not only in agreement with it, but in a
deeply moved agreement.

But the letter goes on to argue the opposite side of the case.

Turning to a few special points, . . . The line of argument you yourself
take depends on the very doubtful assumption that planning is not

more efficient. Quite likely from the purely economic point of view it is efficient. That is why I say that it would be more in line with your general argument to point out that even if the extreme planners can claim their technique to be the more efficient, nevertheless technical advancement even in a less planned community is so considerable that we do not today require the superfluous sacrifice of liberties which they themselves would admit to have some value.

... I come finally to what is really my only serious criticism of the book. You admit here and there that it is a question of knowing where to draw the line. You agree that the line has to be drawn somewhere, and that the logical extreme is not possible. But you give us no guidance whatever as to where to draw it. In a sense this is shirking the practical issue. It is true that you and I would probably draw it in different places. I should guess that according to my ideas you greatly under-estimate the practicability of the middle course. But as soon as you admit that the extreme is not possible, and that a line has to be drawn, you are, on your own argument, done for, since you are trying to persuade us that so soon as one moves an inch in the planned direction you are necessarily launched on the slippery path which will lead you in due course over the precipice.

I should therefore conclude your theme rather differently. I should say that what we want is not no planning, or even less planning, indeed I should say that we almost certainly want more. But the planning should take place in a community in which as many people as possible, both leaders and followers, wholly share your own moral position. Moderate planning will be safe if those carrying it out are rightly orientated in their own minds and hearts to the moral issue. This is in fact already true of some of them. But the curse is that there is also an important section who could almost be said to want planning not in order to enjoy its fruits but because morally they hold ideas exactly the opposite of yours, and wish to serve not God but the devil ...

What we need therefore, in my opinion, is not a change in our economic programmes, which would only lead in practice to disillu- sion with the results of your philosophy; but perhaps even the contrary, namely, an enlargement of them. Your greatest danger ahead is the probable practical failure of the application of your philosophy in the U.S. in a fairly extreme form. No, what we need is the restoration of right moral thinking – a return to proper moral values in our social philosophy. If only you could turn your crusade in that direction you would not look or feel quite so much like Don

Quixote. I accuse you of perhaps confusing a little bit the moral and the material issues. Dangerous acts can be done safely in a community which thinks and feels rightly, which would be the way to hell if they were executed by those who think and feel wrongly.

Yours ever, KEYNES

Even amongst Keynesians ideological commitment lowered the level of self criticism. It was not until 1980 that Kaldor pointed out that the theory that the rate of interest is determined by liquidity preference and the supply of 'money' is both unconvincing and unnecessary.[8]

To begin with, any proposition about *the* rate of interest, as opposed to the general level and pattern of interest rates, is bound to be unrealistic and misleading. Only in textbook models is there a single rate of interest, uniform for all types of loans and all types of borrowers. Next, there is not a clear cut distinction between the stock of money in active circulation and that which is held as a store of wealth. Many middle-income salary earners keep part of their wealth in a deposit account at a bank, receiving low interest, which can readily be transferred to a current (checking) account when payments have to be made.

Keynes, of course, was perfectly well aware of all this, yet he enunciated the theory that *the* rate of interest 'is the "price" that equilibrates the desire to hold wealth in the form of cash with the available quantity of cash' (*General Theory*, p. 167).

As Kaldor points out, the banks are never 'fully loaned up'; they hold part of their funds in short-dated gilt-edged securities at a lower yield and are always ready to provide overdrafts to old, or what they judge reliable, clients at a more renumerative rate. The amount of cash in circulation regulates itself according to the demand for it.

Thus Keynes theory of demand and supply of liquidity is quite unconvincing. It is also unnecessary. Each national banking system has the power to regulate its level of interest rates, but each one has to take account of the level of the others.

I believe that near the end of his life Keynes had reconsidered several aspects of his theory, the theory of interest among them, but at an early stage he was convinced it was correct and important. When we were disputing about some point he wrote to me: 'You do not seem to realise that if you are right the whole theory of liquidity preference has to be thrown overboard.'[9] I had not the self-confidence to reply. So much the better.

It is a serious fault in the exposition of the *General Theory* that it is often not made clear whether a particular argument is to apply to a closed system (an isolated country or the capitalist world as a whole) or to one country in trading and financial relations with others.

This difficulty arises, as we have just seen, in connection with the analysis of interest rates. It is even more serious in relation to employment policy. As the British have found, to raise employment by stimulating home investment and consumption without an increase in exports adequate to match the consequent increase in imports leads to disaster. It is much to be regretted that when the development of sources of oil in Britain gave an unexpected strength to the balance of payments, the opportunity to make a successful employment policy was lost since Mrs Thatcher's government preferred to reduce employment in a vain attempt to cut inflation.

There was a Keynesian revolution in price theory just as important as the revolution in employment theory, though Keynes himself did not take much interest in it.

Keynes did not bother much about 'micro-theory' – the prices of particular commodities (though he started my career by recommending enthusiastically to Macmillans my *Imperfect Competition*) and his idea of 'user cost' did not take on.

Hypotheses about the formation of prices of particular commodities have to be found in terms of the type of market. In markets formed by dealers, who buy to sell again, supply and demand rules, from season to season and over longer swings. Here monopoly or oligopoly of buyers is a common form. The sellers have to accept the prices that they are offered and struggle in vain to increase their share.

The extraction of minerals requires more capital investment than either peasant or plantation production and may be regarded as intermediate between agricultural and industrial production. In none of these cases is there any reason to expect an equilibrium to be established. Changes in demand and in technology may be slow and continuous or abrupt, new sources of supply are discovered or old ones exhausted.

The most interesting case is that of 'administered prices' of manufactures. Here the hypothesis is that a distinction is drawn between prime or direct costs – wages, materials and power – and overhead costs. To find overhead cost per unit of output it is necessary to postulate a standard rate of output, say per annum, and to divide the total overheads by this rate so as to find the gross margin which will permit costs to be covered with some profit. When output and sales exceeds the standard rate, super-normal profits are accruing. Sales below the

standard rate may make it necessary to raise prices but this phenomenon is generally considered to be rare.

With this type of pricing there is not a clear cut distinction between
monopoly and competition. A group of firms producing a range of
similar goods may adopt the system of accepting a price leader so that
all react together to a change in unit prime costs. (The notion of
imperfect competition was a necessary step in liberation from orthodoxy but to say that the ratio of prices to prime costs is determined
by the degree of monopoly is not enlightening.) All this provides
merely a frame within which inquiries can be conducted; when they
are, many anomalies and curious relationships come to light.

There is an obvious sense in which the prices of commodities are
governed by their costs of production but there is also a sense in which
costs are determined by prices. At any moment in any market there is a
price ruling and a business which wants to increase its production must
look round for some line in which the cost can be tucked in underneath
the ruling price so as to yield a net profit.

The system of industrial pricing generates a chronic tendency to
inflation. Any rise in money–wage rates causes prices to rise, which
reduces real wages and sets up pressure for a further rise in
money–wage rates. An initial rise in prime costs may come from a rise
in the price of an essential input – as in the case of oil – or from a rise in
money–wage rates ahead of productivity so that the vicious spiral is
set going. To prevent money–wage rates from rising would mean a
progressive fall in real wages which cannot be accepted. The notion
that inflation is a monetary phenomena and that it can be prevented by
refusing to allow the quantity of money to increase is to mistake a
symptom for a cause. Mrs Thatcher's policy of attempting to cut
inflation by refusing to allow the quantity of money to increase is mere
idiocy: with bitter pain and strife it may be possible to slow down the
rise of money-wage rates but this is not of much use unless money-
costs are reduced relatively to demand so as to allow real consumption
to increase. By cutting expenditure and cutting down employment it
may be possible painfully to slow down the rise of money–wage rates
but there cannot be any satisfaction in limiting the rise in money
incomes by reducing real demand and real output. There is a known
remedy – a general treaty to limit the rise of wage rates – but once
bitterness and distrust have been generated this remedy cannot work.
Inflation is a political problem not a 'monetary' one.

In an important sense money wages are determined by costs – the
cost of living. Keynes recognised very clearly the role that the cost of

living played in underpinning money wages and the length that organised labour would go to defend their living standards. This realisation played a principal part in Keynes's opposition to the return to gold in 1924. Thus in the wake of the return to gold he wrote:

Our export industries are suffering because they are the *first* to be asked to accept the 10 per cent reduction. If *every one* was accepting a similar reduction at the same time, the cost of living would fall, so that the lower money wage would represent nearly the same real wage as before. But, in fact, there is no machinery for effecting a simultaneous reduction. Deliberately to raise the value of sterling money in England means, therefore, engaging in a struggle with each separate group in turn, with no prospect that the final result will be fair, and no guarantee that the stronger groups will not gain at the expense of the weaker.

The working classes cannot be expected to understand better than Cabinet Ministers, what is happening. Those who are attacked first are faced with a depression of their standard of life, because the cost of living will not fall until all the others have been successfully attacked too; and, therefore, they are justified in defending themselves. Nor can the classes which are first subjected to a reduction of money wages be guaranteed that this will be compensated later by a corresponding fall in the cost of living, and will not accrue to the benefit of some other class. Therefore they are bound to resist so long as they can; and it must be war, until those who are economically weakest are beaten to the ground . . .

Mr Churchill asked the Treasury Committee on the Currency to advise him on these matters. He declared in his Budget speech that their report "contains a reasoned marshalling of the arguments which have convinced His Majesty's Government". Their arguments – if their vague and jejune meditations can be called such – are there for anyone to read. What they ought to have said, but did not say, can be expressed as follows: –

Money wages, the cost of living, and the prices which we are asking for our exports have not adjusted themselves to the improvement in the exchange, which the expectation of your restoring the gold standard, in accordance with your repeated declarations, has already brought about. They are about 10 per cent too high. If therefore, you fix the exchange at this gold parity, you must either gamble on a rise in gold prices abroad, which will induce foreigners to pay a higher gold price for our exports, or you are committing yourself to an policy of forcing down money wages and the cost of living to the necessary extent.

We must warn you that this latter policy is not easy. It is certain to involve unemployment and industrial disputes. If, as some people think, real wages were already too high a year ago, that is all the worse, because the amount of the necessary wage reductions in terms of money will be all the greater.

The gamble on a rise in gold prices abroad may quite likely succeed. But it is by no means certain, and you must be prepared for the other contingency. If you think that the advantages of the gold standard are so significant and so urgent that you are prepared to risk great unpopularity and to take stern administrative action in order to secure them, the course of events will probably be as follows:

To begin with, there will be great depression in the export industries. This in itself will be helpful, since it will produce an atmosphere favourable to the reduction of wages. The cost of living will fall somewhat. This will be helpful too, because it will give you a good argument in favour of reducing wages. Nevertheless, the cost of living will not fall sufficiently, and consequently, the export industries will not be able to reduce their prices sufficiently until wages have fallen in the sheltered industries. Now wages will not fall in the sheltered industries merely because there is unemployment in the unsheltered industries, therefore you will have to see to it that there is unemployment in the sheltered industries also. The way to do this will be by credit restriction. By means of the restriction of credit by the Bank of England you can deliberately intensify unemployment to any required degree until wages *do* fall. When the process is complete the cost of living will have fallen too and we shall then be, with luck, just where we were before we started.

We ought to warn you, though perhaps this is going a little outside our proper sphere, that it will not be safe politically to admit that you are intensifying unemployment deliberately in order to reduce wages. Thus you will have to ascribe what is happening to every conceivable cause except the true one. We estimate that about two years may elapse before it will be safe for you to utter in public one single word of truth. By that time you will either be out of office or the adjustment, somehow or other, will have been carried through.[10]

In these discussions Keynes recognised that both the absolute and relative levels of pay posed problems. He saw that in general workers

would resist a reduction in their living standard and he broadly
supported their stand.[11] But he was also only too aware that in a system
typified by sectional bargaining it was impossible to secure the necessary reduction in money wages to offset the effect of an appreciating
pound without seriously reducing the real wages of at least some
sections.

In the *General Theory* Keynes somewhat modified his position
arguing that although workers would resist a '*relative* reduction in real
wage' (p. 14), resulting from an attempt to reduce their money wages,
workers in general would not resist a reduction in real pay resulting
from a rise in the price of wage goods. Now, whilst it is true that
workers do not put in a wage claim everytime the price of one item in
their basket of goods goes up, there is no doubt that the cost of living is
the most important single element in the *periodic* wage claim, and
Keynes came fully to recognise this. The tortuous argument about
wage movements in the *General Theory* were made necessary by the
retention of a Marshallian ideology of the working of the labour
market reflected in the adherence to the downward sloping demand
curve for labour based on diminishing marginal productivity. This
meant that a move to full employment was only possible if real wages
could be brought down and Keynes was out to show that this was
possible without undue difficulty. However the more realistic assumption that productivity remains constant and probably increases with
the level of activity removes the need for the apparently contradictory
views that whilst groups of workers will resist a reduction in their
relative real wage, all workers taken together will acquiesce in general
to reductions in their living standard.

In his work on wages subsequent to the *General Theory* Keynes
emphasised the inflationary consequences of any general attempts to
reduce living standards. In 'How to Pay for the War' it was the lag in
the response of workers to price increases, rather than their failure to
respond, which restrained inflation. Moreover in his advice during the
Second World War he continually warned against the inflationary
threat of attempts to reduce living standards, even gradual reductions,
and in his advice to the Treasury during the war he showed a deep
understanding of the issues:

It is, I find, more usual in the memoranda which are in circulation to
argue that the proper price for the stabilisation of the cost of living is
an undertaking by the trade unions to stabilise wages. Certainly this
would be desirable in itself. But the arguments of those who think

that such a demand would be impolitic, are convincing. Mr Leggett of the Ministry of Labour has put it in conversation that the *possibility* of a rise in wages is an essential safety valve. If the trade union leaders now in authority were to agree to divest themselves of the power to demand higher wages, an agitation would arise to replace them by others not thus restricted. There can be no justification in wartime for a *general* rise in wages, except a rise in the cost of living. But this may not be true of every particular industry. It is difficult to draw the line between wage adjustments and wage increases. Anyway the freedom of the wage bargain is the Ark of the Convenant for the trade union movement, which it is not wise to call in question except for grave and unavoidable cause. My advice to the Chancellor of the Exchequer is, therefore, to stabilise the cost of living without asking for the stabilisation of wages, but to insist that it should be paid for by higher direct taxes.

The policy would be, so to speak, to put the trade unions and the Ministry of Labour 'on their honour'. Experience so far does not suggest that this would be imprudent or surely doomed to disappointment. It is sometimes said that the Treasury has not been rewarded for the existing food subsidy. But the claim of the Ministry of Labour to the contrary can be, I think, largely substantiated. I share Sir Horace Wilson's 'impression that, so far, the wage situation is less unfavourable than we at one time feared'.

and later

It is suggested in some quarters that a very gradual rise in the cost of living index would be comparatively harmless in its effect on wages. I distrust this view. A gradually rising tendency will create the wrong atmosphere. And no one can predict at what point a general movement to raise wages will break loose. I believe it would be better to adopt the contrary policy, fully offsetting rises in some directions by declines in others, even to the point of a slight reduction in the cost of living index when the new policy is introduced.[12]

Keynes's emphasis was on the historical development of trade unions and collective bargaining and the impact of this on the possibilities of the rapid adjustment. 'The old principle of *laissez-faire* was to ignore these strains and to assume that capital and labour were fluid. ... Fifty years ago this may have been a closer approximation to the truth than it is now.'[13] The main thrust of the incorporation of Keynes's work in orthodox theory has been to ignore this aspect of his work, and in particular, with respect to wages, to regard the Keynesian approach as a special case of downward rigidity of real wages. What Keynes said was that because of the historical development of trade union organisation, the reduction of real wages was impracticable and so the theories resting on that belief were redundant. The time which has elapsed since Keynes's work on wages has done nothing to shake his position. However the almost continuous inflationary pressure since the 1940s has done much to shape the historical evolution of trade unions and wage bargaining:

> Most labour market groups have well-defined aspirations founded on strong notions of an appropriate pattern of life which changes as real living standards adapt to economic growth. These are generally respected by employers and indeed are often encouraged by them. The degree to which the economic system is capable of fulfilling these aspirations in practice influences labour relations, the development of trade unions and the pattern of wage fixing.
>
> Periods of sustained wage inflation are caused by worsening inconsistency between workers' aspirations and the level of real wages which they actually receive. In Britain such circumstances have always led to a strengthening of formal bargaining through trade unions. Thus in the century from 1851 to 1951 there were two periods of rapid inflation – the first from about 1895 to 1920 and the second from 1933 to 1951. In both periods there was a substantial growth of trade union membership amongst blue-collar workers and growth of national collective bargaining covering large parts of the economy.[14] By contrast non-inflationary periods were marked by constant or declining trade union membership and less change in the pattern of bargaining. Much the same has been true since 1951. During the 1950s when real wages increased steadily the rate of increase in money wages slowed down and trade unions were quiescent. In the 1960s when real wages grew more slowly the rate of inflation began to rise, trade union membership increased (particularly amongst women and white-collar workers), and in many industries national wage bargaining began to be replaced by plant and company bargaining. In the public sector where national bargaining continued to prevail there was a sharply increased incidence of industrial disputes.
>
> This historical record leaves little doubt that, while trade unions can cause inflation, inflation can also cause changes in trade union

membership and organisation. A fall, or slowdown, in growth of real wages tends to increase money wage claims by the well-organised. This need not accelerate inflation if the real wages of less well-organised groups are reduced to compensate. But any squeeze on living standards of less-organised groups tends to induce a strengthening of their organisation. As inflation continues, organised wage bargaining spreads and the interval between negotiations shortens.

The development of collective bargaining in Britain can therefore be seen as an evolution of increasingly comprehensive wage indexation which has advanced more rapidly whenever real wages have been squeezed. Government attempts to curb this process by introducing incomes policies have ultimately been counter-productive because they have depressed the real wages of many groups, especially in the public sector, provoking a militant response which has caused increased inflation as incomes policies have broken down.[15]

The background to this history of wage indexation and extension of trade union organisation is the underlying pattern of labour market organisation described earlier. Workers and employers have generally cooperated in formalising this pattern of organisation and extending the role of trade unions within formal bargaining machinery. The possibility of dramatically reducing this power of organised labour by political and legal means seems unlikely. Since the legitimisation of trade union activity in the 1870s periodic attempts have been made both by the courts and by parliament to reduce the degree of protection afforded to organised labour. Such legislative action, was however, subsequently reversed by parliaments more sympathetic to the aspirations of working people.[16] Governments in the past have played a central role in establishing improved conditions of employment and in setting the legal framework for effective bargaining by trade unions. The evolution of the British system of collective bargaining has been both an industrial and a political process. Working people have influenced the outcome of the collective bargaining process both directly through changing their industrial organisation and indirectly by giving electoral support to political parties. Thus the evolution of the British system of collective bargaining and its forms of representative government are closely related. The fundamental question at stake in any proposals for change is why labour markets are organised on the basis of largely non-competing groups with well-defined aspirations and how this type of organisation has evolved and is maintained.[17]

To an important degree therefore the strong historical trend in both wage and price formation has been towards institutionalisation. In both cases the tendency has been to 'mark-up' on the basis of costs – costs of production in the case of prices and cost of living in the case of wages. But because wages are a cost of production and price increases which increase cost of living are determined by cost of production, the interaction of institutionally determined wages and institutionally determined prices is chronically inflationary. The inflationary process is therefore essentially about the distribution of income. There are, on the other hand, prices which are not a part of this process and vary more with fluctuation in supply and demand. These include food and raw materials. Such prices influence the institutionalised wages and prices because they are inputs into that sector. A sharp rise in raw material prices increases institutional prices and the price increase then becomes fully incorporated into the price and wage levels in the institutionalised sector. On the other hand reduction in prices from the unorganised sector may have the effect of easing price increases where they are organised. However, recent political and economic developments have tended to reduce this overall degree of price flexibility by extending radically the sectors in which prices are institutionally determined. OPEC which largely determines the price of energy in the world has the policy of fixing its prices to keep them in line with the price of manufactured goods – which are largely cost determined. Moreover the entry of Britain into the EEC in 1971 has broken the link between the world and British prices for food which persisted since the repeal of the Corn Laws in the 1840s. Thus the prices for their output is now fixed by a bargaining process in which the cost of agricultural production and the cost of living for farmers play the major part.

As the proportion of economic agents whose incomes are determined on a cost-plus basis becomes larger so the recycling of inflation becomes more complete. Further the more complete the automatic recycling of inflation the less relevant becomes the 'market' solution. As inflation is essentially negotiated between groups so must be the end to inflation.

At the end of his life Keynes was very unhappy at the prospect of inflation through wage bargaining and he had no remedy. He foresaw that, with continuous high employment, irresistible wage demands would run ahead of growing productivity. Economic science has produced no solution to Keynes's dilemma. It has ignored the emphasis Keynes and Keynesians have placed on the historical trend towards cost-plus price and wage determination. Within orthodox thought Keynes's system has been relegated to a special case of wage and price inflexibility and Keynesian policies have been increasingly regarded as additional interferences with the 'invisible hand'. By advocating the adjustment of the money supply as the answer to inflation and by offering 'market' solutions to unemployment, the economics profession has progressively abandoned logic for ideology and set us back precisely where we started.

NOTES

1. See, for example, J. E. Roemer, *Cambridge Journal of Economics*, vol. 3, no. 4, December 1979.
2. Engels makes these points in a chapter which he supplied to fill a gap in the manuscript for vol. III (chap. 4, 'The Effect of the Turnover on the Rate of Profit').
3. Piero Sraffa (ed.), *Works and Correspondence of David Ricardo*, vol. 1, p. 5.
4. *Principles of Economics*, 1st edn (1890) p. 614.
5. Joseph A. Schumpeter, *Capitalism, Socialism and Democracy*, (London, Allen & Unwin, 1943).
6. In the USA the quantity equation is written $MV = PQ$ where Q is real income. This is not vapid, but untrue.
7. Keynes, vol. IX, pp. 106–7.
8. Professor Lord Kaldor, *Origins of New Monetarism* (University College Cardiff, 1981).
9. Keynes, vol. XIV, p. 146.
10. Keynes, vol. IX, 211–15.
11. Keynes, vol. XIX, 444.
12. Keynes, vol. XXII, 227–8 and 223.
13. Keynes, vol. XIX, p. 228.
14. For an analysis of development up to 1920 see Tarling and Wilkinson, 'The movement of real wages and the development of collective bargaining in the period 1855 to 1920' in *Contributions to Political Economy*, supplement to the *Cambridge Journal of Economics*, 1982.
15. See Tarling and Wilkinson, 'The Social Contract: Post-War Incomes Policies and Their Inflationary Impact', *Cambridge Journal of Economics*, 1977.
16. Thus the legal immunity afforded to trade unions by the 1906 Trade Disputes Act resulted from a landslide victory of the Liberal Party resulting directly from anti-trade union activity of the courts culminating in the Taff Vale judgement. Moreover Labour Governments of 1945–51, 1964–70 and 1974–79 took legislative action both to restore rights eroded by legal or statutory changes and further to improve the position of labour.
17. Roger Tarling and Frank Wilkinson, *Inflation and Unemployment – A critique of Meade's Solution*, CEPR, vol. 8, no. 1, April 1982.

6 J. M. Keynes: Society and the Economist*

JOSEF STEINDL

I THE PARADIGM

What was it that Keynes stood on its head in economics? Perhaps an idea of it can be conveyed in simple words. The analogy between the individual household and society as a whole which many economists as well as laymen use in their reasoning is misleading. Conclusions drawn from this analogy, Keynes showed, are false. Thus for the individual household saving (spending less than one's income) leads to an accumulation of assets. For society as a whole when people spend less they reduce each other's income and the wealth of society is reduced. That for the economy as a whole the relations are different, that spending determines income and not the other way round, is not immediately accessible to common sense which bases itself on the day by day experience of the household. The truth of the matter is revealed only by studying the circular relations in a society (spending – income – spending). This shows that there are feedbacks which for the individual household or firm are unimportant because of its small scope but which for a large unit, such as for example the public sector, will be very important. In economics as in other fields the scope of reasoning is enlarged beyond the field of everyday experience and intuition and produces results in flat contradiction with it.

The instrument for analysing the circular relations in an economy are the national accounts. They are a double entry book-keeping for the society, whole groups like households, business or government

* Acknowledgements are made to Dr Alois Guger and Dr Ewald Walterskirchen of the Austrian Institute of Economic Research for helpful comments and discussions.

being represented by separate accounts, as are also activities like investment, consumption and so on. The systematic development of national accounting received its great impetus from Keynes and his theory. The style of theorising which made use of the concepts of national accounting became widespread only through Keynes although it was known to Quesnay and Marx. Known as macroeconomics it became crucial for the discussion of economic policy problems. It offers a convenient way between the sterility of the Walrasian general equilibrium and the limited scope of the partial analysis of Marshall, because it is couched in terms of variables which are statistically measurable and at the same time relevant for national economic policy.

A special case of circular interrelations in the economy concerns wages. Here it is the analogy between the firm and the economy as a whole which gives rise to the usual faulty reasoning: for a single firm, if it could pay a lower wage rate, the advantage were obvious and would probably lead to an expansion of output. But how different are the relations in the economy as a whole! The general level of prices is strongly influenced by costs and in a closed economy with no foreign trade costs consists mainly of wages. A general increase or decrease in wages will therefore, on simple assumptions, be passed on to prices. Thus, Keynes concludes, workers and trade unions in a closed system will not be in a position to determine the general level of real wages. This shows the lack of realism of the neoclassical view that workers could always bring about full employment if they are prepared to reduce the level of real wages sufficiently.

For Keynes the volume of employment is determined not by real wages but by demand for goods. The variability of production in the cycle is evident and the bottleneck which limits production is most of the time demand.

Let us turn to another characteristic of Keynes's thinking. For him the only real economic constraints which limit our policy options are scarcities of real resources – of labour, skills, machines, factories, land, raw materials, exhaustible resources. If we cannot make use of them this must be due to institutions, superstition or to our own stupidity. We should be wary therefore of the argument 'There is no money for it' and always ask whether there is any real scarcity involved or not. This naturally leads to a critical attitude towards institutions, especially financial ones. Institutions, this is definitely Keynes's view, have to be such as to make possible the full use of the available real resources.

They will not do so automatically or on the basis of very simple precepts such as proposed by Hayek (neutral money) or the monetarists. Keynes therefore had no respect for the tenets of financial orthodoxy – the gold standard, balanced budgets, sound finance – in so far as they merely hindered a rational use of available material resources.

Reference has been made above to the circulation of flows in the economy (transformation of cost into income, income into spending, spending into cost again). This stream is not kept moving by itself, it is always in danger of draining away into leakages constituted by savings. The driving force which replenishes the stream and keeps it moving is investment in plant, equipment etc. The central role of investment as the prime force of accumulation is one of the most distinctive characteristics of the Keynesian view of the economy. The strategic position of investment is due to the length of life of equipment and structures and to the uncertainty of the return. Investment thus depends on expectations which in the last resort can not be fully justified by calculation because of basic uncertainties, so that ultimately investment is based on a kind of optimism ('animal spirits'). Investment, unstable by itself, is rendered even more unstable by the apparatus of finance which is interposed between the saver and the investor. The speculative element in investment is reinforced by the speculative character of the markets for financial instruments, claims of all kinds based on debt. Instability is therefore a basic feature of the system.[1]

Every theory rests on simplification. A characteristic simplification of Keynes is the closed system. It is easy to see why: the circularity of the relations is evident only in the closed system, while in the open system it is interrupted.

But there is also a moral behind it. In a closed system the conflicts of interest between different countries are eliminated, one nation cannot gain at the expense of another. One is therefore thrown back on devices other than sponging, robbing and stealing. The closed system represented the world as a whole.

There is no denying that Keynesian policies meet their greatest difficulty at the point where the system is open, in the balance of payments. There are two ways of confronting these difficulties: the one is to close the country more or less by suitable protectionist measures. The other is to unite all countries in a common international order which will safeguard their interests by the establishment of suitable rules.

II AMNESIA

Conventional wisdom tells us that short of a real cataclysm the technical achievements of a society cannot be lost again. Yet most economists seem to have completely forgotten what Keynes as well as the experience of several decades taught them about full employment. They talk in terms of the treasury view of 1930 ('crowding out'), of budget deficits creating high interest rates, of increasing employment by lowering wages internationally. It is a collective cultural amnesia. Only the system of national accounts remains standing as a lasting monument of the era, difficult to destroy because it was so elaborately built over the whole world.

III THE IMPACT ON HISTORY

A technique that has been forgotten? But was it ever tried? It may be – and it has been[2] – argued not quite unconvincingly that the high employment experienced in the decades after the war has materialised largely without the active help of government policies consciously based on Keynesian economics; and that on the first occasion these policies were really badly needed worldwide – in 1974–75 – they were not applied.

It is true that the high level of post-war employment was partly due to fortuitous circumstances which might perhaps have produced it even had Keynes never existed, namely

(a) The re-armament in the US and Europe following the outbreak of the Korean war in 1950.
(b) The spin-off from war time and post-war military developments leading to or facilitating the introduction of new products which required large investments.
(c) The massive transfer to Europe of old technology from the US to which the Continent had practically had no access in the interwar period and during the war: this was facilitated by the Marshall plan and it led to considerable investment activity.
(d) The international economic cooperation which was the corollary of the military alliance of the West and which removed the balance of payment constraints standing in the way of expansion.

The same kind of skeptical view is also suggested by the fact that Schacht and the economic administration of Nazi Germany quite successfully applied full employment policies when the *General Theory* had not yet been published. Yet all this will not suffice to settle the issue.

IV KNOWLEDGE AND HISTORY

The question is whether employment techniques and theories are similar to technological knowledge. That this played a role in history can hardly be in doubt although it is a tricky task to describe it.

When we consider the relation of knowledge and material development of history we must free ourselves of primitive ideas of unilateral causation. We may get some help from the concept of feed-back and perhaps also from the view that an idea plays a role in history only when 'the time is ripe for it'. What would this mean? Presumably it means that the idea or knowledge must combine with other events or developments in order to become relevant ('it must fall on fertile ground'). We must also remind ourselves that the idea itself arises from a certain historical background which is fairly obvious in the case of the Keynesian ideas. Thus the idea (consciousness) exists between a flow of history which produces it and another flow of history which receives it as seed.

The economics of Keynes whether he wanted it or not in the course of time has become successively associated with one or another of the great streams of events and policies of our time.

In the first place it became associated with the finance of the war in Britain. It was in this context that the system of national accounts was developed by E. Rothbarth, J. E. Meade and R. N. Stone. Keynes and his friends intended to use this in order to overcome the inhibitions of the orthodox bankers and treasury officials against war finance by borrowing: The accounts would show them how the deficits were duly covered by a corresponding amount of saving.

The association of Keynesianism and war finance did not stop there. It was relevant to the post-war rearmament in so far as it removed the scruples of orthodox finance and instead pointed to the benefits obtained in increased employment, prosperity and industrial profits. It may be controversial how far these considerations contributed to armament, but it seems plausible that the military–industrial complex in the United States was somehow wedded to a Keynesian ideology.[3]

A different and hardly controversial association is the welfare state. This ideology arose as a reaction against the horrors of the war and a sign of newly awakened social consciousness in the élite of a society which had been rather impervious to the suffering of the victims of the pre-war depression and which felt darkly how much this had contributed to the war. It represented also a re-assertion of the newly gained political consciousness of the workers.

In Britain it found its first expression in Sir William Beveridge's work on social security and his 'Full Employment in a Free Society' as well as a series of government papers.

The welfare state in the course of time was realised in all industrial countries. It involves a large increase in the public sector and a good deal of built-in stabilisation: This means that a large part of any additional spending comes back in increased revenue and that tends to stabilise the economy.

Another ideological stream which recruited Keynes as an ally or used him as an instrument was of wider political significance. It arose from the need of western capitalism, tainted by the pre-war experience, to change its image so as to be able to face up to the competition of communist propaganda in the cold war. In fact, Keynesian economics was ideally suited for that purpose: it promised an effective reform of capitalism which freed it from some of its most ugly features. The idea that capitalism could be salvaged by Keynesian thought was eagerly embraced by social democrats and somewhat less vociferously by the conservative business community. The best witness to this was the enthusiasm for consumption which dominated the post-war business world. The bitter denunciation of Keynes by established Marxism only reflected these attitudes.

The business community accepted the Keynesian paradigm in spite of their innate dislike of some of its features (role of the state, association with welfare policies).

On the basis of these considerations we can understand the spirit of the Keynesian era: the prevailing ideology of growth and of consumption, and a tremendous optimism which becomes evident and striking once we compare it with the pessimism which took hold of the same strata of society in the 1970s. It was as if by a kind of Aladdin's lamp Keynes had posthumously called up the 'animal spirits' which in his view were the prime movers of the investment process.

It appears then that the earlier quoted arguments about the irrelevance of Keynesian innovations to the post-war development are not the full story. On a balanced view they had a profound influence though this rarely took the form of government deficit spending.

V   NOT A RETIRING SCHOLAR

The novel and unorthodox ideas of Keynes were laid down systematically in his *General Theory of Employment, Interest and Money* (1936) which together with two earlier books, *A Tract on Monetary Reform* (1923) and *A Treatise on Money* (1930) formed the bulk of his theoretical output. Preceding this, however, over a long time beginning in 1919, there was a vast amount of work of a more practical nature dealing with problems of economic policy which arose from the events of the time. It has to be realised that a large part of Keynes's working time and interest was taken up not by the university in Cambridge but by an active engagement in the formulation of economic policy, either in an official capacity, mainly during and after the two world wars, or as an independent writer, lecturer and expert, mainly between the two wars. There was no lack of challenging problems: The condition of Europe after the war, the special problems of post-war Britain – the high burden of war time debts and the need for structural adjustments, mass unemployment which never ceased to be a problem until the second world war, the return to the gold standard at an over-valued rate for the pound sterling (1925), which could be maintained only at a heavy cost in high interest rates and unemployment and was finally given up in 1931 in favour of a floating pound, and in the further course the shift of British policy from free trade to protectionism.

It is surprising that the work of Keynes on these policy questions, apparently guided by a very strong intuition and acute observation, anticipated to a very large extent the results he reached much later and by tortuous routes in his academic work on a theoretical plane.

In fact he advocated public works as a remedy for unemployment consistently and strongly from 1924 onwards.[4] To finance the public works he proposed that the money should be taken out of the sinking fund. There he immediately came into conflict with Treasury views. In view of the crushing burden of the public debt the Treasury was trying to accumulate a surplus year by year in order to repay some of the debt. They were not willing to let Keynes raid their fund.

The works Keynes had in mind concerned transport, communications, electricity transmission, docks and ports and housing. He wanted to include in these schemes also private investment financed by treasury loans or guarantees and subject to technical advice and guidance by a semi-public authority.

Keynes also considered as a source of finance the rechannelling of the considerable funds which year by year were flowing into foreign investment. Of the funds raised on the capital market five times as much was going into foreign investment than into home investment. He argued that the effect of these foreign investments on export and thus on employment in Britain was small whereas an investment of the same sums in Britain would to a very large part increase output and employment there. Keynes was not very explicit about the methods to be employed; he did not clearly advocate a control of capital movements. Needless to say he was touching one of the most neuralgic points of the City. His arguments suggest that he hoped to make the home investments so much more profitable that the foreign investment would be 'crowded out'.

In carrying on his campaign for an active employment policy Keynes felt again and again the need to defend himself on a very general philosophical ground against the accusation of heresy: 'I bring in the State; I abandon *laissez-faire*, – not enthusiastically, not from contempt of that good old doctrine, but because, whether we like it or not, the conditions for its success have disappeared.'[5] He pleaded that private initiative was lacking in the execution of the big projects he had in mind and which would yield from 5 to 9 per cent (he was obviously thinking of the risks involved).

In his lecture 'The End of *Laissez-Faire*'[6] he pointed to saving and investment as activities which could not be left to the free play of the market but which necessitated the intervention of the State.

Another recurring theme is the contrast between enterprise and thrift:[7] 'It should be obvious that mere abstinence is not enough by itself to build cities or drain fens. . . . It is enterprise which builds and improves the worlds' possessions'. In social terms the contrasting pair may be translated into: Industry *versus* the rentier. It is obvious where Keynes's sympathies lay and how acutely he felt the oppressive consequence of a crushing and prolonged debt on an economy and a country. One of the main elements in his proposed post-war settlement was the cancellation of all war debts.[8] Later in a discussion of the financial situation of France, a country which carried the heavy burden of an excessively large rentier class, he recommended price inflation as a way out of the impasse.[9]

And, of course, cheap money policy was a natural concomitant of Keynesian concern for investment and government borrowing. This leads to one of the greatest issues in the inter-war economic policy debates: The return to the gold standard. Keynes, almost alone, passionately opposed it. It corresponded to the interest and the opinion of the City of London that the return should take place at the pre-war rate to the dollar, an issue in which the prestige of the City was at stake. Keynes argued that at this rate the pound would be over-valued by about 10 per cent; a deflation of the wage and price level would be necessary to maintain an equilibrium of payments at this level, with unpleasant economic and social consequences: the existing unemployment would be increased. In fact, on a plain reading of the subsequent events the fears were fully justified. Britain had to keep the rate of interest high in order to prevent an ever pressing outflow of money to New York and this as well as the heavy damage to exports, especially in the critical case of coal, led to great unemployment and to the general strike in 1926. Keynes's opposition against the gold standard was, however, not confined to the particular rate: He had from the beginning developed a policy preference for devaluation as against deflation. He wanted priority to be given to internal policy concerns and not to the establishment of fixed currency relations. The gold standard, he said, bound the City to Wall Street both with respect to interest rates and to price developments.

Faintly visible behind this debate is a fundamental issue which divided and distinguished Keynes from his compatriots and contem-poraries. It is the theme of a lesson which he tried to teach them untiringly, beginning with the famous chapters on Europe in the *Economic Consequences of the Peace*. He said that the world was not the same after this war and that it would never again be the same. He did not share the nostalgic sentimentality of the British middle class who imagined that it was possible to return to the pre-war Britain where they had been so happy.[10] A special part of this illusion was that the City of London would reconquer and maintain its former place in the world. Keynes destroyed this illusion in a cutting passage of merciless logic.[11]

In the last resort when Churchill called in outside experts to state their case, Keynes remained completely isolated.

The most mature statement of employment policies from that time is contained in the pamphlet *Can Lloyd George Do it?* written jointly with Hubert Henderson. The Treasury view that public works would merely crowd out private investment is countered by a *reductio in absurdo*: since large private investment projects are not different from public investment why should they not also crowd out other invest-ment? The Treasury view thus seemed to imply that employment could never be increased at all. In reality there were three sources of finance for the public investment: the saving in payments to the former unemployed; the reduction in foreign lending (this argument apparently here applied to the export surplus); and 'the savings which now run to waste through lack of adequate credit'.[12] This tormented expression of the fact that there are potential savings which are not tapped for lack of investment illustrates the terrific struggle for adequate expression of an insight grasped intuitively. In the same pamphlet there are also vague statements of the multiplier effect (p. 106). There is also reference to the structural maladjustment which was then complicating the problem of unemployment. The change in structure required a shift of manpower from declining to growing industries. But the necessary condition for such a shift from the declining industries, argued the authors of the pamphlet, is that 'jobs have first been created elsewhere, and employers are crying out for men' (p. 90). In another paper[13] there is a foretaste of the Keynesian theory of a general shift in wages: '... if wages are cut all round, the purchasing power of the community as a whole is reduced by the same amount as the reduction of costs'; a change in wage cost extending to all industries and all countries leaves everybody where he was before.

When the recession came Keynes abandoned his free trade principles in favour of protectionism. To most people this seemed a *volte face*; but it might be said that he was only developing a principle which he had asserted before when he expressed his preference for devaluation against deflation: the priority of the internal equilibrium and employment of a country in its relation to the outside world. We shall meet this theme again in the discussions on the international currency order.

The preceding selection of points and arguments from the writings on economic policy may serve as an introduction to a more general observation.

The genesis of the *General Theory* offers a good illustration for the view that important innovations in economic theory are distilled from intuitive solutions of the economic policy problems of the day. The revolutionary content of the *General Theory* was pre-established in the economic policy writings which arose from the deep and passionate engagement of Keynes in the issues of his day.[14]

Moreover the writings on economic policy show a very continuous and consistent line of development up to 1936 with an impressive constancy of certain themes and principles. By contrast, the development on the theoretical plane was erratic, with wild jumps and turn rounds by 180 degrees. Keynes had very little respect let alone awe in front of the great bankers, the City men, the civil servants and politicians or the paraphernalia of their trade. He felt a master in this milieu. But when he entered the maze of academic thinking he was burdened by traditions from which he gained his freedom only after a long struggle. He wrestled with the quantity theory through two books and did not completely extirpate it even in the third. He based his *Treatise on Money* on the assumption of constant total output, an assumption which was underlying most of the faulty reasoning of the 'classical' theory and which blocked the way to the *General Theory*.

The contrast between the two worlds is shown also in the style. The style of Keynes is at its best not in his theoretical work but when he writes on economic policy. His power to reduce an analysis to its essentials, to give concrete shape to abstract considerations so that you feel you can touch and hold them is superb. He gives his best when he tries to speak to the general public.

VI THEN AND NOW: ANALOGIES AND PARALLELS

Can the economic issues which were the subject of heated debates in the 1920s be of any interest to us today? The distance which separates us from this time is thrown into light if we consider that radio broadcasting was introduced in 1921, that the first flight over the Atlantic by Lindbergh took place in 1927; television, computers and robots were subjects of science fiction and atomic power the term in an equation in a new fangled physic's theory which nobody could understand. But the issues which Keynes and his opponents debated have a surprising and terrifying resemblance to similar issues today.

We have again to do with mass unemployment today, although the victims are now better cared for than they formerly were. And it is again the dominant wisdom that it is due to excessive wages that they cannot be employed.

Then and now the arguments against effective action include 'crowding out' and the burden of the public debt. This burden, interestingly enough, is today much lower than at the time of Keynes: in the UK the interest payments were 24 per cent of central government expenditure in 1920 and rose to 40 per cent in the late 1920s.[15]

After the Second World War, up to a few years ago, they were less than 14 per cent. The change was in the same direction in other countries.

It is quite true that this burden is bound to increase. The reason is not so much increased borrowing of governments as high interest rates. And here there is a very strong parallel between Britain in the twenties and Britain, as well as Europe, today. Lord Kaldor considers the two periods as the first and second reign of the monetarist dogma (using the term in a rather wide sense).[16] In both cases vital interests were sacrificed on the altar of an exotic deity: the interest rate was kept high in order to prevent the outflow of funds. In the first period, though, the policy was decided inside the country, while in the second case it was imposed on Europe from outside, and very difficult to avoid in the circumstances.

Another parallel strikes the eye if we think of Keynes's attitude to capital exports. He had complained that the financial apparatus was predominantly geared to the needs of other countries and not of home investment. Today the foreign investment of Britain is by far less important than it was; the great foreign lending of the British banks is offset by borrowing abroad. But the complaint remains that the banks are neglecting the interests of home industry. In addition its international involvement makes the system extremely unstable. Incidentally, it would be highly amusing if we had a comment from Keynes on the functioning of the joint stock system today, with the take-over movement as its central feature.

Notwithstanding all the analogies, there is one difference which distinguishes our time: inflation. While for that reason one argument against expansion – that it would lead to rising prices and wages – is more credible now that it was in the deflationary inter-war years (it was used nonetheless even then) we must not blind ourselves against the immense harm that deflation did in those years. By reducing the value of real estate and other tangible assets as well as cash flows, it increased the number of foreclosures and insolvencies.

Today, it is true, the high interest policy together with decreasing inflation rates tends to produce a similarly depressing effect on the value of real assets.

Turning now to the wider aspect of social attitudes: Can we not find analogies today to the nostalgia which Keynes found in the British middle class who were longing to go back to pre-war times? In a nostalgia, that is, for the pre-welfare state? It would seem to be equally utopian, but it can explain the strength of neo-conservativism in US and Britain. Perhaps there is at least a small bit of topicality in the remarks which Keynes made about the capitalists of the time after the First World War: 'They allow themselves to be ruined and altogether undone by their own instruments, governments of their own making, and a Press of which they are the proprietors'.[17]

And the inability of politicians, conservative as well as social democratic,[18] to grasp the least bit of Keynes's ideas or to share his distaste for the stupid waste of humanity and ruin of his country? Alas, the analogies abound.

VII   THE OPEN ENDS OF THE GENERAL THEORY

The *General Theory* is not always a paragon of clarity, unequivocal and unambiguous, nor does it represent a very complete and consistent system. As Keynes said '. . . the whole book needs re-writing and re-casting'.[19] The gaps in the argument of the *General Theory* stand out in relief very distinctly when we compare it with the work of M. Kalecki[20] which otherwise offers a close parallel to it.

The book does not contain any distribution theory and distribution is rarely mentioned in it. In consequence the propensity to save is defined so as to refer to the income of the nation as a whole, in other words to a kind of average behaviour. The importance which the distribution of income has for the propensity to save is completely left in the dark although it is perfectly sure that Keynes was only too well aware of it.[21] Aggregation is definitely carried too far here. The distinction between retained profits of business and saving of rentiers and other people outside enterprises is obscured although it is relevant for Keynesian arguments.

The importance which this omission has for the later exegesis of the *General Theory* will soon become obvious. In this connection it is also noteworthy that monopoly in all its forms is largely absent from the scene except for the trade unions. In the discussion of money and real wages perfect competition is explicitly assumed. As an implication of this Keynes was still carrying with him a part of the ballast of the 'classical' tradition the bulk of which he had successfully discarded: he believed that an increase in demand must necessarily lead to increased prices of manufacturing goods with the implication of inevitable fall in real wages in the upswing of the cycle. It was later shown by J. G. Dunlop and L. Tarshis that a negative correlation between real wages and the cycle did not exist.[22]

A second and perhaps the most important point concerns the method and the meaning of the *General Theory*. Is it a general equilibrium theory which describes the relations within a system which would keep it at rest provided it were not disturbed from outside, or is it a process analysis which shows step by step how a system starting from given initial conditions develops from one day to the next? The general equilibrium is a state to which the system ineluctably strives wherever it may start from and which it will reach provided there is no outside interference. Where does this concept come from?

In problems of mathematical physics we often have to do with a transitory solution to a differential equation which, starting from given initial conditions, vanishes after a certain span of time and leaves only the permanent solution which is independent of the initial conditions and determined only by the parameters of the equation. This permanent solution seems to correspond to the equilibrium which economists have in mind when they speak rather vaguely of 'dominant and permanent forces'. But in physics the whole process lasts only a small fraction of a second. In economics long term equilibrium requires years or rather decades to work itself out.

In the intervening time the conditions of the system change repeatedly so that equilibrium has no chance of ever being reached. In view of that there is hardly any empirical basis for the statements about long-term equilibrium. The basis is largely *a priori* and, one suspects, often ideological. The situation may be rather better for short period partial equilibrium.

Now in its essence the Keynesian thinking was not concerned with general equilibrium. For one thing his practical mind militated against it. How indeed should one use such a theory in dealing with problems of practical economic policy? His famous dictum 'In the long run we are all dead'[23] shows what he thought of long term equilibrium. When he explained the volume of investment by the state of expectations and discussed their instability he was evidently thinking in terms of process analysis. Yet he has not been sufficiently consistent and clear in pursuing this line. We miss in his work the systematic use of lags which we find in Kalecki and which must necessarily be an essential feature of a process analysis in economics. Thus the lag between investment decisions and investment is for Kalecki a reason why investment determines saving and not the other way round. Again one has to think of the decisive role of lags in the cobweb or in any other cycle.

At the same time we find Keynes talking in terms of equilibrium concepts such as in chapter 18 ('The General Theory of Employment Re-stated') and also in connection with the aggregate supply and demand functions. By this lack of complete clarity he opened the door through which the Trojan horse of the neoclassical synthesis could enter.

A further problem concerns the failure to distinguish between short and long term rates of interest which is puzzling to the reader. By rate

of interest he meant the long term rate, and his alternative to investment in bonds (consols) was only money. The short term assets had
then to be considered as money[24] unless he disregarded their existence
in the context altogether. The last interpretation is the more plausible
one; since Keynes introduced the money supply as an exogenous
variable he could not plausibly include short term assets in it.

Kaldor has drawn attention to the fact that the quantity of money is
always exogenous in Keynes's exposition of the theory of interest and
he sees in this a survival of the quantity theory of money. In so far as the
quantity of money (ultimately also of base money), and not only its
velocity, responds to the amount of transactions, increasing in boom
and declining in recession, it is endogenous in character. This side of
the picture is never seen in Keynes, because he implicitly always deals
with open market operations in his exposition of interest theory.

Conspicuous by its absence from the *General Theory* is a theory of
the trade cycle. Bits and pieces relevant to the subject are strewn all
over the place but they do not amount to a theory. It would be unfair to
blame Keynes for this omission; but one cannot help contemplating
how much more committed to dynamics the book would have looked
had he gone further in this direction. There are two further subjects
which are under-represented in the book although Keynes had plenty
to say about them in his practical policy writings: the open economy
and long-term development. Both are so extensive and so complicated
that Keynes had every justification to leave them out. They are
mentioned here only because it has become fashionable to dwell on
them, especially on the failure of Keynes to extend his theory to the
long run. The tacit implication of this criticism is that he ought to have
gone into general equilibrium theory. It was to his credit that he did
not.

VIII THE COUNTER-ATTACK

The dismantling of the *General Theory* started as soon as it was
published if not before, and with the prominent participation of some
of Keynes's friends and colleagues. The method was to prove that the
new theory did not differ as much as Keynes claimed from the
conventional ('classical') equilibrium theory, that it was only a special
case of it, or applicable only under narrowly restricted circumstances.

The attackers naturally profited from the weaknesses pointed out
above. Thus Harrod[25] blatantly asserted that the marginal efficiency of

capital was nothing else but the marginal productivity known to neoclassical theory, and in this way assimilated the *General Theory* to the neoclassical distribution theory. He could do this only because Keynes had been so vague and uncommitted with regard to distribution theory. The identification was a travesty. Marginal productivity relates specifically to factor substitution. Marginal efficiency, by contrast, relates primarily to an expansion of output capacity; it depends on the state of demand and on the exploitation of new technical know how. The broader meaning of Keynes's concept results from the fact that it refers to an economy in which there is no full use of resources and in which the dynamic possibilities of new technical methods come into play. These influences are embodied in the concept of expectations.[26]

The review of Harrod as well as that of Hicks[27] which was destined to become very influential, uses, however, a more fundamental way of attack by addressing itself to the very meaning of the *General Theory*.

The method is to misunderstand and misinterpret the *General Theory* as an equilibrium theory, a procedure which as we have seen has been facilitated by Keynes himself.[28] By this trick all the distinctive and revolutionary features of Keynesian theory vanish and dissolve into thin air. What sense is there in a system of mutually dependent variables to argue that investment determines saving and not the other way round? The concept of effective demand as an active agent looses its meaning for the same reason. It is true that Keynes did talk of a long-term equilibrium with a 'relative stability'.[29]

What he described there – and it is worth re-reading – is a tendency to long-term unemployment characteristic of our system, and he added that it must not be taken as a necessity but should be changed.

The specific line taken by Hicks in his interpretation is directed towards money and interest. His main concern is to insist that an increased inducement to invest or an increase in the propensity to consume would raise the rate of interest *via* an increased demand for money on account of the transactions motive. How could Keynes, he asks, maintain that the rate of interest would not rise in these circumstances (when more money would be needed for the increased volume of business transactions)? The answer is probably that Keynes assumed the long term rate of interest to respond only very slowly to a change in the conditions of the money market (which corresponds to experience). But however that may be, the conclusions drawn by Hicks are quite amazing. He does not deny the essential Keynesian position that the rate of interest is a monetary phenomenon depending on institutions only and determined by banking policy. Yet he maintains that by demonstrating that the rate of interest must rise in the circumstances described above he has approximated the Keynesian system to that of the 'classics'. But for the 'classics' the rate of interest is determined by material scarcity, of capital or of saving, not by institutions or policy. Yet for Hicks the Keynesian system is now, after his 'corrections' concerning the rate of interest, different from the traditional classical system only under special circumstances: It is a 'slump economics' (op. cit., p. 158) or also: 'the general theory of employment is the economics of depression' (p. 155).

It is a puzzle why Keynes did not defend himself against the interpreters who no sooner than his theory was born endeavoured to replace it by a changeling of the most doubtful character. In fact, he thanked Harrod for his review. But those who at that time underwent the conversion from 'classics' to Keynes can still remember what a strenuous intellectual adventure it was. It must be realised that Keynes was surrounded by complete incomprehension of a public stunned by the novelty of his ideas. It may be that Harrod wanted to be helpful by dressing up the bogey man in impeccable academic clothes, and that Keynes took it in this way. What neither of them realised at that time was that the distortions of the first hour would grow into a ruling system called neoclassical synthesis. This theory dominated the universities in the decades in which full employment ruled in the outside world. It said that in the long run a *laissez-faire* system would re-establish and maintain full employment and that the deviations from it were temporary and unimportant.

Members of this school tended to be split personalities, putting on in turn the Keynesian hat when they advised the Administration on economic policy of the day, and the neoclassical hat when they wrote on highbrow economic theory.

A particular subspecies of the neoclassical synthesists was wont to argue that since full employment was safeguarded in any case by the Keynesian demand management, it was fully legitimate to apply neoclassical reasoning to the present world.

In this way the thought of Keynes was gradually undermined so that the take-over of the university departments by a combination of pure neoclassicists and monetarists could proceed fairly quickly. The appropriate moment for this was dictated by events outside the universities: The calling off of Keynesian policies by the leading powers.

IX   HAVE KEYNESIAN POLICIES FAILED?

Before the 1970s what impressed the observer of the post-war scene was how much fuller employment was maintained than Keynes had ever expected.

When Sir William Beveridge[30] had put the full employment target at 3 per cent Keynes wrote to him: 'No harm in aiming at 3 per cent unemployment but I shall be surprised if we succeed.'[31]

The post-war unemployment rate in Britain, and in most European countries as well, was of the order of 2 per cent or less until the 1970s. In the US the figure was rather larger. The high levels of employment were realised with – what seems to us now – relatively moderate rates of inflation (of the order of 3 per cent in the 1950s and 4 per cent in the late 1960s). It has to be borne in mind, though, that this favourable result was facilitated by an improvement of the industrial countries' terms of trade in relation to the third world.

For quite a long time, therefore, the maintenance of high levels of employment succeeded much better than Keynes himself had expected.

To understand the crisis of the 1970s fully we have to realise, that even before the overt difficulties of that time certain unfavourable factors were active behind the façade of prosperity.

One of them was the fact that in some countries Keynesian policies had never been wholeheartedly adopted. The US had only a fleeting relation to full employment. Congress could be reconciled to it only when it was bound up with the military–industrial complex. The adherence to full employment policy therefore weakened in 1969.

Germany had been forced into full employment in the early fifties from outside, by an export boom. In the later sixties she pursued a restrictive monetary policy which contributed decisively to the weakening of private business investment since that time.

Great Britain departed from the cheap money policy of the early post-war years in 1951; monetary controls played a larger role since then. Full employment policy in Britain was qualified by the recurrence of balance of payments crisis (sometimes provoked by the refusal to devalue when it was necessary – in 1964) which were partly due to a structural weakness of the foreign balance and partly due to a tendency of wage levels to run ahead of those of her competitors. While in the earlier period (up to the middle sixties) the economy was overstrained owing to large defence spending, it later lost its impetus because private investment flagged.

But the weakening of investment may not have been exclusively a result of the policies pursued, it may also have come from certain structural changes in the capitalist system. The concentration of business proceeded and this tended to increase the fear of excess capacity and a cautious attitude to investment. A symptom of the weakening interest in real investment was the take-over movement, a growing interest in financial manipulation as opposed to production.[32] The weakening of private investment was the direct cause of the growing budget deficits, a development which reached its climax after the recession of 1974–75.

If Keynesian policies are said to have failed in the 1970s this can only mean that continuing full employment has proved impossible because it has led to insuperable difficulties. Most prominent among these difficulties is the tendency for 'efficiency wages' (as Keynes termed wages per unit of output) to drift upwards and thus to cause inflation. This has always been stressed by the close followers of Keynes, Joan Robinson, Lord Kahn and Lord Kaldor. Keynes himself foresaw the difficulty, and stated that this was a political question.[33]

This is indeed confirmed by the observation that restraint on wage levels operates in a climate of social consensus (Sweden, Austria, Germany, Switzerland) whereas wage inflation is uncontrollable in a climate of social confrontation (Italy, Great Britain, France before De Gaulle and after 1968). It appears that inflation is the expression of a latent conflict about income distribution which is carried on continuously, with everybody passing on the bill which nobody wants to pay. It may also be more than a coincidence that wage inflation characteristically dominates in countries with unstable government: Great Britain has only once in the post-war period had a government (Macmillan) which lasted longer than five years. The 'see-saw' is bound to act as a de-stabiliser on economic calculations. Italy with a permanently unstable government is another example.

The wider socio-political aspects of full employment policy no doubt would deserve close study. The long period of full employment and prosperity has wrought considerable social changes; sometimes these changes have come, in typical Marxian fashion, in conflict with existing rigid structures, and social and political tensions have resulted. An outbreak of such tensions occurred in 1968 with the student movement and militant workers' unrest, simultaneous in a number of countries, in France verging for a moment on social revolution. The wage explosion 1968–70 followed in the wake of these signs of social impatience. By way of a feedback process (wage–price–wage spiral) a wage explosion confined to one year increased also the inflation rates of the following years. The effects of the wage explosion might still have been managed if it had not been for subsequent events: the transition to fluctuating exchanges removed an important restraint on wages, and the divergence of inflation rates in different countries was thereby increased. To this was further added the *hausse* in commodity prices in 1973 and the oil shock at the end of that year.

After the recession in 1974–75 had started it soon became obvious that the US and Germany had given up full employment policies. This was a political choice. These countries had not done all they could to explore alternative ways, such as an incomes policy based on social consensus instead of confrontation. Moreover, by letting the dollar drift downwards, US inflation was powerfully stimulated. Nor is it clear that inflation would have been worse than it actually was if the US had pursued a policy of expansion to absorb the excess of labour supply. This would have avoided the loss in productivity growth which drove up the wage cost per unit of output, and which resulted from stunted growth of GDP and low capacity utilisation.

But while the preoccupation with inflation was understandable in the US where owing to less social security private saving is more widely important than in Europe, giving up full employment in Europe represented a more surprising change of policy. Some countries such as France were holding out for an expansionist policy in 1975, and they were ultimately forced to give it up only because of Germany's restrictive policies. Thus the ultimate victory of the restrictionist policy almost everywhere resulted not from independent decisions of the different countries, but was to a large extent brought about by the pressure which the creditor countries with their low inflation rates brought to bear on the rest of the industrial world.

This leads to a subject which has to be treated separately in detail. It concerns the worsening in international economic relations which started in the late 1960s. That the foreign balance was the neuralgic point in his policies Keynes knew only too well and in his later years he was entirely occupied with this complex of questions.

X THE DEFEAT

The war changed the position of Keynes: from an outside critic he became a member of the establishment, holding a highly responsible office in the Treasury. He was concerned with war finance on which he had written an analysis which became the basis for a new understanding of this subject.[34] In particular he introduced the concept of the inflationary gap, the difference between the amount of effective demand and the available supply, as a measure of the degree of inflation.

The policy of cheap money pursued during this war was due to his influence and in consequence it became known as a 3 per cent war as opposed to the 5 per cent war 25 years earlier. The easy money policy and the large treasury borrowing was made possible by the strict controls of the British war economy which created a dam for the large excess of incomes over available civilian supplies, channelling it off into saving: beside exchange control there were the physical controls at home – raw material controls and extensive rationing of consumer goods. Curiously enough, rationing did not meet with the approval of Keynes. It competed with his own 'deferred payment' scheme of taxes to be repaid after the war. This scheme was applied in practice only to a very limited extent, and rationing which corresponded more nearly to the strategy proposed by Kalecki,[35] became the effective instrument for dealing with the inflationary gap. In this question Keynes was less advanced than the war time civil service which, driven by necessity, came to understand very well the administrative and socio-politic advantages of the strategy of rationing ('fair shares').[36]

The main concern of Keynes was, however, external finance. This involved, in particular, the negotiations with the United States which, from the Mutual Aid Agreement over Bretton Woods to the Financial Agreement were carried out by him.

In the Keynesian work of these war years two different but interwoven themes were present: One was ensuring the survival of Britain by procuring finance for its pressing needs day by day. The other was to lay the plans for a new international order of currencies, applying Keynesian thinking on a world scale. The two were, unfortunately, not unrelated. Britain, completely drained of reserves by 1940 and having sacrificed two-thirds of her exports, was dependent on supplies offered by the United States as 'Lend and Lease' which was granted on the understanding that Britain would 'pursue a policy, in cooperation with the United States, for world recovery and prosperity'.[36]

American ideas on what this policy was to be were coloured by the free trade ideology of the State Department and its leader Cordell Hull. This corresponded to the interests of a creditor country of great industrial efficiency. A special bugbear was discrimination, one of its forms being non-convertibility of currencies. A ban on discrimination was the chief content of the 'consideration' demanded of Britain. After being first mentioned in the Atlantic Charter it became Article VII of the Mutual Aid Agreement. This was directed against Britain's Imperial Preference and it also would have rendered impossible any bilateral practices. Convertibility was insisted on in the Bretton Woods Agreement with a period of grace of 5 years which was reduced to two years in the Financial Agreement of 1945 (the conditions for the post-war loan).

Now to the Keynesian vision of an international order. It started from a specific problem, the prospective difficulties of post-war Britain, but it had a much more general significance.

Keynes had already in 1933[37] thought of an international currency order which would secure abundant liquidity and therefore obviate the aggressive scramble for gold or equivalent reserves which destabilised and depressed the level of world trade and which forced weaker countries into a deflationary policy of unemployment. In the early stage of the war Keynes considered two alternative ways of avoiding a recurrence of the conditions of the interwar period: Britain, with American assistance, could employ Keynesian remedies for unemployment and trade depression on a world scale.[38] This involved also measures for stabilising commodity prices by means of Buffer Stocks, proposed in a Memorandum for the War Cabinet on the International Regulation of Primary Products.[39] Proposals for the finance of the Buffer Stocks were also contained in the plan for the Clearing Union. (These plans were gradually lost sight of in view of the pressure of currency problems and also owing to Keynes's illness.[40] Or else, Britain, thrown back on her own devices, would have to make use of the bilateral techniques developed in Germany by Schacht. Pursuing the first alternative Keynes set to work from 1941 on to develop his famous plan for an International Clearing Union.[41] Its idea was to base the international monetary order not on gold but on a central fund into which each country (in accordance with a quota settled for each country) would pay in its own currency and from which it would obtain the right to draw within certain limits whatever currencies it needed to balance its foreign accounts. In this way the fund would act as a clearing house for the countries of the world, it would settle surpluses and deficits in their balance of payments by a general reckoning up.

The most important aims pursued by the plan for a Clearing Union were the following:

(a) Adequate reserves were to be created and an equitable and reasonable distribution of these reserves was to be guaranteed.

(b) Arrangements were to be made to counteract the existing bias against the debtor countries and in favour of the creditor countries, which favoured depression. Not only persistent debtor countries but equally also persistent creditor countries were to be forced to contribute their part to the adjustment whenever a disequilibrium arose. In this way the bias in favour of depression characteristic of the present system was to be avoided.

(c) It was to be recognised that adjustment of exchange rates were necessary and reasonable in certain circumstances. Therefore rigidity of exchange rates was not proposed, but the opposite extreme, fluctuating exchanges, was also excluded.

The aim was not only to start the countries off on expanding trade, but also to prevent disequilibria from arising, or to correct them if they arose, and to maintain a continuing expansionist climate. The plan was criticised for not going far enough by Kalecki and Schumacher.[42] But no doubt the plan offered a chance for the revival of world trade after the war.

At this point, however, the harsh realities of the other preoccupation of Keynes came into play. The United States had drawn up a rival plan, the White-Plan, which was strongly based on gold, did not provide adequate reserves and did not correct the bias in favour of the creditor.

After negotiations in September–October 1943 a Joint Statement of the United States and Britain was published in April 1944 which leaned essentially on the US proposals. It constituted the defeat of Keynes's aims. In Britain it was passionately opposed by Hubert Henderson, Joan Robinson and Thomas Balogh. The Joint Statement was the basis for the Bretton Woods conference in July 1944 and the Savannah conference 1945 from which the International Monetary Fund and the World Bank emerged.[43]

Bretton Woods involved nothing essentially new. The ruling system became a gold–dollar exchange instead of a gold–sterling exchange. As predicted by Henderson, Balogh and Joan Robinson the system was not in a position to stand up to the post-war strain which resulted from the contrast between the demand of an impoverished Europe and the output capacity of the US and led to a large excess demand for dollars. This danger had been soft-pedalled by Keynes who had made himself the defender of his own undoing. When Britain, in an attempt to carry out the obligation contracted against the loan of 1945, introduced convertibility in 1947, the Bretton Woods system effectively broke down, because this move failed instantaneously. In the further course of events, the international payments system was kept going only owing to massive American loans and investments and chiefly to Marshall aid which constituted in a way a realisation or substitute for Keynesian plans for the recovery of the world.[44]

It seems that Keynes was beaten by historical necessity, in so far as he happened to represent a waning power (although this was not essential for the principles he stood for). This interpretation is not generally shared. Lord Kahn thinks that the British position was stronger than it seemed and that a great part of the concessions might have been avoided.[45] Keynes had been a very sick man which affected his stamina and his whole outlook. (He died four weeks after return from the Savannah conference).

The defeat of Keynes is still felt today. From Bretton Woods and Savannah a wide arch is spanned to our own time. The countries of Europe, trusting in the existence of a working international order, have been induced to open themselves up with regard to trade and payments. But, it is obvious by now, a workable international order does not exist. Countries find themselves helplessly thrown about by arbitrary movements of capital and exchange rates. They are, as Keynes had warned on the eve of the return to gold, bound to Wall Street in their interest rate policy. A house of cards – the Euromarket – has been built up, which is exempt from any kind of national or international control. It is the ultimate triumph of *laissez-faire* in the matter of finance. Where is the lender of the last resort to which, on an international level, banks will be able to turn if this structure starts crumbling?

The decisive defeat of Keynesian policies did not come in the domestic sphere of wage policy, it occurred in the international field. Indeed, the two digit inflation in industrial countries which is widely regarded as the rock on which Keynesian policy had been ultimately stranded was itself merely the consequence of uncontrolled *laissez-faire* in the international commodity markets. This regime was pleasant enough for the industrial countries in so far as it turned the terms of trade in their favour in the 1950s and 1960s. But the low commodity prices led to neglect of investment in the plantations and mines, so that the output could not cope with the sudden increase in demand in the world boom of the early seventies.

The point of Keynes's Buffer Stock Scheme had been precisely to avoid this: by maintaining adequate and stable prices it was to secure a steady development of supplies.

In a different way also the case of oil demonstrates the consequence of *laissez-faire*: the excessively low prices of the pre-OPEC times made the industrial world wasteful of oil and drove it into an extreme dependence on oil producers who then took revenge on their former exploiters. Here too, international agreements between producers and consumers might have avoided the extreme changes of the terms of trade. Moreover, the Clearing Union would from the start have prevented frustration of development countries by giving them adequate credits for investment. This should have reduced the latent tension between North and South and therefore the likelihood of 'ganging up' on either side.

The 'invisible hand' has certainly not left traces of any kind of rational ordering; instead the visible heavy hand of creditor countries has imposed their policies on others.

If Keynes was defeated, it was not on the plane of logic: It was on the plane of power. Was he then, was the Clearing Union and the Buffer Stock Scheme, utopian? Yes, and it looks even more so today. Yet it is said that utopians are the greater realists. We are today faced with the same questions which confronted Keynes in the years 1939–41 in his thinking on international relations. We have practically not got any further in the meantime. If we want to start anew, we have to start where Keynes left off.

NOTES

1. See H. P. Minsky, *John Maynard Keynes* (New York Columbia University Press, 1975). P. Davidson, *Money and the Real World* (London 1972).
2. R. Matthews, 'Why Britain Has Had Full Employment Since the War', *Economic Journal*, vol. 78, September 1968, pp. 555–69, and the discussion in *Economic Journal*, March 1970. He says there were no budget deficits and there was buoyant private investment, but he admits that at least the absence of 'perverse reactions' of the government could be attributed to an advance in know-how due to Keynes. Matthews completely neglects that the vastly increased government spending was partly financed by increased profit taxes which cut into company savings and therefore acted much like a budget deficit.
3. See L. J. Griffin, M. Wallace, J. Devine, 'The Political Economy of Military Spending: Evidence from the United States', *Cambridge Journal of Economics*, vol. 6, March 1982.
4. 'Does Unemployment Need a Drastic Remedy?', *The Nation*, May 1924.
5. R. F. Harrod, *Life of J. M. Keynes, pp. 405–6.*
6. *Essays in Persuasion Coll. W.*, vol. IX, pp. 272–94.
7. *Treatise on Money, Col. W.*, vol. VI, p. 132.
8. *The Economic Consequences of the Peace, Coll. W.*, vol. II.

9. 'The French Franc'. *Essays in Persuasion, Coll. W.*, vol. IX.
10. Donald Winch, *Economics and Policy* (London: Fontana books, 1972) pp. 85.
11. *Coll. W.*, vol. IX, pp. 198–9.
12. *Coll. W.*, vol. IX, pp. 116–17, 120.
13. 'The great slump of 1930'. *Coll. W.*, vol. IX, p. 128.
14. This has been noted by others including J. A. Schumpeter according to whom generally '. . . vision of facts and meanings precedes analytic work . . .' *History of Economic Analysis*, (New York: 1954) p. 1171, which he illustrates by the example of Keynes of whom he says: 'The whole period between 1919 and 1936 was then spent in attempts, first unsuccessful, then increasingly successful at implementing the particular vision of the economic process of our time that was fixed in Keynes's mind by 1919 at the latest' (p. 42).
15. D. Winch, op. cit., p. 105. In proportion to GNP these interest payments were 5.4 per cent in 1920 and 7 per cent in 1930, compared with 4 per cent after the Second World War.
16. Nicholas Kaldor, *The Scourge of Monetarism* (Oxford, 1982) p. ix.
17. Keynes, *The Economic Consequences of the Peace*, p. 150.
18. D. Winch, op. cit., p. 126–34 and Appendix.
19. *Coll. W.*, vol. XIV, p. 47.
20. M. Kalecki, *Theory of Economic Dynamics* (London, 1954).
21. This becomes evident in *How to Pay for the War* (1939).
22. J. G. Dunlop, 'The Movement of Real and Money Wage Rates', *Economic Journal*, Sept. 1938; L. Tarshis in *Economic Journal*, March 1939. The response by Keynes is reprinted in *Coll. W.*, vol. VII, appendix 3, p. 394.
23. *A Tract on Monetary Reform, Coll. W.*, vol. IV, p. 65.
24. N. Kaldor, *The Scourge of Monetarism* (Oxford, 1982) p. 74.
25. R. F. Harrod, 'Mr. Keynes and traditional theory'. *Econometrica*, Jan. 1937, vol. 5, pp. 74–86.
26. The above paragraph echos the arguments of Fausto Vicarelli, *Keynes* (Milano, 1977) pp. 178–9.
27. J. R. Hicks, 'Mr. Keynes and the Classics': a Suggested Interpretation', *Econometrica*, April 1937, vol. 5, pp. 147–59.
28. In recent years Sir John R. Hicks has come to admit this misrepresentation: 'Some Questions of Time in Economics', *Evolution, Welfare, and Time in Economics*. Essays in honour of Nicholas Georgescu-Roegen, ed. A. M. Tang, F. M. Westfield and J. S. Worley (Massachusetts, 1976), pp. 140–1).
29. *Coll. W.*, vol. VII (1973) pp. 249–54.
30. Sir William Beveridge, *Full Employment in a Free Society*.
31. Lord Kahn, 'Unemployment as Seen by the Keynesians', in G. D. N., Worswick, (ed.): *The Concept and Measurement of Involuntary Unemployment* (London, 1976) p. 30.
32. For the case of Italy see Giangiacomo Nardozzi, 'Sviluppo e stagnazione dell' economia italiana, 1951–1971', *L'industria*, 1974.
33. Lord Kahn, *On Re-reading Keynes* (London, 1975) p. 29.
34. *How to Pay for the War. Coll. W.,* vol. IX.

35. 'General Rationing', in *Studies in War Economics* (Oxford: Oxford University Institute of Statistics, 1947).
36. Harrod, *Life of John Maynard Keynes*, p. 584.
37. 'The Means to Prosperity', *Coll. W.*, vol. IX.
38. Harrod, op. cit., p. 586.
39. *Coll. W.*, vol. XXVII: 'Activities 1940–46: Shaping the Post-War World: Employment and Commodities', 1980, pp. 168–94.
40. *Coll. W.*, vol. XXVII, 1980, pp. 196–7.
41. *Coll. W.*, vol. XXV, 1980.
42. 'New Plans for International Trade', *Institute of Statistics Oxford; Bulletin*, vol. 5, supplement no. 5, August 1943. It was claimed there, *inter alia*, that without exchange controls to limit international capital movements the functioning of the plan would not be guaranteed.
43. *Coll. W.*, vol. XXVI, 1980.
44. 'Lord Balogh, Keynes and the International Monetary Fund', in A. P. Thirlwall (ed.), *Keynes and International Monetary Relations*. The second Keynes's Seminar held at the University of Kent at Canterbury 1974 (London: 1976) esp. pp. 79–80.

    In the sense of a system of fixed exchange rates the Bretton Woods system did of course last until the US stopped converting dollars into gold at the end of 1971. The contention of Lord Balogh is that this system functioned only thanks to factors essentially extraneous to it, namely the Marshall Plan, the US direct foreign investments, the civil and military assistence to allies and finally the military expenditure abroad which together created abundant reserves throughout the period. In the end this abundance of dollars became too great a blessing so that the readiness of the world's central banks to hold them became doubtful, and this meant the end of the gold-dollar system.
45. A. P. Thirlwall, op. cit., pp. 58–9.

7 The *General Theory:* Critical Reflections Suggested by some Important Problems of Our Time

PAOLO SYLOS LABINI

I THREE TYPES OF CRITICISM OF MODELS OF ECONOMIC THEORY

The risk of a new 'Great Depression, the 'crowding-out' of private investment by public spending, and inflationary stagnation, are the important problems of our time referred to in the title. Before setting out some critical reflections on the *General Theory* suggested by these problems it will be useful to make a number of more general, or as it has become customary to call them, 'methodological' considerations.

A theoretical model may be criticised either from the point of view of its logical coherence, or with reference to the hypotheses upon which it derives its results. These hypotheses, in their turn, can be judged invalid either because they did not apply even in the historical period in which the model was proposed, or because even though they were then valid they no longer are relevant to today's changed conditions. The latter is frequently the case for the very simple reason that economic theory is historically conditioned. Hypotheses may thus be criticised because they are unacceptable for either logical or historical reasons.

The model worked out in Keynes's *General Theory* has been the subject of all three types of criticism. In terms of logical coherence, Alvin Hansen has, for example, levied criticism regarding the influ-

126

ence that variations in income might exert on the rate of interest. It would have been a valid criticism if Keynes's system were interpreted in terms of simultaneous equations, but it is clearly invalid if the system is interpreted in terms of causal sequences.[1] The greater part of the other criticisms belong to the second and third types. I myself have advanced criticism of both types at different times referring to (a) the essentially psychological character of the assumptions upon which Keynesian theory is founded, (b) the hypothesis that the quantity of money is exogenous, and (c) the assumption that the labour and product markets all react in the same way to variations in demand (Keynes supposed that increases in demand would not produce significant variations in either prices or wages as long as there was unemployment in the system.[2])

The criticisms under points (a) and (b) are in large measure independent of historical changes. The criticism under point (c), on the other hand, is affected by such changes in a number of different ways. More precisely, for product markets it was important to distinguish, even in Keynes's day, between markets for primary commodities, agricultural products and minerals on the one hand, and the markets for industrial products on the other. For the former, in the short period which was Keynes's subject, prices depend on demand and supply, while for the latter prices vary with costs and are in large measure independent of demand in conditions of excess productive capacity. As far as the labour market is concerned, from the beginning of time the distinction between manual and intellectual labour has been of importance, although many economists – Keynes among them – have reasoned as if it were not. After the conspicuous increases in average individual incomes which has occurred in the industrialised world after the second world war, which has also made possible important improvements in the conditions of the unemployed, there has been an increasing tendency for workers in the industrialised countries to refuse repetitive and disagreeable labour. Such jobs have thus been eliminated in part by automation, and in part allocated to immigrant workers from the less developed countries. Today it is thus necessary to distinguish among three types of occupation: (a) primarily manual, repetitive and disagreeable work, (b) work which is still manual, but with an increasing technical or specialist component, and (c) primarily intellectual work, in offices. Compensation in labour markets for the first type of work – wages – is directly affected by changes in the demand for labour, particularly if there is free immigration of foreign labour. In markets for the second type of labour, compensation – also wages – is much less sensitive to variations in the demand for labour and is only affected by very large movements. Compensation in markets for the third type – salaries – hardly responds at all to changes in demand (the reader is reminded that the discussion refers to money payments). The well-known 'Phillips curve' which has, quite rightly been considered as compatible with Keynesian theory, always refers to wages, not salaries. However, on account of the bargaining power that trade unions have acquired it is now some time since unemployment has been the unique, much less the major factor determining changes in wages; the other factor is the cost of living, so that rather than a single Phillips curve it would be more appropriate to think of a whole 'family' of them. With the conspicuous increases in the average family income, the extension of, and increase in, unemployment benefit coverage, and the further growth of trade union power, not even the two variables just presented – unemployment and the cost of living – are any longer capable of explaining changes in wages. The explanatory power of the 'so-called' Phillips curve is thus further reduced. At the same time the proportion of workers receiving salaries, in large part independent from changes in the demand for labour, has sharply increased.

Keynes considered the labour market as relatively homogeneous, with the qualification that when the economy nears full employment increases in the demand for labour would encounter 'bottlenecks' that would cause increases in the wages of certain categories of labour. For the reasons given above, the Keynesian assumption concerning the homogeneity of the labour market could be considered as acceptable in his time and for the initial post-war period. Today, for 'historical' reasons, it no longer seems acceptable. Let us see why.

According to Keynes, the volume of employment could be made homogeneous, 'by taking an hour's employment of ordinary labour as our unit and weighting an hour's employment of special labour in proportion to its remuneration; i.e. an hour of special labour remunerated at double ordinary rates will count as two units'.[3] This criterion, which is also that adopted by the Classical economists, presumes that relative wage rates are constant, at least in the short period. In the past, when wage rates were very close to subsistence this assumption may have reflected reality. But, in our times, with the growing refusal of labour to take on repetitive and disagreeable occupations this assumption is no longer valid, for we observe a tendency for the relative wages of disagreeable employments to increase, at least in the short period, so Keynes's criterion is no longer valid. The relative increase in wages in such occupations can always be partially offset by offering employment to foreign workers, but in such a case an increase in the demand for a certain type of labour leads to an increase in immigration and not in the employment of domestic labour. Thus, taking immigrant labour into account, the volume of unemployment does not fall although total employment may rise.[4]

II   TWO REFERENCE MODELS

In difference from the criticisms regarding the internal logical coherence, those concerning the logical or historical acceptability of the hypotheses are convincing only if one is able to point out a viable alternative, even if it is not fully developed. I will try to satisfy this requirement by means of two models, the first setting out the Keynesian position, the second incorporating alternative hypotheses which it is necessary to introduce in order to discuss the above mentioned problems. It should thus be kept in mind that the two models are applicable only for the purposes of this essay. The first model can be interpreted as a system of simultaneous equations and, from this point of view, it is similar to the IS–LM model worked out by Hicks and accepted by Keynes (although it is doubtful that it correctly represents his theory). The second model, in which the variables are directly or indirectly dated, cannot be interpreted as a system of simultaneous equations; it excludes the concept of static interdependence and presupposes a process analysis.

I   *Keynesian Model*

Income:	$Y_w = C_w + I_w$	(1)
Consumption:	$C_w = a_1 + b_1 Y_w$	(2)
Investment:	$I_w = a_2 + b_2 (R^*/K^*) - c_2 i$	(3)
Rate of Interest:	$i = a_3 - b_3 M_w + c_3 Y_w$	(4)
Employment:	$N = a_4 + b_4 Y_w$	(5)
Price level:	$P = a_5 W$	(6)
Wages:	$W \equiv \bar{W}$	(7)

Where Y = income, C = consumption, I = investment, R = total profits, K = capital, i = rate of interest, M = quantity of money, W = wage level, N = employment, P = price level, $*$ = expected values. The subscript w indicates measure in wage units: for example $Y_w \equiv Y/W$.

In addition to equation 1 for income we may also write equation 1a $Y_w = \alpha N$ which results from $Y = \alpha\ WN$ on the assumption that the distribution of income does not change and therefore money incomes are proportional to money wages ($\alpha > 1$). Equations 6 and 7 hold under conditions of widespread unemployment. In conditions of near full employment we should substitute as follows:

Prices: $\qquad\qquad P = a_6\ W + b_6\ N$ $\qquad\qquad\qquad$ (6a)

Wages: $\qquad\qquad W = a_7 + b_7\ N$ $\qquad\qquad\qquad\quad$ (7a)

It should not be necessary to point out that 7a is equivalent to the Phillips relation.

II *Alternative Model*[5]

Investment:	$I = a_1 + b_1\ R/Y_c + c_1\ UT + d_1\ i$	(1)
Prices (rate of change):	$\hat{P} = a_2 + b_2\ \hat{W} - c_2\ \hat{\pi} + d_2\ \hat{P}C$	(2)
Profits (share):	$R/Y_c = a_3 + b_3\ P - c_3\ W + d_3\ \pi - e_3\ PC$	(3)
Capacity Utilisation:	$UT = a_4 + b_4\ C + c_4\ I + d_4\ E$	(4)
Consumption (current prices):	$C_c = a_5 + b_5\ W + c_5\ NW + d_5\ N$	(5)
Consumption (constant prices):	$C = C_c/P$	(6)
Cost of Living:	$\hat{V} = a_6 + b_6\ \hat{P}$	(7)
Employment:	$N = \alpha\ \hat{C} + \beta\ \hat{I} - \hat{\pi}$	(8)
Wages:	$\hat{W} = a_7 + b_7\ \hat{N} + c_7\ \hat{V} + d_7\ UP$	(9)
Income:	$Y = C + I$	(10)
Rate of Interest:	$i = \bar{i}$	(11)

Key to additional symbols: UT = rate of capacity utilisation, PC = prices of primary commodities, π = productivity of labour, E = exports, NW = other non-wage incomes, V = cost of living, UP = union pushfulness. A circumflex indicates a rate of change. Y, C and I are given in terms of constant prices, except when given the subscript c for current prices.

The given variables in the first model are the expected rate of profit (R^*/K^*) which expresses long-term expectations, the wage rate and the quantity of money (fixed exogenously by the Monetary Authority). In the second model the givens are productivity, prices of primary commodities, other non-wage incomes, union pushfulness and exports. The rate of interest is given exogenously by the Monetary Authority.

There are differences between the two models in the equations for investment, prices and employment. In addition the equations for profits and capacity utilisation do not appear in the first model, nor does the quantity of money appear as a variable. We will return to the importance of this omission in section VI. Here I would like to emphasise that one of the fundamental differences between the two models is in the investment equation which in the second model depends, in addition to other determinants, on the distribution of income and more precisely on the share of profits in income.

Formally it may appear that the difference is not great considering that variations in the rate of profit (R/K) are proportional to variations in the share of profits in income if the short-period capital–output ratio (K/Y) is constant, a reasonably realistic assumption if we accept, as Keynes seemed inclined to do, that expectations are often of an extrapolative character so that as a rule movements in the current rate of profit can be considered as an index of the expected rate. In reality, however, the difference between the two models on this point is important since the rate of profit in the second model does not depend in any essential way on psychological factors (such as the long-term state of expectations) but on the interaction of prices, wages and productivity, an interaction – one might add – that in its turn depends on a number of forces including those coming from abroad, especially from imported primary commodities and extra-economic factors such as those produced by economic and social conflicts that influence wages. But the basic difference results from the fact that only the second model exhibits the antithetical, two-sided role of wages: an increase in wages stimulates investment by increasing the demand for consumption goods and thus for investment goods (equations 9, 5, 6, 8, 4, 1), but an increase in wages tends to reduce the share of profits[6] which has a negative influence on investment (equations 9, 2, 3, 1). Whether the positive or negative influence tends to predominate will depend on the intensity of the increase in wages and on the value of the coefficients. All this suggests that there is a problem of an optimum in the rate of increase in wages (and a corresponding problem of an optimum rate of profit).

III THE GREAT DEPRESSION OF THE 1930s

Let us start by examining the first of the three great problems cited above, the risk of another Great Depression. I should first point out that for this problem, as well as for the problem of inflationary stagnation, the first and the third criticisms outlined in the first section (the weakness of the psychological assumptions and the hypothesis concerning the homogeneity of the different markets) are of most importance, while for the third problem – the crowding-out of private activity – it is above all the second criticism (the exogeneity of the quantity of money) which is most relevant.

The question of the psychological hypotheses underlying Keynes's theory is strictly linked to the question of expectations, or better, a part of it. In order to avoid misunderstanding let me start by saying that I do not intend to deny the relevance of expectations or, more in general, the importance of psychological or subjective factors. However, if the economist wants to avoid usurping the field of competence of the psychologist and if he wants to avoid pseudo-explanations that dissolve into circular reasoning he must be able to explain *why* certain expectations are formed rather than others. Only if (and to the extent which) determining factors are outside his field of study can they be assumed as given data. The criticism arises when expectations are assumed to be the *primum mobile* or rather, when the reasons that are the foundation of expectations or other movements of the spirit are described in vague and generic terms or not really explained at all.

The Stock Market Crash of 1929 and the economic crisis which followed were attributed by Keynes to a fall in the marginal efficiency of capital, an expression of the state of long-term expectations which depends not only on psychological factors but also on other factors such as the actual and foreseen size and composition of the capital stock and consumers' tastes. However, Keynes attributed so much importance to psychological factors that he felt it necessary to point out – *excusatio non petita*: 'We should not conclude from this that everything depends on waves of irrational psychology'[7]

Whether the waves that Keynes evokes were rational or irrational, they were without explanation; since the cycle, according to Keynes, depends on variations – themselves cyclical – in the marginal efficiency of capital, the Keynesian explanation of cycles and crises in general, and thus of the spectacular crisis of 1929, must be judged, in the last analysis, an exemplary case of the category of pseudo-explanation.

This does not imply that Keynes's analysis of the Great Depression is without value. The fact is that this historical event presents the economist with questions of various kinds: (a) Why did the Stock Market Crash, which signalled the initiation of the Great Depression, occur? (b) Why was the depression, despite fluctuations, so persistent? (c) Of what benefit were the various measures proposed for curing the crisis, in particular (i) reductions in money wages, (b) expansionary monetary policy, and (iii) expansionary fiscal policy?

Keynes responded to the first question by reference to the marginal efficiency of capital and variations in the state of expectations. As indicated above, and as we shall see more clearly below, such a response is not satisfactory. To the second question Keynes responded with his analysis of effective demand (there was nothing to guarantee, in his view, that the point of intersection of the aggregate demand and supply functions should correspond to full employment income). To the third question Keynes gives several arguments to suggest that reductions in money wages will be inappropriate for recovery and to deny, in conditions of deep slump, the efficacy of expansionary monetary policy. He rather supported the necessity of expansionary fiscal policy in the form of decisive increases in public spending in excess of government revenues; the deficit would, in fact, act to support aggregate demand.

Keynes's response to the first question – the reason for the Stock Market Crash which marked the beginning of the Great Depression – is clearly evident in the following quotation:

If I may be allowed to appropriate the term *speculation* for the activity of forecasting the psychology of the market, and the term *enterprise* for the activity of forecasting the prospective yield of assets over their whole life, it is by no means always the case that speculation predominates over enterprise. As the organisation of investment markets improves, the risk of the predominance of speculation does, however, increase. In one of the greatest investment markets in the world, namely, New York, the influence of speculation (in the above sense) is enormous. . . . Speculators do no harm as bubbles on the steady stream of enterprise. But the position is serious when enterprise becomes the bubble on a whirlpool of speculation. When the capital development of a country becomes a by-product of the activities of a casino, the job is likely to be ill-done. The measure of success of Wall Street, regarded as an institution of which the proper social purpose is to direct new investment into the most profitable channels in terms of future yield, cannot be claimed as one of the outstanding triumphs of *laissez-faire* capitalism . . .[8]

The Wall Street Crash, which represented the conclusion of an unmitigated speculative orgy and created some important preconditions for the depression, should rather be attributed – this is the thesis that I support in opposition to Keynes – to three 'objective' factors which interact one with the other: the extraordinary changes in the distribution of income, the effects of important technological innovations, and the profound changes in market form with the diffusion and consolidation of oligopoly and monopoly in industry, finance and certain areas of trade.

The rigidity of prices with respect to demand which became widespread after the First World War is the factor which initiates our explanation. As a consequence of the process of concentration of firms in a number of important branches of production large corporations began to emerge capable, within certain limits, of influencing prices. An analogous situation may be discovered in those sectors where product differentiation was developed as a result of mass means of communication and their use for publicity purposes. In these markets prices became progressively less sensitive to changes in demand, varying rather in relation to costs, and in particular to fixed costs. However, in countries in which foreign competition plays very little role – as was, and to a large extent still is, the case in the United States – reductions in prices may be appreciably below reductions in direct costs.[9] This is precisely what occurred in the years immediately before the Crash (see Table 7.2, Appendix, p. 153, columns 2, 3, 4, 8 and 9). As a consequence unit margins in industry increased and total profits rose both for the reasons given here as well as from the increase in production which has a doubly positive effect on profits: the reduction in indirect unit costs with the consequent increase in net unit margins and the multiplication of that higher margin on a larger number of units.

Such a process appears in a particularly accentuated form in the public utility companies, especially in the electric industry and the railroads, which in the United States were private but subject to public control. These controls had been introduced before the First World War with the intention of calming price movements and holding down profits in these two important sectors. After the war the paradoxical result of these controls was to reinforce the market power of the companies operating in the two sectors and to cause profits to rise by more than in any other industrial sector. In fact, the controls had been introduced in a period of rising prices and the objective was to slow the rate of increase in prices or to bring them to a halt in the two sectors concerned. After the war conditions were different, the price of petroleum fell substantially (due to the extraordinary progress in methods of geological prospecting, the discovery of new fields and progress in methods of extraction) and oil is the major energy source in both the electricity industry and the railroads. In addition, the fall in the price of petroleum also caused the price of coal to fall. Furthermore, unit labour costs also fell. Thus, costs were clearly falling, while the controls were acting to stabilise tariffs and charges in both the electricity industry and the railroads. The result was a strong increase in profits in both industries.

An analogous phenomenon, if less pronounced, occurred in other industries. In general the prices of raw materials were stable and money wages grew only moderately (11 per cent from 1922 to 1929) but, as a result of technological innovations of various sorts, productivity grew strongly (+ 30 per cent). In spite of this fact, 'by some not very well understood form of witchcraft' as Einaudi put it,[10] prices of industrial products remained constant with a consequent swelling of industrial profits (see Table 7.2, Appendix, p. 153, columns 3, 5, 8 and 9). In reality the relative stability of prices was the result of market power – 'spontaneous' and 'artificial' – which had been greatly reinforced in the preceding two or three decades. Thus gross unit margins increased. At the same time, with the expansion of production, indirect costs per unit of output tended to fall and profits tended to rise as a result of both the rise in the net margin and from the increase in quantity produced. It is precisely this shift in distributive shares which is at the origin of the Wall Street Crash, not the exhaustion of the (unexplained) wave of optimism, followed by an (unexplained) wave of pessimism. It is not that waves of this sort do not occur, but for each of them the factors that generate them must be identified. In the case that we are considering the crucial factor was the conspicuous share of profits which continued to grow and thus generated expectations of further growth.

Most economists maintain that increasing profits in a capitalist system can only bring benefit and increased growth to the economy, no matter how iniquitous or socially unjust they may be from other points of view. But things are not that simple. Smith had already rejected – rightly – such a point of view. The truth is that in any given situation, as already pointed out, there is an optimum to the share and the rate of profit, particularly in the industrial sector. A falling rate, at least after a certain point, acts as a break on accumulation. This is the traditional position. But, an increase in the rate of profit is normally accompanied by a fall in the share of income going to labour, which must eventually be reflected in a reduction in the rate of increase in the demand for consumption goods, and thus indirectly in the demand for investment goods, stalling the entire growth process. Taking into consideration income other than profits and wages of industrial workers – such as the incomes of managers and those of family businesses – does not substantially modify the sequence of events described here.

In its essential characteristics, the contradictory sequence spelled out here can be made explicit with the help of the second model. An increase in wages has a positive effect on investment (equation 1) through the increase in the demand for consumption goods (equation 5) and the degree of capacity utilisation (equation 4) given the level of employment. On the other hand, the increase in wages has a negative effect if this causes a reduction in profits (equations 2, 3, 4) because prices do not rise or do not rise sufficiently. The reverse sequence tends to result from reductions in wages, or if productivity increases given wages and the level of employment (this is a more complex process which equations 8, 5, and 1 help to clarify).

Considering the empirical evidence, occasions of exceptional increases in profits and in other non-wage incomes are clear and numerous (cf. Table 7.2, Appendix, p. 153, column 10).[11] With respect to changes in output it should be noticed that changes in basic consumption goods such as food products and textiles show minimal expansion, as does the wage bill (cf. Table 7.1, Appendix, p. 152, column 5 and Table 7.2, Appendix, p. 153, column 5; from 1922–23 to 1928–29 food products increase by 2 per cent and textiles by 9 per cent).

On the other hand, production of durable goods such as automobiles and private housing, goods acquired by those receiving average and above average incomes, expand at a much more rapid rate. It is important to note that the greatest activity occurs from 1922 to 1926 and after that dies out rather rapidly (Table 7.1, Appendix, p. 152, columns 3, 6). Even though there are no disaggregated data available we can suppose that in the residential construction sector activity was concentrated in the provision of housing for the middle and upper classes located in the new suburban developments made possible by the beginning of the automobile age.[12] As the opportunities for productive investment became more scarce, for the reasons already outlined, the mass of investible funds resulting from the high profits and the growth in other non-wage incomes was redirected, first (until 1927) toward high risk investments in foreign countries[13] (see Table 7.3, Appendix, p. 154, column 4), and then to the Stock Market to purchase shares whose prices were rising precisely because profits were rising. After a certain point the increase in prices became explosive because the funds coming from the profits of the productive sector were joined by speculative funds from the financial community and the very profits resulting from stock market speculation (Table 7.3, column 5). The wave of speculation should be viewed in these terms and not in essentially psychological terms as is usually the case.

At the origin of this process we can then identify the enormous redistribution of income which subsumes and gives expression to the two grand accompanying changes, that of market form and technological innovation.[14] As we have pointed out above it was not only profits, in particular industrial profits, which benefited from this redistribution, but other non-wage incomes as well; in particular mixed incomes in the non-agricultural sector and the income of managers, especially those who participated directly or indirectly in the profits of the medium and large-size firms. All things considered then, the great prosperity of the 1920s did not concern more than 20 per cent or at maximum 30 per cent of income recipients; the others had to be content with rather more modest benefits from the 'new era'[15]

Not only the analysis of the cycle and crises, but the entire Keynesian construction is based – it must be repeated – on psychological hypotheses. The three pillars of that construction, as is well known, are the long-term state of expectations, the propensity to consume (which expresses a fundamental 'psychological' law) and liquidity preference. Having made this choice it must have seemed natural to Keynes to assume given the state of technology, the distribution of income, and the form of the market ('the intensity of competition'), i.e. the three factors which are essential, in the opinion of this writer, to the understanding of the conditions which brought about the Great Depression and, more generally, for interpreting the most important lines of development of modern industrial capitalism.

It might thus appear that anyone who accepted such a position would be obliged to reject the entire Keynesian analysis. But this is not the case if we recognise that the relevance of a particular set of hypotheses depends on the problem being analysed. When we move from the problem of the origins of the Depression to different problems such as the analysis of the mechanisms governing the variations in effective demand, the choice of one set of hypotheses or another takes on a lesser importance.

IV   THE REDUCTION OF WAGES AND EXPANSIONARY MONETARY POLICY

Let us start by examining these two measures, postponing for a moment to the next section consideration of the measure which Keynes considered vital, the expansion of public expenditure. It will be useful for this discussion to refer to our first model.

The reduction of wages tends to produce a proportionate reduction of prices (identity 7, equation 6) and of monetary demand without any effect, in the first instance, on the level of activity. In other words, Keynes highlights the role played by wages in variations in demand, a role that is essentially denied by traditional theory. While it is also possible to identify the other role of wages, in determining changes in the distribution of income, in the 'Alternative Model' this role cannot be discovered in the traditional Keynesian model.

According to Keynes, however, in conditions of general unemployment, a reduction in wages would not be without effect. Since the quantities are expressed in terms of wage units, a reduction in W, given M, leads to an expansion in M_w ($= M/W$) and thus to a reduction in i (equation 4) and therefore an expansion in I_w, Y_w and N (equations 3 and 1a). Thus, in conditions of widespread unemployment a reduction in W can increase the level of activity only through the tortuous path of increasing the 'real' quantity of money. But in this event it is far simpler to adopt an expansive monetary policy directly without reducing the wage unit: 'Having regard to human nature and our institutions [among which are included the trade unions] it can only be a foolish person', writes Keynes, 'who would prefer a flexible wage policy to a flexible monetary policy. . .'. He adds, 'It is only in a highly authoritarian society, where sudden, substantial, all-round wage changes could be decreed that a flexible wage policy could function with success. One can imagine it in operation in Italy, Germany or Russia, but not in France, the United States or Great Britain'.[16]

Policy to reduce wages is thus inadequate to the task of curing the depression. Would expansionary monetary policy, polemically suggested by Keynes's discussion of cuts in wages, be a better alternative? Keynes responded that in conditions of deep depression with the rate of interest near 'liquidity trap' levels monetary policy was nearly or completely useless. In such conditions only a policy of expansionary public spending could be of help, even if this produced deficit spending.

V   THE QUESTION OF CROWDING OUT

Before completing his *General Theory* Keynes made several attempts to discredit the traditional position that every increase in public spending, and the more so if it was deficit spending, produced an equal reduction in private spending without effect on either income or employment because borrowing by the government for public works implied a reduction in the fund of private savings available for private investment. These attempts had met with little success and he eventually became convinced that he could only prevail by going to the roots of traditional theory. It is probable that this is the immediate origin of the *General Theory*. One of the most important ideas to emerge from the book is that in conditions of widespread unemployment neither additional investment nor additional public sector deficit spending take away available savings, rather they generate savings. Only in conditions of near full employment would increased saving be necessary to avoid inflation and what is today called 'crowding out'.

If we consider the qualification just noted it seems obvious that the crowding out hypothesis, today so much in vogue, is not necessarily in contradiction with the Keynesian point of view. However, it appears that it is possible to have inflation and crowding out even in the presence of widespread unemployment. It is precisely the co-existence of these phenomena – crowding out, inflation and unemployment – that has appeared to be in contradiction with Keynes's construction. Here is the source of what Hicks has called the 'Crisis' of Keynesian theory.

What is the cause of this co-existence? There are a number of different reasons. First is the non-homogeneity of the labour market and the product markets discussed above: the pressure of demand for labour can increase the wages for disagreeable jobs, or increase immigration without producing any significant effect on the level of employment. On the other hand, wages may rise, for any given level of unemployment, as a consequence of an increase in the cost of living. And the cost of living can increase, even if indirectly, as a result of the pressure of demand (which tends to push up the prices of agricultural products and other primary products); but it can also increase for other reasons such as increases in indirect taxes, public utility charges, or for legal reasons (for example, changes in rent control laws) as well as from factors with their origin abroad. Finally unions, thanks to the conspicuous bargaining power acquired in recent decades, are capable of pushing up wages even in the presence of widespread unemployment: wages also push up prices through a process similar to that sketched out by Keynes.

Having introduced foreign factors, a possibility that is precluded from the traditional Keynesian model by the hypothesis of a closed system,[17] we must recall that the public deficit, by increasing internal demand and thus imports, will tend to produce a foreign deficit and that a payments deficit puts downward pressure on the exchange rate which causes the prices of imported goods to rise in terms of domestic currency. All of these causes of increasing prices are independent of the pressure of demand as such.

But, it is argued that the public sector deficit tends to 'crowd out' private investment. Now once the increase in demand tends to make itself felt in increasing prices, as if the economy were near full employment, it is no longer possible to criticise Keynes on these grounds. The problem is to discover why one can describe such a situation as if it were the equivalent to full employment even though the level of unemployment is very high. I have already indicated some of the elements capable of explaining this fundamental question; others will be given below, but first some additional observations on the public sector deficit are in order.

In general the problem has up to now been discussed with reference to the short period or even within simultaneous equilibrium systems such as Hicks' IS–LM. But it is necessary to extend the discussion to the long period. In fact, if the medium and the long-period tendencies of expenditures and receipts are similar there are certain consequences, while if they tend to diverge, on the other hand, the consequences are completely different.

When we start from conditions of equilibrium in the government

budget and the rate of increase in expenditures systematically coincides with the path of receipts no permanent deficit can occur. But, it is
normal for income to fluctuate: when it is declining receipts also tend
to follow the same path while expenditures tend to move in the
opposite direction because unemployment benefits tend to rise as do
other costs associated with alleviating the economic and social problems caused by recession. For these reasons deficits tend to occur in
phases of recession and to disappear in phases of expansion, or even to
produce surpluses. Such deficits, because they are temporary, serve a
very useful function because they support demand during the recession
and act as a parachute for falling incomes. The government deficit, in
the 1950s and the 1960s was thus seen as playing the role of 'automatic
stabiliser'. Such a point of view appears as a natural corollary of
Keynesian theory and it was justified as such.

Problems started to arise in the 1960s, became persistent in the
1970s, and in the last two or three years have gone from bad to worse.
The fact is that inflationary conditions have existed on a world level
since 1971. Since then the process of growth has been sharply reduced
in all industrialised countries including Japan, even if the Japanese
economy has at least up to the present performed much better than the
others. But, despite the weakening of growth, expenditures – particularly those of a social nature – have continued to grow at a rate which is
similar to those experienced during the period of sustained growth,
and in some cases at even higher rates because they are determined by
legislation introduced in the 'fat years', and also because of the fact,
already demonstrated in previous recessions, that certain expenditures
grow most rapidly in precisely those periods when economic performance is poor. Receipts, however, tend to follow movements in
income rather closely and if the rate of increase in receipts, even
though declining, remains above the rate of increase in income this is
evidence of 'fiscal drag', a result of the progressivity of the tax system
in combination with inflation which provokes strong economic and
social tensions. In any case, expenditures tend to increase at a rate that
is systematically higher than revenues. The stabilising effect falls into
the background and, progressively, the destabilising factor takes the
upper hand.

The growing deficit in fact usually requires recourse to the creation
of money as well as sales of government debt. But in conditions such as
those recalled above, the expansion of the money supply tends to have
decidedly inflationary effects (which cannot be fully explained by

means of the relations evoked in the monetarists' theory). Now, on the basis of what has been said here, it is probable that even in the presence of under-utilised resources, increases in demand will fall primarily on prices (or that there is an increase in monetary demand as a result of an increase in prices) without any increase in the level of activity and the volume of savings. In such conditions the government, selling debt, must compete with other uses for savings and thus drive up the rate of interest, making the crowding out phenomenon more than evident. The rising rate of interest acts as a brake on investment and contributes to the weakening, and in some cases to the disappearance, of real growth. The deficit tends to increase at an accelerating rate on account of the increase in interest that the State must pay on its debt. This results both from the increase in the rate of interest as well as from the increase in the size of the debt offered to the public in the bond market.

In the long period – this is a very important point – the gap between the growth in spending and the growth in revenues depends, at least in part, on the composition of spending itself. If the share of expenditure destined to productive uses is high, income will tend to increase at a higher rate than it would have had there been a lower share of productive spending. Remember that Japan alone among the industrialised countries avoided the 'fiscal crisis of the State', not so much because public expenditures grew at a lower rate than in other countries, or at a lower rate than income, as from the fact that the share of expenditure directed to productive ends was higher than that observable in the other industrialised countries. I believe that this is a very important consideration in explaining how Japan succeeded in maintaining a rate of growth above zero even in highly adverse international conditions.

Keynes was not preoccupied with these problems. The public sector deficit was of minimal size and the more important political and economic problem was unemployment which depended primarily on bankruptcy and lay-offs, not on the failure to absorb new labourers. His practical intention, already followed in previous writings, was to demonstrate the utility of decisive expansion of public expenditure to promote recovery. These are the motives which led Keynes to adopt a 'short-period' point of view in the sense that he considered the immediate determinants of effective demand, neglecting the durable consequences of investment and the variations in productivity. Today, however, conditions are profoundly different and that point of view can no longer be justified.

VI   THE MOTIVES FOR MONETARY CREATION

The question of the destination of public expenditures, production or consumption, brings us back to the question of the motives which determine the creation of money. Keynes, as Friedman, assumes money to be exogenous; there is never any question of why money is created by the banking system. This assumption is inexact in the case of the monetary base (principally, currency of the Central Bank) and completely beside the point in the case of bank money in the strict sense (current account deposits).

In the pre-Keynesian text-books it was usual to distinguish money issued for 'commercial' causes, not only for firms operating in domestic and international trade, but also for firms directly or indirectly involved in production, from money created for, or directly by, the State. Speaking of money I refer to the two categories cited above, the monetary base and bank money. The Central Bank, however, which issues bank notes did not normally (and does not) have direct relations with private enterprises, but only with commercial banks which sought (and still seek) loans from the Central Bank against the debt instruments issued by firms. In addition, in difference from commercial banks, the Central Bank has a direct relation with the Government, upon which it ultimately depends, and to whom it furnishes bank notes as 'advances' or as a 'sinking fund'. In the ancient texts, either implicitly or explicitly, it was supposed that money created for commercial purposes was used for productive expenditures, while that created for the State was directed toward consumption. Such presumptions were not correct, simply because it is not the intentions but the results that are of importance: firms that fail do not in general repay their loans so that money created by loans to them has the same effect as money created for consumption.

On the other hand, the money issued for the account of the State can be used for productive as well as unproductive uses, as was noted above. With regard to the second category of money, it might appear that deposits are only created for commercial purposes, but this is not the case, for more than a few public bodies borrow money from private commercial banks. These latter, however, have direct links to the private firms, and it is thus that it is via the commercial banks that the 'production cycle' combines with the 'credit cycle' to borrow the adept analytical expression of Marco Fanno.[18]

The difference between the creation of money for productive purposes and the creation of money for consumption purposes resides in the fact that in the first case, when the production cycle closes, the means of payment return to the banks as the firms repay interest and principal (this is the process that Schumpeter called 'auto deflation'), while in the second case the means of payment remain in circulation. In the case of money created for productive purposes, when the firms contracted loans in order to acquire means of production there is an inverse process, which might be called 'auto inflation', the increase in the quantity of money and in demand acting in markets for goods with flexible prices starts a process of inflation which tends to spread, while in the markets for goods whose prices are not sensible to demand the additional demand has the sole immediate effect of calling forth increased production. Once the firm reaches the end of the 'production cycle' and throws the increased output on the market, production continues to increase, while the pressure of demand is lessened in the markets for goods with flexible prices.

The assumption that money is exogenous should be rejected because it impedes the examination of the motives, and thus the destination, of the newly created monetary means. This is particularly damaging to an analysis of medium or long-period factors. From the arguments given above it should be clear that the assumption may have partial validity as it applies to the monetary base, while there is no validity whatsoever in the case of bank money. It is this partial validity which is the real source, I believe, of the assumption here under criticism. But, the validity is only partial, for while it is true that the Central Bank has a non-negligible discretionary power in the creation of bank notes, its power is asymmetrical (it is greater in the case of restriction of the monetary circulation). Further, the forces that tend to provoke the emission of bank notes comes from the firms, even if indirectly, or from the Government. The Central Bank can either permit or counter these impulses, but it cannot create them. The variations in bank money, on the other hand, are more directly linked to the activity of firms than is the monetary base. It is precisely the variation in bank money that is to be found behind the phenomena of 'auto inflation' and 'auto deflation'. It should thus not be surprising if variations in economic activity are fully reflected in variations in bank money, while the movements in the monetary base are much less closely related to the movements of the economy.

In sum, in the examination of variations in the total quantity of money (currency and deposits) it appears that as a first approximation it is correct to neglect the discretionary power of the Monetary Authority, which is, on the other hand, very important in consideration of the rate of interest. For this reason, following a suggestion by Kaldor,[19] I have included equation 11 in the Alternative Model.[20] However, it should be kept in mind that the discretionary power of the Monetary Authority regarding the rate of interest is great, but not unlimited because the Central Bank has to contend with two constraints, one determined by the supply of public debt and the other by the rates of interest of the major economies whose level influences international capital movements.

The considerations expressed above are in complete agreement with the statistics relating to the two categories of money for the period 1922–33 (cf. Table 7.3, Appendix, p. 154, columns 1 and 2). It appears that the monetary base in the period 1926–31 varies little, while M_1 (currency plus demand deposits) undergoes violent fluctuation. But, if things are as they appear from these statistics and if it is true that the fundamental instrument of monetary policy is the monetary base and not bank money (as Friedman himself argues) it is then impossible to attribute a decisive role to monetary policy among the events that led to the Great Depression.[21]

This criticism of the assumption that money is exogenous applies equally to Keynesian theory and to the monetarist approach, but the criticism is more damaging to the second approach for two reasons. In the first place such an assumption appears to be vital in Friedman's theory, while it is not vital in Keynesian theory; and in the second place Keynes appears to have been the more nearly correct in crediting monetary policy with a minimal influence on the events surrounding the Great Depression.

VII SOME OBSERVATIONS ON INFLATIONARY STAGNATION AND THE RISK OF A NEW GREAT DEPRESSION

The world inflation that we are now experiencing cannot be satisfactorily understood by means of either a Keynesian or a monetarist type of analysis, although the first is in certain cases capable of some useful insights into the process. I have elsewhere proposed that the origin of this process is to be found in the crisis of the international monetary system, while the explanation of inflationary differentials requires examination of the movements of the cost of labour and public sector deficits in each particular country.

As a consequence of the crisis in the international monetary system the speculative factor has come to play an ever-increasing role in world markets for primary commodities because the weakness of the dollar as a store of value has caused some raw materials to replace it in this role. After the adoption of flexible exchange rates speculation has become even more prevalent and has spread to foreign exchange markets. In addition, simultaneously with the persistence of inflation, growth rates of the world's industrial countries taken as a whole have fallen markedly.

In fact, every world economic expansion tends to bring with it a substantial increase in the prices of raw materials which in its turn tends to produce (or aggravate) deficits in the payments balances of the industrialised countries. In order to reduce these deficits the governments of these countries usually adopt restrictive monetary or restrictive fiscal policies. As a result a world economic downturn becomes inevitable. This, in my view, is the reason why expansion and contraction have succeeded one another with even greater rapidity than in the past (every 2–3 rather than 5–6 years) since 1971. Each recovery has been accompanied by a substantial and rapid increase in raw materials' prices (much more accentuated than those which occurred before 1971) and thus by increasing current account deficits in the majority of the industrialised countries. Each downturn, such as that we are currently experiencing, has been accompanied by a reduction in the prices of raw materials. It also appears that each increase is of greater magnitude than the previous reduction. It is also apparent that reductions now only concern rates of increase of industrial prices and not their absolute levels because, among other things, money wages continue to rise more rapidly than productivity. Taken together the results of these developments are inflation (which continues without interruption, although at diverse rates) and a weakening of the growth process due to the fact that the phases of expansion have a tendency to become shorter while the phases of contraction become ever longer.

To escape from this unfortunate situation of inflationary stagnation it will be necessary for the principal industrialised countries to formulate a common strategy which should be divided into two phases. In the first it will be necessary to bring about a dynamic restructuring of public sector finances and to formulate an agreement for the reform of the international monetary system: a new Bretton Woods agreement will be required. In the second phase national economic policies will have to concede priority to economic policy on an international scale because the growth of any one country crucially depends on the expansion of all the others. For the reform of the international monetary system, which plays the central role in his strategy, an attentive study of Keynes's plan for a Clearing Union presented to the Bretton Woods Conference and which he felt to be of major importance should be a first priority.[22]

The question of world inflation is thus closely connected with the grave and persistent difficulties that the growth process has exhibited in recent years. It is these difficulties that have led some economists to speak of a possible repetition of the 1929 crisis and a subsequent prolonged depression.

It is, however, more than evident that current conditions are radically different from those of the late 1920s. It is not necessary to demonstrate that on the demand side there is a clear excess, not a deficiency. There is weakness, however, on the side of profits, especially in the industrial sector and this factor not only acts as a brake on the growth process; it also prevents the outbreak of any speculative waves such as occurred in 1928–29. The weakness of profits is further aggravated by the heighth of interest rates. Inflation should be favourable to firms for it lightens the real burden of outstanding debt, but this advantage, which benefits the capital account, in most cases is more than offset by weakness in the profit and loss account because, on the one hand, indirect costs per unit of output tend to rise systematically and, on the other, in periods of inflationary pressure in many sectors prices tend to rise less than in proportion to costs,[23] primarily because of the pressure of foreign competition. In certain sectors (petrochemicals, steel) this has produced conditions of real crisis.

As for the banking system, the present situation in the principal industrialised countries is very different from that of the 1920s and 1930s. In those times the banking system did not have the series of administrative and legislative constraints and supports that were subsequently introduced and which more or less exclude the possibility of a chain of bankruptcies.

The high rates of interest which were mentioned above depend on diverse factors, among which the competition of the Government in the market for private savings should be recalled. They also depend on the monetary policies of the major industrialised countries, and especially the largest of these, the United States, which has adopted a sharply restrictive policy with respect to industry (but much less so with respect to government agencies). This policy has pushed up interest rates around the world and with particularly damaging effects on the heavily indebted underdeveloped countries.

It is possible to argue that such a policy is based on a fundamentally flawed analysis of the problems of the economy, that even the budgetary policy is flawed because it attempts to reduce the deficit by means of expenditure cuts which in fact increase the deficit by causing income to stagnate and further reduces government revenues (what is needed is not cutting expenditures, but rather to change its composition similarly to the policy followed by the Japanese). However, considering the pragmatism that usually characterises North American policy it is possible that the United States will change its position before long.

To sum up, a tendency to stagnation or to weak growth performance is very likely, a collapse of dramatic proportions is not. Whether growth should turn out to be very weak and frequently interrupted by decline or even should proceed at a rate substantially below that of the previous two or three decades, but superior to that of the most recent years, will depend on the strategy adopted by the most important industrialised countries, starting with the United States.

VIII BRIEF CONCLUDING CONSIDERATIONS

As will be clear from the above, this writer, in agreement with a number of other economists, attributes a part of our current economic difficulties to errors of North American policy which can be more accurately credited to Friedman than to Keynes. It is to Keynes, on the other hand, that we attribute, within certain limits, the blame for those excesses in public spending which have been one of the basic causes of the 'monetarist counter-revolution'. And if in the United States the excessive growth in public spending depends more on military expenditures, which are obviously unproductive expenditures, than on social security expenditures, not even the expansion in these expenditures, which are also unproductive although in a different sense, have been sufficiently restricted to keep them within the bounds of the reduced rate of growth of real incomes. In European countries there can be little doubt that the excessive spending has been primarily of a social character. It is not difficult to see that the policies of generalised social security covering even those families above the level of real need has gone too far. I believe that the tendency, exhibited by Keynes, to pay scarce attention to long-period effects (a tendency which among other things led him to approve, even if in paradoxical terms, of projects to 'dig holes in the ground') has made easier the tasks of governments intent on using social expenditures for purely political purposes.[24]

There is also in this case a question of an optimum. Up to a certain point the support of demand – even that coming from social expenditure – not only assures improvements in the quality of life, but also promotes income growth. It is, however, necessary to avoid excesses of one type without falling into the opposite extreme. It is not a question of reducing the total level of expenditures by the public sector, but only their rate of increase by means of reducing expenditures for consumption and increasing productive expenditures.

Thus there are some excesses for which Keynes must be considered responsible. But, everything considered, the rupture that he provoked in traditional theory can be evaluated, in my view, very positively. Without Keynes, and in particular without the *General Theory*, it is probable that the social progress which has taken place after the second world war would have been much more modest, the expansion of production would have been much less rapid, and the diffusion of well-being among the poorest sections of society would have been much slower.

On the analytical plane, it is necessary to emphasise that Keynes is much superior to most economists who were his contemporaries because of the fact that he directed systematic attention – especially in his essay on *The End of Laissez-Faire* and then in the *General Theory* – to one of the fundamental problems of our time, the growing role of the State in economic life. Keynes himself has contributed to this growth; in the final analysis, his *General Theory* can be regarded as a great intellectual effort to see how the State could intervene to save capitalism, making it function in a socially acceptable way.

NOTES

1. Cf. A. H. Hansen, *A Guide to Keynes* (New York: McGraw-Hill, 1953) ch. 8, and L. L. Pasinetti, *Growth and Income Distribution* (London: Cambridge University Press, 1976) ch. 2.
2. I have raised the points of criticism referred to in the text in 'The Keynesians', *Banca Nazionale del Lavoro Quarterly Review*, November 1949; *Oligopoly and Technical Progress* (Cambridge, Mass.: Harvard University Press, 1967); *Lezioni di Economia*, vol. I, *Macroeconomia* (Rome: Edizioni dell'Ateneo, 1979); and 'Rigid Prices, Flexible Prices and Inflation', *Banca Nazionale del Lavoro Quarterly Review*, March 1982.
3. J. M. Keynes, *The General Theory of Employment, Interest and Money* (London: Macmillan, 1936) p. 41.
4. With reference to Great Britain (but the case is similar for most industrialised countries) a partial measure of this factor is given by the share of foreign labour in total employment, around 2% in 1931 (400 000 of 18 million) and between 8 per cent and 9 per cent in 1981 (slightly less than 2

million in 21 million), estimates taken from 1931 and 1981 Census figures.

5. It is an enlarged and slightly different version of a model originally presented in 1967 in 'Prices, Distribution and Investment in Italy, 1951–1966: an Interpretation', *Banca Nazionale del Lavoro Quarterly Review*, December, 1967, and which is in the process of further amplification and elaboration. For equations 2 and 3 see P. Sylos Labini, 'Prices and Distribution of Income in Manufacturing Industry', *Journal of Post Keynesian Economics*, Autumn 1979.

6. See 'Prices and Distribution of Income, etc.', op. cit.

7. Keynes, op. cit., p. 162.

8. Keynes, ibid., pp. 158–9. See also 'The Great Slump of 1930', and 'The Consequences of the Collapse of Money Values', in *Essays in Persuasion*, vol. IX of *The Collected Writings of John Maynard Keynes* (London: Macmillan, 1973).

9. P. Sylos Labini, 'Prices and Distribution of Income', op. cit.

10. L. Einaudi, 'Debiti', *Riforma sociale*, Jan.–Feb. 1934.

11. See J. Schumpeter, *Business Cycles: A Theoretical, Historical, and Statistical Analysis of the Capitalist Process* (New York: McGraw-Hill, 1939) p. 831, and R. R. Keller, 'Factor Income Distribution in the United States during the 1920's: a Re-examination of Fact and Theory', *Journal of Economic History*, March 1973.

12. The production of automobiles in 1929 (4.5 million) was only surpassed in 1949 (5.1 million).

13. Cf. J. K. Galbraith, *The Great Crash* (Boston: Houghton Mifflin, 1961).

14. The basic lines of this interpretation were already set out in my *Oligopoly and Technical Progress*, op. cit. I returned to the question in a brief essay 'On the Optimum Rate of Profit', in *Studies in Economic Theory and Practice: Essays in Honour of Edward Lipinski* (Amsterdam: North Holland, 1981). It has recently come to my notice that a young North American economic historian, who undoubtedly had not seen my book, published a very similar interpretation not too long ago, cf. Keller, op. cit. I should point out that the analysis mentioned earlier concerning the paradoxical consequences of rate control for public utility companies (reinforcing their market power and increasing their profits) was put forward for the first time by Keller.

15. Cf. E. Fano, 'I paesi capitalistici dalla prima guerra mondiale al 1929', in *La crisi del capitalismo negli anni '20*, M. Telò, ed. (Bari: De Donato, 1976).

16. Keynes, *General Theory*, op. cit., p. 268. It should be remembered that Keynes was referring to M_w and not M, thus the 'Fisher effect' (the increase in prices increases the rate of interest) is in general compatible with Keynes's analysis, despite the contrary position held by some critics. Keynes normally reasoned in terms of constant prices, but assumed that when prices varied they moved in step with wages; thus if prices and wages increased for any reason M_w would fall and in such conditions the rate of interest would increase.

17. It has always been a source of wonder to me that an English economist should have constructed a theory on the assumption of a closed system. To be sure, in this way Keynes has greatly simplified his analysis; the cost,

however, has been high, both on the theoretical and practical level.

18. M. Fanno, *La teoria delle fluttuazioni economiche* Turin: UTET, 1957; 1st edn, 1947).

19. N. Kaldor, *Origins of the New Monetarism* (Cardiff: University College Press, 1981).

20. I criticised Keynes on the exogeneity of the quantity of money in my youthful note cited in the first section. I have no qualms admitting to the arrogance and superficiality of that piece. I still believe, however, in the importance of recognising that money cannot be treated as an exogenous factor. Recently Kaldor, who certainly can be considered a great Keynesian, has written in the work just cited: 'Keynes, who ... was not particularly wedded to his liquidity preference theory, might have saved endless trouble to his successors (and the misery of the unnecessarily unemployed) if he had thought about the matter just a little longer, and had not written quite so carelessly about the amount of money or cash being independently determined by the monetary authorities' (Kaldor, op. cit., p. 21). Kaldor criticises Keynes's assumption concerning the exogeneity of the quantity of money in such drastic terms because he sees in it the reason which has allowed the monetarists to gain the upper hand in monetary policy.

21. In his attempt to attribute to monetary policy the major responsibility for the Great Depression Friedman goes so far as to affirm that in the immediately preceding period the Federal Reserve 'imposed or permitted a drastic reduction in the money base' (cf. 'The Role of Money', in *The Optimum Quantity of Money and Other Essays* (Chicago: Aldine, 1969). It is difficult to know how to judge such a statement, which is in direct contrast with the statistical evidence he himself presents in his works written together with Anna Schwartz. I shall leave judgment to the reader.

22. J. M. Keynes, *Activities, 1941–1946: Shaping the Post-War World: Bretton Woods and Reparations, The Collected Writings of J. M. Keynes*, vol. XXVI (London: Macmillan, 1980).

23. P. Sylos Labini, 'Prices and Distribution of Income', op. cit.

24. In his essay in this volume Jan Kregel appears to contradict this point of view when he maintains that for Keynes 'the principal objective of economic policy was the stabilisation of investment', while deficit spending was only admissible as a temporary expedient and as a last resort. However, the contradiction is more apparent than real given that these qualifications regarding deficit spending, as can be seen from the references, were introduced by Keynes in his writings of 1942 and 1943 which were only published in 1980. Such qualifications were not in the *General Theory*, except for the generic 'in conditions of involuntary unemployment'. On the other hand we do find strong support for government deficit spending which is reinforced by picturesque metaphors about digging holes in the ground, the construction of pyramids, earthquakes, wars, cathedrals and funeral masses (cf. section VI of ch. 10). It does not seem right to me to place all the blame on economists and politicians for the application of Keynesian theory which Kregel rightly censures: a part of the responsibility, at the very least for insufficient clarity, must be attributed to Keynes himself.

APPENDIX   SELECTED STATISTICS FOR THE PERIOD 1922–35

TABLE 7.1   Production

	Industrial production	Electrical energy	Consumer goods			Housing	Railways (cars)
			Durables	Semi-durables	Non-durables		
1913–14	80	41	60	17	46	62	255
1922	100	100	100	100	100	100	100
1923	120	116	146	131	116	121	182
1924	113	125	130	122	102	135	227
1925	127	139	176	141	113	149	218
1926	133	154	143	149	116	158	254
1927	133	166	143	132	117	155	182
1928	140	177	156	144	117	150	136
1929	153	192	185	154	119	148	200
1930	127	188	143	105	97	112	136
1931	100	179	86	80	78	82	27
1932	80	162	47	49	56	46	15
1933	100	169	50	56	60	39	–

TABLE 7.2 *Prices and wages*

| | Prices | | | Wages | | | Trade Union membership | Hourly productivity | Unit labour costs | Distribution of income |
| | Agriculture | Raw materials | Finished goods | Hourly | Total | Total salaries | | | | |
	1	2	3	4	5	6	7	8	9	10
1913–14	76	71	70	47				75	62	
1922	100	100	100	100			4.0	100	100	29.0
1923	105	103	103	106	11.0	2.8		98	108	(48)
1924	106	102	100	110				105	105	
1925	117	111	104	110	11.0	3.0		113	97	
1926	110	104	104	110				114	96	
1927	106	101	98	110				117	93	
1928	112	103	99	110				124	90	
1929	112	102	98	114	11.6	3.6	3.4	130	88	33.5
1930	95	88	91	112				132	84	(54)
1931	65	68	80	104	6.9			137	76	
1932	50	57	73	90				130	70	
1933	54	59	73	90	6.6	1.6		136	66	

TABLE 7.3   *Money and finance*

	Money Base	Money (M_1)	Rate of discount	Foreign loans	Shares in industrial companies
	1	2	3	4	5
1913–14	3.5	15.9			
1922	6.3	33.8	4.2	100	100
1923	6.6	36.3	4.2	55	109
1924	6.8	38.0	4.2–3	127	116
1925	6.9	41.3	3–3.7	141	154
1926	7.1	43.3	3.7–4	147	168
1927	7.1	44.5	4–3.5	175	217
1928	7.1	45.9	3.5–5	164	272
1929	7.1	46.1	5–6	88	370
1930	7.0	45.2	4.5–2.3	118	289
1931	7.3	42.0	2.3–1.5	30	189
1932	7.7	34.8	1.5–2.8	4	95
1933	8.1	30.6	2.8–2.2	1	119

NOTES   Base: 1922 = 100.
Table 7.1:1 and Table 7.2:3, 4, 5, 6, 8, and 9: Manufacturing industry.
Table 7.1:3: Includes automobiles.
Table 7.1:4: Shoes and clothing.
Table 7.2:7: in millions (1939: 9; 1970: 21).
Table 7.2:10: % share of income going to the upper 5% of income recipients (from 33.5% in 1929, it falls to 17% in 1972); an estimate of the share going to the upper 20% is given in parentheses (from 54% in 1929, it falls to 43% in 1972).
Table 7.3:1 and 2: millions of dollars (column 2: M_1 = notes plus demand deposits).
Table 7.3:5: 'foreign capital issues (government and corporate) publicly offered in the United States'.

SOURCES   *Historical Statistics of the United States – from Colonial Times to 1970* (Washington: Department of Commerce, 1972); *Statistical Abstract of the United States* (Washington: Department of Commerce, 1934 and 1937). Column 10 of Table 7.2: in addition to the sources already cited cf. the article by M.A. Copeland, 'Determinants of the Distribution of Income', *American Economic Review*, March 1947. Columns 1 and 2 of Table 7.3: M. Friedman and A. Schwartz, *A Monetary History of the United States, 1860–1960* (Princeton University Press, 1964, Tables A1 and B3).

8 From Equilibrium to Probability: a Reinterpretation of the Method of the *General Theory**

FAUSTO VICARELLI

But style is not a careful composition of coherent substances. Often it is an impossible mixture, an absurd craving. . . . Talent is not a guarantee but a risk. It's like a friend who takes you up to a cross-roads without a single road-sign and says: 'all you have to do now is find your way home from here'.

(Vespignani)

I INTRODUCTION

Keynes's interpreters have never questioned his extraordinary ability to face up to the complex and at times dramatic problems of his time. On many occasions however the analysis proposed in the *General Theory* has been considered as having no relation to the vision of capitalism which emerges from his earlier, fundamental works. This has created considerable and, in some instances, insuperable difficulties, both in understanding Keynes's message (the theory) and in the analysis of the functioning of the economic system (the method).

* A previous draft of this paper benefited from useful criticism from Professors M. Amendola, A. Asimakopulos, M. Draghi, C. Gnesutta, J. Kregel, G. Martinengo, G. Nardozzi, A. Roncaglia, S. Parrinello and P. Sylos Labini. Responsibility for any weaknesses or mistakes present in the text is mine alone.

It is above all on this second aspect of the controversy that I would like to concentrate in this paper.[1] The basic problem to which I would like to draw attention is the use of the neoclassical concept of equilibrium in the interpretation of the *General Theory*, and the various attempts to formalise its main propositions. Even in the most generally accepted sense of the term, that suggested by F. Hahn,[2] it is rooted in the tradition of general equilibrium theory and thus in the deductive methodological framework of this approach. It is thus inevitable that interpretations of Keynes based on this concept should lead to similarities with the work of Walras. This view of Keynes must appear paradoxical given his Marshallian background. In many senses it is, yet it was inevitable that Keynes's challenge to traditional theory on the highly delicate ground of its generality was bound to lead to comparisons with the Walrasian paradigm, which J. R. Hicks's works had already introduced into the Cambridge citadel.[3]

There can be no doubt that Keynes himself facilitated this 'normalisation' of his heretical position through his attempts, in certain chapters of the *General Theory*, to dress his message in traditional clothing in the hope of gaining more general acceptance. Nonetheless, the idea that in conditions of perfectly flexible prices and wages all markets, including the labour market, are necessarily in equilibrium, has always been present in theoretical assessments of Keynes's work. This has led to the search for other rigidities such as quantity constraints, lack of information etc. to explain the existence of unemployment.

The most original feature of Keynes's vision of capitalism as a world in which expectations motivate both real and financial economic decisions, has proved difficult to interpret within the framework of neoclassical equilibrium. This has become apparent to both J. R. Hicks and J. Tobin, the two economists who have paid most attention to the theoretical implications of Keynes's message. As a result the former has been led to introduce *ad hoc* hypotheses into his temporary equilibrium concept[4] and the latter has had to accept the existence of divergent prices for the same capital goods.[5]

The *General Theory* however is independent of the concept of equilibrium, not in the sense that it considers situations which are somehow different from Walrasian equilibria but rather in that it is founded methodologically on an analytical philosophy which is completely alien to the neoclassical notion of equilibrium. This philosophy is the same as Keynes had already put forward in his *Treatise on Probability*. It enabled Keynes, on the basis of his observations of those aspects of capitalism he considered to be the most significant, to induce conclusions logically connected to this reality. The degree of belief which it is rational to attach to this kind of conclusion, that is to say, their *probability*, has nothing to do with actual economic events. In its relation to the plan underlying the *General Theory* the comparison between *ex-ante* and *ex-post* values, which it is impossible to avoid within an equilibrium approach, lies at a completely different level of analysis.

The powerful analytical force which the *General Theory* derives from this method is the explanation at the highest possible level of abstraction, of the forces which determine the levels of income and employment at a given moment in time, without reference to 'periods'. Emphasising, as it does, the coexistence, at any given time, of decisions based on short and on long-term expectations, this interpretation shows the incompatibility between Walrasian equilibrium, with full employment of all factors, and Keynes's vision of capitalism.

If it is true that one of the main reasons for the difficulties encountered by economic theory in explaining the present world economic crisis is its inability to distinguish between contingent facts and the forces which determine them, Keynes's inductive method presents an analytical tool of great contemporary significance.

II PROBABILITY, UNCERTAINTY AND EXPECTATIONS

Between two sets of propositions, therefore, there exists a relation, in virtue of which, if we know the first, we can attach to the latter some degree of rational belief. This relation is the subject matter of the logic of probability.[6]

The argument which I want to put forward is that if Keynes had recalled this point from his *Treatise on Probability*, at the beginning of the *General Theory*, its interpretation might have proceeded along very different lines from those represented in the so-called neoclassical synthesis. In my opinion, the Keynesian definition of probability, applied to the *General Theory*, is of significant interpretative value for both its content and method. The questions of content concern expectations and the way in which these show the *General Theory* to be a theoretical expression of Keynes's vision of capitalism; the methodological points regard certain important aspects of the logical process whereby underemployment equilibrium is determined.

In both of these cases it is important to bear in mind the sense in which Keynes considers probability as belonging to Logic. In the *Treatise on Probability* the terms 'certain' and 'probable' indicate the differing degrees of rational belief which differing levels of knowledge allow us to attribute to given propositions. Probability may thus appear to be something subjective. Keynes however is eager to point out that from a logical point of view this is not so. Probability 'is not . . . subject to human caprice'.[7] Once the facts on which our knowledge is based are given the probability of a proposition is something completely objective: 'the theory of probability is logical, therefore, because it is concerned with the degree of belief which it is rational to entertain in given conditions, and not merely with the actual beliefs of particular individuals which may or may not be rational'.[8]

The basis of probability, in other words, and the reason for its belonging to Logic rather than to Mathematics, lies in the fact that it establishes what rational beliefs may be derived from a set of facts with which one is directly aquainted.[9] As a consequence the object of the theory of probability is that knowledge which can be obtained by argument from direct acquaintance with facts. The choice of the facts or propositions used to acquire knowledge by argument is naturally subjective, but 'the relations, in which other propositions stand to these, and which entitle us to probable beliefs, are objective and logical'.[10]

There is thus a close link, in Keynes's conception of probability, between those propositions which are an object of probabilistic knowledge and those which are known and from which the former are logically derived. To claim that a proposition is probable is meaningless if we do not first establish the context to which this evaluation refers: 'No proposition is in itself either probable or improbable, just as no place can be intrinsically distant; and the probability of the same statement varies with the evidence presented, which is, as it were, its origin of reference. . . . We cannot analyse the probability-relation in terms of simpler ideas.'[11]

Ten years after the publication of the *Treasise on Probability*, in a review of a collection of studies by F. Ramsey, published posthumously,[12] Keynes reviewed his position in the light of criticism from the young philosopher. Ramsey had criticised the approach taken in Keynes's *Treatise on Probability* on the basis of a line of thought which led him to make a distinction between 'human' and 'formal' logic.

According to this argument formal logic has as its object the rules of coherent reasoning. 'Human logic', on the other hand, consists of the analysis of certain 'useful mental habits' by means of which the human mind uses the information supplied by perception, memory and other channels to achieve knowledge. Although he believed Ramsey had not succeeded in distinguishing rational degrees of belief from belief in general, Keynes accepted that this concept could enrich probability theory:

> The application of these ideas to the logic of probability is very fruitful. Ramsey argues, as against the view which I had put forward, that probability is concerned not with objective relations or propositions but (in some sense) with degrees of belief, and he succeeds in showing that the calculus of probabilities simply amounts to a set of rules for ensuring that the system of degrees of belief which we hold shall be a consistent system. Thus the calculus of probabilities belongs to formal logic. But the basis of our degrees of belief – or the *a priori* probabilities, as they used to be called – is part of our human outfit, perhaps given us merely by natural selection, analagous to our perceptions and our memories rather than to formal logic. So far I yield to Ramsey – I think he is right.[13]

There is a significant echo of this admission in chapter 12 of the *General Theory*, dedicated to long-term expectations, where Keynes states that the state of long-term expectations depends not only on the most likely predictions but also on the 'confidence' attached to these. Economic decisions have to be taken, not in a context of risk, as in the case of repeated trials where probabilities can be calculated on the basis of frequencies, but rather in a context of uncertainty, characterised by a scarcity of information. 'Human logic' can thus help us in understanding the mechanisms which together go to determine the state of 'confidence', that is to say the complex of conditions to which economic actors attach fundamental importance in their decisions.

Recognition of the validity of Ramsey's criticism thus allows Keynes to enrich the essence of the approach of the *Treatise on Probability* when he comes to apply it. A note to ch. 12 of the *General Theory*[14] in which he states that 'very uncertain' should not be taken to mean 'very improbable' refers directly back to ch. 6 of the *Treatise on Probability*, which discusses the 'weight' of arguments whose probability is to be ascertained. Here the term 'weight' is used as a synonym for 'relevant knowledge' and is clearly distinct from the concept of probability:

As the relevant evidence at our disposal increases, the magnitude of the probability of the argument may either decrease or increase according as the new knowledge strengthens the unfavourable or the favourable evidence; but something seems to have increased in either case – we have a more substantial basis upon which to rest our conclusion. I express this by saying that an accession of new evidence increases the weight of an argument. New evidence will sometimes decrease the probability of an argument, but it will always increase its weight.[15]

As a result the uncertainty which dominates expectations throughout the *General Theory* is expressed, in the language of the *Treatise*, in terms of scarcity of information, that is to say of the slim basis on which conclusions have to be based. Probability, on the other hand, lies at a different, independent level of analysis and remains solidly anchored to the concept of a logical relationship between premises and conclusions. The uncertainty of the elements which go to form expectations reduce 'confidence' but exert a neutral effect on probability and thus on the degree of rational belief which it is possible to assign to future events on the basis of their relationship with events which have actually been observed. The probabilistic approach to expectations, in the sense of the *Treatise*, is thus left unaffected by the importance the *General Theory* attaches to uncertainty.

This conclusion is a very important one in that it allows us to take a new view of the significance of Keynesian theory with respect to the crucial role of expectations in explaining the marginal efficiency of capital and liquidity preference, two key pillars in Keynes's theoretical construction. On publication of the *General Theory* a review by J. R. Hicks[16] immediately grasped the strategic importance which Keynes attributed to expectations. What he emphasised, however, were the limitations and dangers of this approach. In his view these limitations were implicit in the hypothesis of the invariancy of expectations with respect to events occuring, to use his own terminology, within the 'period' considered in the analysis. The dangers lay in the risk that in long-run applications the analytical effectiveness of the expectations method might 'peter out'.[17]

The neoclassical synthesis of Keynesian thought has not paid much attention to expectations, relegating these to the position of exogenous elements capable merely of shifting functional relationships which in all other respects are considered to be stable. The development of macroeconomic theory along so-called neo-neoclassical lines, has led on the other hand, via the rational expectations paradigm, to the incorporation of this aspect of the Keynesian anomaly within the orthodoxy of Walrasian equilibrium. A line of interpretation of the *General Theory* which refers back to the Cambridge tradition accepts the significance of expectations but nonetheless considers these the least essential element in Keynes construction, incapable of preventing traditional theory from reducing the most innovative features of his thought to the prevailing orthodoxy.[18]

The weakness of a theory based on expectations is alleged to consist of the lack of any relation to objective elements and the consequently arbitrary nature of its assumptions and conclusions. Any attempt to explain the workings of the capitalist system without first identifying precise laws showing the tendencies of its forces determining objective conditions is, according to this view, wasted effort, or at any rate devoid of theoretical validity. In this sense then, apart from questions of method, the resort to expectations is alleged to undermine the heuristic content of the *General Theory*.

If however we interpret expectations in the light of Keynes's own conception of probability, we discover that this criticism is unfounded. Let us consider for example the formation of the long-term expectations used in the calculation of the marginal efficiency of capital. Keynes begins – or rather he assumes that the entrepreneur begins – by observing a series of data which is supplied regularly by the market. On this basis he derives those elements relevant to the evaluation of the prospective return on an investment. This is exactly the approach used in the *Treatise on Probability:* the knowledge of particular propositions supplied by the evidence is used to construct a 'reasoned' knowledge of non-observable propositions by application of the logical relationship existing between the former and the latter:

> We are assuming in effect that the existing market valuation, however arrived at, is uniquely correct in relation to our existing knowledge of the facts which will influence the yield of the investment, and that it will only change in proportion to changes in this knowledge: though philosophically speaking, it cannot be uniquely correct, since our existing knowledge does not provide a sufficient basis for a calculated mathematical expectation.[19]

The strength of this conception of expectations thus lies in the way the argument is based on the most objective possible datum, namely observed reality. The subjective factor exists: it lies however in the choice of the aspects of reality taken as a starting point. This has nothing to do with the supposedly arbitrary nature of the conclusions; rather it constitutes the key point in the whole theory. It is unquestionably of key significance that for Keynes it is the intensity of effective demand, the existing quantity of capital goods and trends on the stock market – rather than sun spots or the weather – which entrepreneurs take as reference points in reality when formulating their expectations.

III   VIRTUAL EQUILIBRIUM AT A POINT IN TIME

In his review of the *General Theory* Hicks views Keynes's analysis in terms of expectations as a contribution to formal economic methods: 'From the standpoint of pure theory, the use of the method of expectations is perhaps the most revolutionary thing about this book'.[20] At the same time he warns readers of limitations and dangers that he sees in this 'method of expectations'. At a purely methodological level the problem raised by these limitations and dangers is the meaning of Keynesian equilibrium, undoubtedly one of the most intricate questions in the confused mass of interpretative literature surrounding the *General Theory*.

The leading role in this literature also belongs to Hicks, the author of the IS-LM model, the paradigm which has polarised the interpretative debate, as well as of the most recent and profound discussion of the subject.[21] Hicks, as can be seen in his writings in recent years,[22] has reconsidered the interpretative ability of his original model. In his recent 'explanation' of IS–LM he devotes considerable space to the interpretative difficulties which arise when one reasons in terms of a period. It is on this point that I would like to concentrate my attention.

The idea of summarising the analytical content of the *General Theory* in IS–LM curves derives from an application of Walras' analysis of exchange to the Keynesian markets for goods, labour, money and bonds.[23] Hicks proves that the model can still be coherently applied when wages are given and labour demand and supply are not in equilibrium, and that there is no difficulty in considering the price of goods as fixed. The complications arrive when it is necessary to identify the curves used to determine, in Hicks's terminology, effective demand and employment, the basis for the IS curve. One of these curves showing the dependency of effective demand on employment can be identified immediately: in the *General Theory*, for any given level of investment, effective demand grows in step with the growth of employment as a result of an increase in consumption. The converse relationship, on the other hand, whereby employment depends on effective demand, is in Hicks's view, difficult to identify, once one takes into account the time factor.

The fact that the realisation of production plans requires time, implies that within the period chosen as an object of analysis (Hicks's 'week') current employment is determined with respect to expectations of future demand. It cannot thus be considered a function exclusively of current demand unless it is supposed that the gap between production and current demand is the only factor determining the current input of labour. This hypothesis, Hicks observes, is an arbitrary one and cannot be assumed as a rule of conduct for entrepreneurs. It is unlikely that the latters' behaviour should be uninfluenced by their expectations of conditions in future periods. In Hicks's view, however, taking account of successive periods makes it necessary to abandon an analysis based on single periods and to move towards Lindahl-style, sequential models of analysis, alien to the IS–LM approach.

There is one way to avoid these difficulties, namely to suppose that production plans are actually fulfilled, that is to say that current production is equal to effective demand. In conditions of equilibrium, when demand and production coincide, it is in fact reasonable to consider current demand as a reference point for labour input. The period within which equilibrium is achieved must not however be too short; it has to allow a minimum of time for production plans to adjust to demand (not a 'week', but a 'year'). There is, in any case, a further problem concerning the equilibrium between the supply and demand for money as a stock which underlies the LM curve. Here it is sufficient to bear in mind that stock equilibrium has to be maintained for the whole period which implies the realisation of expectations within the period considered.[24] If, however, expectations are systematically achieved there can no longer be any uncertainty, the principle underlying liquidity preference.

There is no way of escaping from this impasse without resorting to *ad hoc* hypotheses which are equally unsatisfactory.[25] It is thus natural to ask whether there might not be some other way, outside the equilibrium paradigm, of supplying a logical interpretation of the analytical message of the *General Theory*. As in the case of expectations, here also a solution can be found in an interpretation based on Keynes's concept of probability.

Let us concentrate our attention on the fundamental proposition contained in ch. 3 which sums up all the others proposed by the

General Theory, namely that unemployment is a consequence of insufficient aggregate demand. In the light of the *Treatise on Probability* unemployment should be seen as an observed reality, of which we have direct knowledge (a 'secondary' proposition in the language suggested to Keynes by W. E. Johnson). That aggregate demand is insufficient is a proposition known by argument (the 'primary proposition'). The explanation of the economic forces at work, given in the same chapter, is the logical relationship between the observation and the conclusion. As part of a general definition of theory this interpretation might appear to be trivial: any theory reaches its conclusions on the basis of certain premises. If however we consider the consequences of a different, yet substantially similar, formulation of the question, more directly concerned in the debate around the meaning of Keynesian equilibrium, namely that an increase in investment leads to a (more than proportional) increase in income, this is no longer the case.

Here it is the increase in investment which constitutes the evidence on which to base our argument, while the increase in income is a conclusion drawn with a probability determined by the degree of rational belief which can be attributed to the conclusion. This probability, however, has nothing to do with the result effectively obtained in terms of the resulting income level. The conclusion indicated above could be derived with the highest possible degree of probability (that is to say with certainty) and still fail to correspond to factual reality, which is influenced by a vast range of circumstances. The comparison between logical conclusions and factual reality is illegitimate and cannot constitute a decisive element in the evaluation of a theory. An illogical argument could lead to conclusions consistent with reality; this would not be enough however for us to grant it scientific respectability.

If we interpret the *General Theory* as an analysis of what happens within a given period of time, the comparison between *ex-ante* values (conclusions by argument) and *ex-post* values (factual reality) becomes inevitable and the notion of equilibrium appears as the only way of making the comparison innocuous.[26] Although, on this ground, the *General Theory* authorises many ambiguities of interpretation, Keynes' authentic version, dated just one year after its publication, is very clear:

> The expected results are not on a par with the realised results in a theory of employment. The realised results are only relevant in so

far as they influence the ensuing expectations in the next production period. . . . Income on the other hand is realised result. . . . Time relationship between effective demand and income incapable of being made precise. . . . No definite relationship between aggregate effective demand at one time and aggregate income at some later time. This does not matter.[27]

Keynes also recalls how in his lectures at the beginning of the 1930s he had paid much attention to the relationship in time between input and production and how in the end he abandoned this line of analysis as over-complicated but 'mainly because there was no determinate time unit'.[28] As far as the difference which may appear between *ex-ante* and *ex-post* values is concerned he confesses that he realised too late how emphasis on this point might lead to his ideas being misunderstood for 'the theory of effective demand is substantially the same if we assume that short period expectations are always fulfilled'.[29]

This emphasis on the validity of the theory, even in conditions of equilibrium, is the most convincing argument that equilibrium is not required, that the theory is constructed outside an equilibrium framework of analysis. If we read ch. 3 of the *General Theory* without regard for the Marshallian language in which it is written, we see clearly that what Keynes is aiming to do is to identify the forces on which income and production depend at a given point in time. Given that entrepreneurs decide production levels on the basis of their demand and price expectations,[30] it is the forces of demand, summed up in the propensity to consume and the marginal efficiency of capital, which influence the level of production. This proposition is independent of equilibrium. If, at a given point in time, aggregate demand should exceed production, this is nothing more, *ceteris paribus*, than one more element to bear in mind in the formulation of expectations and thus in production plans.

Hicks justifies the price of accepting the equilibrium method with the need for a theoretical formulation capable of explaining historical reality. In order to explain reality we need a model. Given that the variables in the model have to be determined, the model must necessarily be in equilibrium.[31] Certainly we cannot question the fact that the *General Theory* aimed to explain reality, and indeed that this was the most significant element in the whole Keynesian revolution. Keynes warns us, however, that to achieve an understanding of capitalism, we have to be willing to accept a high degree of abstraction. The logical model which he presents is based on the method of induction, as defined in the *Treatise on Probability*. It makes it possible to identify those forces which, at a given point in time, that is to say independently of the passage of time, determine income and employment. The operation of these forces may be formalised in a mathematical model the determinacy of which confirms the logical nature of the process of induction. The solution to this model can be called 'equilibrium'. It is clear however that what we are dealing with here is a 'virtual equilibrium' in which all the magnitudes appear as *ex-ante* values and in which expectations are an exogenous variable.[32] The comparison with the effective values of the magnitudes in question, and verification of whether or not expectations are fulfilled, imply a different level of analysis to which Keynes had no intention of devoting himself.

IV INCOMPATIBILITY BETWEEN EFFECTIVE DEMAND AND FULL FACTOR EMPLOYMENT

The interpretation of the *General Theory* as an analysis of the forces which at a given point in time determine income and employment enables us to clarify an important point in Keynes's logical model, namely the meaning and consequences of the coexistence of short and long-term expectations. Entrepreneurs' production decisions depend on short-term expectations concerning the return on sales achieved on completion of the production process. Decisions to increase productive capacity depend on long-term expectations concerning the net return on investment. The capitalist system is characterised by the fact that at any given time both kinds of decision influence the forces in operation.

The reference to the short and the long term in Keynes's treatment of expectations has nothing to do with Marshall's short and long period. Keynes's distinction refers to the time horizon for decision-making and not, as with Marshall, to phenomena occuring within periods of differing length. This approach places the analysis at a high level of abstraction and the maximum possible level of generality: all the real phenomena considered to be of significance can be taken into account at the same time. In this way we can talk in terms of an analysis in real time, not in the sense that the analysis claims to determine what happens with the passage of time, but in the sense that no phenomenon of relevance to action at a given point of time is ignored.

It is thus incorrect to attribute to the *General Theory* a method based on a short-term analysis in which rates of profit differ, as opposed to a long-term method in which the latter are uniform.[33] The question of whether or nor current rates of profit are equalised belongs to that part of analysis in which *ex-ante* and *ex-post* values are compared, a problem Keynes does not explore. From the logic underlying his analysis we may conclude, however, that the possibility of competitive forces achieving convergency towards a uniform rate of profit does not depend on the passage of time. There are basically two reasons for this and they are not completely independent of each other. Theoretically, the circumstances, the systematic and the non-systematic forces which hinder the operation of competition are always in action, at any given point in time, with the same intensity. No matter how much entrepreneurs may learn from experience, expectations concerning the future return on investment can never be reduced to observed reality. On this last point Keynes is very explicit:

> Express reference to current long-term expectations can seldom be avoided. But it will often be safe to avoid reference to short-term expectation, in view of the fact that in practice the process of revision of short-term expectation is a gradual and continuous one carried on largely in the light of realised results. . . . Nevertheless, we must not forget that, in the case of durable goods, the producer's short-term expectations are based on the current long-term expectations of the investor; and it is in the nature of long-term expectations that they cannot be checked at short intervals in the light of realised results. . . . Thus the factor of current long-term expectations cannot be even approximately eliminated or replaced by realised results.[34]

This passage clearly shows that Keynes is willing to concede that short-term expectations are essentially determined by realised results and may thus be definitively identified with these, but that he completely rules this out as a possibility for long-term expectations.[35]

Bearing in mind Keynes's statement that the theory of effective demand is valid, regardless of the difference between *ex-ante* and *ex-post* values, we may thus consider the play of forces at a point in time on the assumption that short-term expectations are realised. While doing this however we have to take into account an aspect of reality, analysed in the *General Theory*, which has often been neglected: the existence of a market for existing capital goods.[36]

In order to approach this problem in as direct a way as possible it is useful to explicitly suppose that a market for second-hand capital goods exists.[37] A market of this kind is implicit in the analysis of ch. 17

of the *General Theory* in which Keynes returns to the question of 'own' rates of interest, raised by P. Sraffa,[38] using this to point out the specific characteristics of money and of the interest rate on money.

The 'own' rate for a durable good (for example cotton) had been defined by Sraffa as 'the interest on the money required to buy spot 100 bales, plus the excess (or minus the deficiency) of the spot over the forward prices of the 100 bales'.[39] This definition is based on the complete operation of the arbitrage between loans in kind and loans in money and on the existence of a future market for the goods which constitute the object of the analysis. The existence of future markets is not however essential for the relationship between 'own' rates and the monetary rate of interest. Where there are no such markets all that is necessary is to substitute the expected future price for the forward price.

In his discussion of the options open to owners of wealth who have to choose among different existing capital goods, Keynes actually reasons in terms of 'expectations of appreciation (or depreciation)', over the period of time considered, of the capital goods themselves with respect to their 'own' rates of interest. He concludes, pointing out that in equilibrium the 'own' rates, as corrected for expectations of appreciation or depreciation, will be uniform both among themselves and *vis à vis* the rate of interest on money.[40]

Once we have explicitly supposed the existence of a market for second hand investment goods (which, for simplicity, we may take to be homogeneous machines or shares representing them) the possibility of purchasing, or renting existing goods is incorporated among the productive decisions open to the entrepreneur within the time-horizon of short-term expectations.[41] While it is true that these decisions are taken on the basis of productive capacity which, at the system-wide level, has to be taken as given, it is also true that an individual firm may acquire additional productive capacity by buying or renting from other firms or owners of wealth. What characterises this choice, placing it within the realm of short-term expectations, and distinguishing it from the demand for new capital goods, is the fact that the time horizon within which the entrepreneur perceives the need to expand his productive capacity is the same as that applying to production decisions. In other words, the firm believes it worthwhile to expand its productive capacity for just a single stage of the productive process.

If we suppose that virtual equilibrium, as an expression of the forces at work at a given point in time, coincides with traditional equilibrium, then, as Sraffa had already pointed out,[42] there is no reason why spot

prices and forward prices (or current prices and the expected future
price) for capital goods should differ. As a result the price for the
services of machines will be fixed at a level where the 'own' rate will be
equal to the rate of interest on money. The economic system, analysed
in the *General Theory*, is thus characterised, in this context of fulfilled
short-term expectations, by production decisions based on traditional
conditions of equality at the margin and by the presence of exogenous
long-term expectations. It is on the latter that Keynes bases his
innovatory concepts of liquidity preference and the marginal efficiency
of capital. The uncertainty which dominates long-term expectations
continues to play a key role, exerting an essential influence over the
determination of the interest rate and the volume of investment.

If we concede that the system achieves traditional equilibrium this
places us in the best possible position to compare Keynes's conclusions
with those of the traditional or neoclassical theory, the basic paradigm
of which is provided by the Walrasian model. In view of the way in
which Hicks, in his most recent interpretation of the *General Theory*,[43]
and F. Modigliani[44] both insist on the Walrasian basis for the interpretative models they propose, it is worthwhile assuming this paradigm
as the basis for our comparison. What we have to do is to integrate the
IS–LM model with the production function, equilibrium conditions on
factor markets and the relationship between 'own' rates and the
monetary rate of interest.

$$y = y\ (r,g) \tag{1}$$

$$M/p = L\ (y,r) \tag{2}$$

$$y = f\ (N,K) \tag{3}$$

$$N = N\ (W/p) \tag{4}$$

$$K = K\ (v/p) \tag{5}$$

$$v/p = r \tag{6}$$

where y = real income; r = the rate of interest on long-dated bonds;
g = vector of exogenous variables representing autonomous demand;
M = the nominal quantity of money; p = the price level (or, to be more
precise, the price of the homogenous consumption and investment
good, present in the IS–LM model); N = the (rigid) labour supply;
W = nominal wages and v = the price of the service of existing capital
goods; K = the stock of existing capital goods.

Equation 1 expresses the equilibrium condition for aggregate demand and supply (IS). Equation 2 shows the equilibrium on the market for money (LM). Equation 3 is the production function. Equations 4 and 5 express the equilibrium between the supply of labour and of existing capital goods (both taken as given) and their respective demands, obtained from their marginal productivity schedules. Equation 6 shows the equality between the 'own' rate for capital goods (v/p) and the monetary rate of interest.

The model consists of 6 independent equations[45] with 5 unknowns: y, r, p, W, v. It follows that although nominal wages are assumed, in line with the neoclassical tradition, to be completely flexible, the model is nonetheless incapable of determining equilibrium values for the variables except as a coincidence. The comparison between this model and those of the neoclassical tradition shows that the fundamental difference lies in the fact that the above model contains both equation 5 and 6. In neoclassical models based on perfect substitution of assets, equation 5 does not exist, given that it is impossible to distinguish the demand for capital goods from the demand for bonds. In those neoclassical models based on imperfect substitution, on the other hand, it is equation 6 which disappears for the returns on different assets need not be uniform. Within their respective visions of reality these models are thus determinate.

The determinacy of these models sacrifices precisely that aspect of capitalist reality on which Keynes bases his interpretation of the forces in action at a given point in time. As we have seen this consists of the coexistence of three distinct decision-making processes, namely decisions by owners of wealth, decisions by entrepreneurs who plan their combination of factors within the short-term horizon, and decisions by entrepreneurs to create demand for new capital goods[46] on the basis of their long term expectations.

V EFFECTIVE DEMAND IN THE LONG RUN

Despite the exclusion of the 'liquidity trap' and of all other rigidities, the Keynesian forces at work at a given point in time are not such as to allow us to deduce from our initial assumptions, on logical grounds, that all factors are fully employed. As far, however, as explicit comparison between Walras's and Keynes's vision of the workings of capitalism is concerned,[47] this is not the only point of interest. What is also important is to avoid a possible misunderstanding, namely that the argument that the *General Theory* is independent of equilibrium implies that Keynes's message may be interpreted in terms of 'disequilibrium'.[48]

As is well known, the literature on disequilibrium takes Walrasian equilibrium as its point of departure, considering current positions as a temporary shift away from this equilibrium. The argument put forward here is that even in the most favourable circumstances, when short-term expectations are assumed to be fulfilled, the forces acting at a given point in time only by chance can determine the full employment of capital and labour. It follows that it is meaningless to talk in terms of a shift away from an equilibrium which the model, if it takes account of these forces, is incapable of determining. If, as in a Walrasian environment, there is no distinction between the present and the future, so that only current events are of relevance to decision-making and long-term expectations have no role to play, firms would be willing to absorb the total volume of investment corresponding to full employment savings. In terms of the model described above this would mean that in equation (1) income y and the rate of interest r are predetermined by the full-employment solution resulting from the rest of the system, but that despite this the equality between production and aggregate demand would be ensured by a suitable adjustment of the volume of investment. This would supply the missing endogenous variable needed to make the model determinate.

The exogenous nature of investment, that is to say, the way in which it depends on exogenous long-term expectations, constitutes, together with liquidity preference, the most important fruit of the heresy of the *General Theory* with respect to the dominant neoclassical theory. First, it is a fruit of Keynes's programme of research: the study of a monetary economy considered necessarily in conditions of uncertainty; and secondly of his approach: to achieve his conclusions inductively, on the basis of observed facts. Investment decisions may prove to be right or wrong, the *General Theory* tells us nothing about this. If they are wrong, the mistake will influence the formation of expectations at some future point in time. Even if they are correct, however, this does not mean that decisions will be repeated (for example that the volume of investment or the rate of increase in capital stock will remain the same). There exists no 'normal' level of investment or 'normal' rate of accumulation or plant utilisation to which long-term expectations tend to comply.

It is here that we discover the analytical power of Keynes's inductive method as compared to the deductive method used in neoclassical equilibrium. To argue that in the course of time the rate of profit and investment will tend to certain 'normal' values on the presumption that the forces which hinder this trend will tend, in time, to be neutralised, implies the definition of postulates from which one deduces which forces are to be considered temporary and which permanent. In classical economic thought this distinction might have been justified on the basis of the theoretical and institutional environment, character- ised by the identification of centres of savings with centres of invest- ment. Today, however, the distinction is purely arbitrary, facilitating the neoclassical interpretation of the *General Theory* in which long term expectations are an endogenous variable.[49]

Does this mean that Keynes was not interested in the long-run future of the economic system?

'In the long run we are all dead. Economists set themselves too easy, too useless a task if in tempestuous seasons they can only tell us that when the storm is long past the ocean is flat'.[50]

This well-known sentence cannot be interpreted, as has been done so often, as a reply in the negative. If anything it expresses a severe condemnation of tautological statements, devoid of analysis of the causal links underlying current events.

Actually Keynes relegates the long term prospects for capitalism to the last chapter of the *General Theory*, dedicated to the 'social philosophy' underlying the work. This is not a change in the method used – from an analysis of a point in time to one in the course of time. Rather it consists of an enunciation of normative propositions derived from the positive economic reasoning of the rest of the book. At the basis of Keynes's 'philosophy' lies a deep dissatisfaction with an economic society incapable of providing full employment, and in which the distribution of wealth and income is 'arbitrary and unjust'.

The traditional theory, Keynes observes, justifies interest and the unequal distribution of income and wealth as functional to the forma- tion of savings. It is possible that within certain limits a degree of inequality has an active role to play in stimulating economic activity. Nonetheless the justification given for interest is wrong, at least as long as full employment has yet to be achieved. Given that savings depend on investment what we ought to hope for is a fall in the rate of interest. Unless there is an adequate increase in the propensity to consume the maintenance of full employment, once this has been achieved, will depend on their being an appropriate rate of accumulation, presuma- bly requiring a reduction in the interest rate.

In the long run therefore what is required is the 'euthanasia' of the rentier:

Now, though this state of affairs would be quite compatible with some measure of individualism, yet it would mean the euthanasia of the rentier, and consequently, the euthanasia of the cumulative oppressive power of the capitalist to exploit the scarcity-value of capital. Interest today rewards no genuine sacrifice, any more than does the rent of land. The owner of capital can obtain interest because capital is scarce, just as the owner of land can obtain rent because land is scarce.[51]

This however is Keynes's desire rather than the logical conclusion of the analysis extended to the long run. Keynes clearly states that the disappearance of the rentier is part of the order of events which he is 'supporting'.

Meanwhile the hope for an adequate fall in the interest rate does not imply the conception of a stable level of investment or a transition towards a state of the economy capable of doing without the role of the firm, considered, to use an effective expression of Shackle's,[52] as 'imagination in action'. Investment will always require a subjective evaluation of expected return and thus the contribution, to decision-making, of 'animal spirits'. At the same time, however, a low rate of interest will make it possible to achieve a volume of investment adequate to ensure full employment, even when, as capital becomes more plentiful, highly remunerative investment opportunities become less common.

Actually, even in the long run, Keynes considers the instability of the marginal efficiency of capital as the greatest threat to full employment. He believes that a policy of low interest rates is a necessary, but not a sufficient, condition to achieve the desired volume of investment. It is from this view that he derives his policy of 'socialising' investment, an idea which comes to the surface in other parts of the *General Theory* and which he believes to be fully compatible with his free-enterprise vision of the economy:

... it seems unlikely that the influence of banking policy on the rate of interest will be sufficient by itself to determine an optimum rate of investment. I conceive therefore, that a somewhat comprehensive socialisation of investment will prove the only means of securing an approximation to full employment; though this need not exclude all manner of compromises and of devices by which public authority will co-operate with private initiative ...

Whilst, therefore, the enlargement of the functions of government involved in the task of adjusting to one another the propensity to consume and the inducement to invest, would seem to a nineteenth-century publicist or to a contemporary American financier to be a terrific encroachment on individualism, I defend it, on the contrary, both as the only practicable means of avoiding the destruction of existing economic forms in their entirety and as the condition of the successful functioning of individual initiative.[53]

Keynes expresses just one doubt, confirming that he entrusts the long term to his normative hopes rather than to tendencies already at work: 'Is the fulfilment of these ideas a visionary hope? Have they insufficient roots in the motives which govern the evolution of political society? Are the interests which they will thwart stronger and more obvious than those which they will serve?'[54]

NOTES

1. As far as the content of Keynes's message is concerned see my own *Keynes: the Instability of Capitalism* (Macmillan, 1984).
2. 'An economy is in equilibrium when it generates messages which do not cause agents to change the theories which they hold or the policies they pursue' (F. Hahn, *On the Notion of Equilibrium in Economics*. An Inaugural Lecture (Cambridge University Press, 1973) p. 25.
3. It is sufficient to observe that Hicks's review of the *General Theory* is already centred around the legitimacy or otherwise of the use of the adjective 'general'.
4. See in particular, J. R. Hicks, 'IS–LM: an Explanation', in J. R. Hicks, *Money, Interest and Wages, Collected Essays in Economic Theory*, vol. II (Oxford: Basil Blackwell, 1982).
5. J. Tobin, 'A General Equilibrium Approach to Monetary Theory' in *Journal of Money, Credit and Banking*, February 1969.
6. J. M. Keynes, *Treatise on Probability*, 1921, in *Collected Writings of J. M. Keynes (CWK)*, vol. VIII, pp. 6–7.
7. *Ivi*, p. 4.
8. Ibid.
9. Keynes's conception of probability is thus a much broader one than that based on the statistical frequency of a phenomenon. Keynes, recalling the evolution of philosophical and mathematical thought on probability, emphasises how the dominance of frequency-based theory has restricted the application of probabilistic theory to repeatable events, identifying probability with its quantitative measure. There can be no doubt that economists are familiar precisely with this frequency-based approach and that they nearly always reason in terms of probability distributions attaching economic significance to means, variance etc. The *Treatise on Probability* calls for a broadening of conceptual horizons, inviting economists to reason in terms of the logical relationship between direct and indirect knowledge.

10. Ibid.
11. *Ivi.*, pp. 7–8.
12. J. M. Keynes, *Essays on Biography, CWK*, vol. X.
13. *Ivi.*, pp. 332–3.
14. J. M. Keynes, *The General Theory of Employment, Interest and Money, CWK*, vol. VII, p. 148.
15. J. M. Keynes, *Treatise on Probability*, op. cit., p. 77. On this line see E. R. Weintraub, 'The 4,827th reexamination of Keynes's system', ch. 3. *Microfoundations* (Cambridge University Press, 1979).
16. J. R. Hicks, 'Mr Keynes's Theory of Employment', *Economic Journal*, June 1936, in *Collected Essays*, op. cit.
17. In order to understand the effective importance of these comments on expectations it should be borne in mind that Hicks was interpreting the *General Theory* in the light of G. Myrdal's approach. The latter's method, based on the distinction between *ex-ante* and *ex-post*, had been reviewed by Hicks ('A Review of Myrdal', in *Collected Essays*, op. cit.). See J. A. Kregel, 'Microfoundations and Hicksian Monetary Theory, in *de Economist*, vol. 130, no. 4, 1982.
18. See in particular P. Garegnani, 'On a Change in the Notion of Equilibrium in Recent Work on Value: a Comment on Samuelson' in M. Brown, K. Sato and P. Zarembka (eds) *Essays in Modern Capital Theory* (Amsterdam: North Holland, 1976).
19. J. M. Keynes, *General Theory*, op. cit., p. 152.
20. J. R. Hicks, 'Mr Keynes's Theory of Employment', op. cit., p. 86.
21. J. R. Hicks, 'Mr Keynes and the 'Classics': a Suggested Interpretation', in *Econometrica*, January 1937, and J. R. Hicks, 'IS–LM. An Explanation', op. cit.
22. See in particular, J. R. Hicks, *The Crisis in Keynesian Economics* (Oxford: Basil Blackwell, 1974) and J. R. Hicks, *Casuality in Economics* (Oxford: Basil Blackwell, 1979).
23. See J. R. Hicks, 'IS–LM: an Explanation', op. cit., pp. 320–1.
24. See J. R. Hicks, *Capital and Growth* (Oxford University Press, 1965).
25. See J. R. Hicks, 'IS–LM: an Explanation', op. cit., pp. 329–30.
26. That Keynes's method of expectations has nothing to do with the analysis of the Swedish school has been argued very lucidly by J. A. Kregel in 'Economic Methodology in the Face of Uncertainty: the Modelling Methods of Keynes and the Post-Keynesians', *Economic Journal*, June 1976.
27. J. M. Keynes, *CWK*, vol. XIV, pp. 179–80. The passage is contained in a series of notes with the significant title 'ex-post and ex-ante', prepared by Keynes for his lectures in 1937.
28. *Ivi.*, p. 180.
29. *Ivi.*, p. 181.
30. If we assume perfect competition individual firms' expectations can only be based on the expected market price. See on this point S. Parrinello, 'The price level implicit in Keynes's effective demand', *Journal of Post-Keynesian Economics*, Autumn 1980 and C. Casarosa, 'The microfoundations of Keynes's Aggregate Supply and Expected Demand Analysis', *Economic Journal*, March 1981.
31. J. R. Hicks, 'IS–LM: an Explanation', op. cit., p. 327.

32. F. Hahn's 'conjectural' equilibrium seems the closest concept to what is meant here by 'virtual' equilibrium. See F. Hahn 'On Non-Walrasian Equilibria', in *Review of Economic Studies*, February 1978. It seems to me that the logical approach is fully coherent with the concept of 'contemporary causality', recently proposed by Hicks. (See J. R. Hicks, *Causality in Economics*) and used to conduct his 'explanation' of the IS–LM model. The avoidance of any form of period analysis makes it possible nonetheless to keep faith with Keynes's principle of given expectations.

33. There is an interesting discussion of this point in A. Vercelli, 'Equilibrio e disequilibrio nella Teoria Generale di Keynes: il ruolo dei salari monetari e le difficoltà di un metodo di puro equilibrio' in A. Graziani, C. Imbriani, B. Jossa (eds), *Studi di Economia Keynesiana*, (Naples: Liguori 1981).

34. J. M. Keynes, *General Theory*, op. cit., pp. 50–1.

35. There is a clear contrast here with the theory of rational expectations, developed over the last ten years on the basis of contributions by R. E. Lucas. In its most general formulation this theory is based on the hypothesis that decision-makers' subjective probability distribution with respect to the future values of variables coincides with the objective distribution, based on the information supplied by the model. As a result any systematic gap between forecasts and reality has to be identified and explained. For Keynes, on the other hand, while decision-makers' forecasts are assumed to be logical, the probability of the conclusions (long-term expectations) has nothing to do with whether the events actually happen (as pointed out in note 9 on p. 174 above Keynes's concept of probability is not measured in terms of the frequency of events). In this view it is the lack of systematic errors which deserves an explanation.

36. The works of P. Davidson, H. P. Minsky and J. Tobin are significant exceptions to this rule.

37. The *General Theory* explicitly discusses the market for shares (the Stock Exchange). In the definition of the marginal efficiency of capital (chapter 11) there is a clear distinction between the 'supply' or reproduction price of newly produced capital goods and the market price for existing goods of the same kind. In a reply to criticism from R. Hawtrey, Keynes makes it clear that 'where the investment is not irrevocably fixed to the ground, there generally is a second-hand market, e.g. even in cotton spindles and looms' (J. M. Keynes, *CWK*, vol. XIII, p. 630).

38. P. Sraffa, 'Dr Hayek on Money and Capital', *Economic Journal*, March 1932. Keynes's term 'own rates' refers to what Sraffa had called 'natural or commodity rates'.

39. *Ivi.*, p. 50.

40. J. M. Keynes, *General Theory*, op. cit., p. 227–8.

41. The development of leasing companies in recent years makes the hypothesis of a market for the services of capital goods into a very realistic one.

42. Sraffa, op. cit., p. 50.

43. J. R. Hicks, 'IS–LM: an Explanation', op. cit., pp. 320–32.

44. F. Modigliani, 'Liquidity Preference and the Theory of Interest and Money' *Econometrica*, 1944.

45. Following Walras's law we ignore equilibrium on the market for bonds.

46. The price of existing capital goods is assumed to be the same as that of newly produced capital goods. It might be objected that this is not completely correct in that existing goods are used in the current phase of production whereas newly produced goods are employed only in a subsequent phase. If this were thought necessary it would be possible to take account of this distinction introducing a separate price for newly produced goods thereby following Keynes. Given however that there is a necessary relationship between these two prices (in equilibrium the difference might be equivalent to the price of services for a single productive phase) this would not change the substance of the argument. If, on the other hand, one accepts the hypothesis of J. Tobin's general equilibrium model ('A General Equilibrium Approach', op. cit.), namely that the two prices are completely independent, one arrives at different conclusions. For a critique of this approach see C. Gnesutta, 'Equilibrio del conto capitale e meccanismo di trasmissione degli impulsi monetari' in F. Vicarelli (ed), *La Controversia Keynesiana* (Bologna: Il Mulino, 1974).

47. This comparison has recently been made by M. Morishima. See M. Morishima, *Walras' Economics* (Cambridge University Press, 1977). The results are only apparently similar to those of the author (see F. Vicarelli, 'Introduzione' in *La Controversia Keynesiana*, op. cit.: F. Vicarelli, *Keynes: the Instability of Capitalism*, op. cit.

48. There now exists an extremely broad literature on disequilibrium. Here it is sufficient to recall the pioneering works of Don Patinkin, *Money, Interest and Prices*, New York: Harper, 1965); R. W. Clower, 'The Keynesian Counter-Revolution' in F. H. Hahn and F. Brechling (eds) *The Theory of Interest Rates* (London: Macmillan, 1965); R. J. Barro and H. I. Grossman, 'A General Disequilibrium Model of Income and Employment', *American Economic Review*, March 1971.

49. The impossibility of reducing long-term expectations to past and present events is upheld with force by J. Tobin in his critique of the theory of rational expectations. See J. Tobin 'Asset Accumulation and Economic Activity' (Basil Blackwell, Oxford: 1980).

50. J. M. Keynes, *A Tract on Monetary Reform*, CWK, vol. IV, p. 65.

51. J. M. Keynes, *General Theory*, op. cit., pp. 375–6.

52. G. L. S. Shackle, 'New Tracks in Economic Thought, 1926–1939' in S. Weintraub (ed.) *Modern Economic Thought*, (University of Pennsylvania Press, 1977).

53. J. M. Keynes, *General Theory*, op. cit., pp. 378–80.

54. *Ivi*, p. 383.

9 Aggregate Income Distribution Theory

SIDNEY WEINTRAUB *

Two major themes provide the focal centre for this study: (a) the wage-unit as numéraire, which has the unique quality of imparting price and money dimensions to the economy, and (b) the theory of distributive shares.

Keynes was as lucid and forthcoming as any mortal writer might be in communicating the wage-unit concept, which gave coherence and dimension to his theory, making it apt even for the modern stagflation age. Yet Keynes's reminders were swept aside by perfunctory Keynesians who attached a unidimensional fiscal policy employment orientation to his theory, in an astonishing haste to by-pass Keynes's price level and monetary underpinnings. Only a half-loaf of Keynes was pounced on for dissemination as the stuff of Keynesianism.[1] Errors of commission in this respect were not of Keynes's making; the onus instead falls at the Keynesian doorstep which took it upon itself to breed an alien, and mechanical, thought imposter. Small wonder that Keynesianism has petered out while Keynes's ideas are still much alive, if not wholly in vogue because of the caricatures that masqueraded in his name; the monetarist flailing at the straw man they erected has not facilitated understanding.[2]

On the theory of income distribution Keynes was, at best, laconic and yet some crucial issues are at stake: ultimately controversy and conflict over income shares divide the community and abet its tensions. Analytically, the distributive aspects contribute to settle the income and employment out-turn. While Keynesians have contributed little to

*The author is Professor of Economics at the University of Pennsylvania. The paper was written while he was Visiting Professor at the Faculty of Economics of the University of Rome.

evolving the theory it has remained for those working more or less on Keynes's lines, such as Kalecki, Kaldor, Joan Robinson, to advance our understanding.

At the outset I want to underscore my debt to Keynes and his methods which, I think, are rather apparent in *my work*: I came to honour Keynes and not to denigrate his memorable, rarely matched and even less seldom surpassed achievements in a discipline now over two centuries old. This assessment should be praise enough in a volume dedicated to commemorating Keynes's birth, manifestly an event to the great benefit of our civilization.

My own approach, with occasional simplifying departures, has been erected on Keynes's Aggregate Supply and Aggregate Demand apparatus which, unfortunately, appeared only fleetingly in his chapter 3 with more detail (to be mentally filled in by the reader) in ch. 20, and clinging only fitfully elsewhere. Clarity would have been served by reiterating the concepts in the course of the full *General Theory* exposition. But this is to ask more from the work that has already given so much.[3]

At the time of writing (late 1982) there are over 30 million unemployed in what we are pleased to call the 'advanced' and 'mature' western world. Economists disclose an incredible capacity to tolerate other people's misfortunes with complacency and equanimity, to the shame of the profession's ethics, ideology, or comprehension of well-being. Keynes's teachings have still not been absorbed; too many of his analytical insights still defy the professional grasp.

I THE SIGNIFICANCE OF INCOME DISTRIBUTION

Most of this chapter will be devoted to repairing the singular omission of the *General Theory* (hereafter *GT*), namely, the matter of income distribution. Recognition of the theory of relative shares simplifies, and enhances, Keynes's *opus*. Clearly, Keynes could manage without it, but his theme is fortified by its presence. Not least, income distribution emerges as a vital foundation for the elegant and mobile superstructure of the macro theory.

Keynes mentions income distribution in summarizing his theory (p. 245) and in his concluding plea *for* income inequalities 'but not for such large disparities as exist today' (p. 374). There may be another line or two of reference, an almost aside on the consumption function (p. 11) but they are not easy to find; peculiarly, they do not strike the eye – as I think they should – in the theory of the consumption function and the multiplier, both of which were pioneered by Keynes with notable assistance from Kahn on the multiplier gadget. Bearing on the point, Keynes conjectured the *euthanasia* of the rentier – in those days of low interest rates – with sparse regret (ch. 16). Interpreted as a prediction in the current era of usurious interest rates, with new rentiers benefiting egregiously from the historic interest rate peaks of the last 14 years, Keynes's devout observation must rank as unfortunate and as erroneous as Karl Marx's expected immiseration of labour through real wage decline because of the augmentation of the ranks of the army of unemployed.

Keynes was hardly the only culpable one in his studied neglect of the distribution of income. In countless studies – so-called – of the consumption function the words scarcely appear although the relations are crucial in ascending from an individual to an aggregative relation: change the income division and the purchase relations are bound to be altered except in very special instances. The theory gets slap-dash treatment as the typical neoclassical orientation, with the only novel wrinkle showing in concepts of 'investment in human capital' where the recognition is soon poisoned by some forced makeshifts to lend econometric sustenance to some vague and spurious concepts of marginal (or even average in this context) productivity. The data are invariably described as 'not disproving' the theory; further study is always advocated. Many of our most prestigious neoclassical economists have persisted in exhorting students to master the marginal concepts though, so far as I am aware, no neoclassicist has explained to the class how to measure an academican's marginal product. (If, as I suspect, it is often nil or negative then the measurement issue dissolves). The theory seems today, as in J. B. Clark's time, to require that economists buy tickets to observe some farmer working a land plot somewhere out in Wyoming, perhaps spreading manure over the land, as economists watch *en masse* as witnesses in some vast spectator sport.[4]

Marginal productivity theory, in mature economies where the service sector has been expanding, has become even more vulnerable: measurement vagueness compounds the haziness, and indeterminateness, always identified in the monopolistic or oligopolistic industrial world where the estimate of the marginal revenue product has long been recognised as a defective weak sister. With the more recent work of Sraffa explaining that in his system a marginal product 'just would not be there to be found' (preface, p. v, *Production of Commodities By Means of Commodities*), and the reswitching dispute which put some given bends in the relation between the demand for capital equipment and the rate of interest, the sanguine operativeness of the old time marginal productivity religion has become even more mythical. Wreckage abounds at the very centre of neoclassicism: Keynes's omission may be characterised as a fortuitous happenstance of benign neglect, its inclusion, as in fidelity to Marshall, would have created what others would later have had to eradicate.

Yet distribution, for all its neglect by Keynes, still remains the main bout and the central fascination of economics – or it should be, as Karl Marx discerned. For truly, even for the unemployed, it is not work itself that they crave, for much of it is monotonous, arduous or plainly distressing to people who would prefer to do other things. What they do miss instead is the income which work brings, along with the ego-trip of being found useful. Being knocked down the income ladder, to the null income of the unemployed group, must always arouse resentment at the 'injustice' of the impersonal market or capitalistic system. Social tensions, hates and hostility, tax disputes, political and even racial acrimony, are more often than not linked to matters of income shares. Quoting Marx: 'The English Established Church, e.g., will more readily pardon an attack on 38 of its 39 articles than on 1/39 of its income.'(*Capital*, vol. I, author's Preface to the first edition.) Generously interpreted, the remark is neither atheistic nor sacriligous, but instead a powerful maxim on the very human motive of income protectiveness that marks so much of our daily conduct. Inflation, like unemployment, has a severe distributive pinch, with the anguish and frustration attributable to the real income loss by those who have been 'mugged', by finding their real earnings lagging the price indicators – bitterness becomes rife as past expectations are disappointed.

There is no need to pile up instances of the domineering importance of income distribution, concretely. Very touchy motives of envy and self-interest are transparent as soon as the matter is broached; it is only economic theorists who dismiss it as secondary and not urgent enough for theoretical resolution.

II THE LACK OF HISTORY IN THE PRODUCTION FUNCTION

One analytic criticism will be made of the typical neoclassical production function which has often aroused Mrs Robinson's ire for slipping in several illegitimate assumptions. Disapprobation here will be registered on slightly different grounds, arguing that there is more history, evolution, goodwill and generosity, and psychology, embedded in the innocent appearing mathematical functions than neoclassical economists have ever been eager to admit.

For example, consider:

$$Q = Q(N, K, L) \tag{1}$$

where Q = physical output, N = labour, K = capital equipment, L = land or natural resources

Neglecting all the issues surrounding the measurement of K, so far as labour is concerned its marginal product would be written as $(\delta Q/\delta N) > 0$; the marginal product, for any $N = \overline{N}$, would be accredited as determining labour's real-wage.

Nonetheless, equation 1 is replete with hidden assumptions. In effect it supposes that regardless of how labour was paid in the past, of how well or poorly it was fed, or of how healthy it is now as a result of its income, its contribution to production will be the same, utterly unspoiled or unaffected by history. Likewise, it is presumed that regardless of how well labour *expects* to be paid in the future, and wholly unrelated to its emerging real income, its production contribution will remain neat, regular, and unsullied.

It is on notions as rarified as these that marginal productivity theory has cast its somnolent spell, divorced from a past history or an expected future. The mathematical expositions effectively recite: grab a handful of productive factors and, no matter how you have treated them in the past or what they expect in the future, the productive results will be the same.

III   A BASIC LINEAR MODEL

Taking leave now of criticism of the neoclassical affront in income distribution theory, the constructive aspect of the emphasis on macrodistribution can be derived from a simple linear Aggregate Demand–Aggregate Supply model that captures the essence of Keynes's thinking. Thus:

Aggregate Supply: $Z = kwN = wN/\theta$ $\hspace{2cm}$ (2a)

Aggregate Demand: $D = D' + D''$ $\hspace{2.5cm}$ (2b)

where w = the average wage (and salary), N = employment, k = the markup of prices over unit labour cost and θ = the wage share = l/k

Further Z = GBP, or Gross Business Product rather than the more familiar Gross National Product for we are dealing with the capitalistic enterprise sector of the economy. Too, D' = nominal consumption outlays or the more conventional C , not in real terms but in nominal sums. Likewise, D'' = nonconsumption outlays including private investment, government purchases from the private sector, and the net export–import balance, with the entire total being in nominal terms in contrast to the usual 'real' magnitudes given in $I, G, (X-I_m)$.

Generalising an insightful celebrated thought credited to Kalecki and used extensively by Kaldor and Joan Robinson, we can write the $K-K-R$ hypothesis as:[5]

Consumption Outlay: $D' = \alpha wN$ (2c)

The Equilibrium Juxtaposition

Putting these relations in an equilibrium context it follows:

$$D = Z \qquad N = [D''/w(k-\alpha)] = [\theta D''/w(1-\alpha\theta)] \qquad (3)$$

Quite obviously, from the presence of k or its θ reciprocal, the level of employment depends keenly on the size of the wage share: income distribution is a job determinant.

For the equilibrium money income aggregate, also derived from $D = Z$ and assuming that $Z = kwN$, we have:

$$Z = [kD''/k-\alpha] = [D''/(1-\alpha\theta)] \qquad (4)$$

Thus money income, too, is contingent on the wage share θ . Further, inasmuch as $D'' = k''w''N''$, then the money wage in the investment sector (w'') imparts the nominal dimension to the income aggregate. As a simplification we shall suppose that $w'' = w$, or that the average money wage in both the C and I sectors of the economy is precisely the same.

Equation 4 is the 'average' money income multiplier while equation 3 is the 'average' employment multiplier. It is possible to link-up equation 4 to the usual version of the average multiplier by invoking equation 2c, and dividing by $Z(=D)$ in order to insert the wage share. Thus:

$$c = \alpha\theta \text{ and } (1-c) = s \tag{5a}$$

where c = the average propensity to consume and
$\quad\quad s$ = the average propensity to save.

$$S = s_wW + s_rR \quad\quad s = s_w\theta + s_r\pi \tag{5b}$$

where S = savings, $W = wN$, R = non-wage income π = the non-wage share.

Thus it follows that:

$$Z = [D''/(1-\alpha\theta)] = [D''/(1-c)] = [D''/s] = [D''/(s_w\theta + s_rw)] \tag{5c}$$

Considering equation 5c, off to the right, it is clear that any shift in the distribution of income must have an impact of consequence on the income aggregate so long as there is a significant discrepancy in the average savings (or consumption) propensities. Parenthetically, the same analysis can be mobilised if, instead of distinguishing between wage and nonwage income – everything but wages and including depreciation allowances – we were to separate income by income classes, as Under $3000, then $3001 to $5000, and $5001 to $7000, etc. How income is disbursed will effectively help determine how much income there will be to dispense.

As a further indication of the potency of income distribution in income determination, and as an obvious deduction from the K–K–R simplifying hypothesis that 'wage earners spend all and nonwage earners save all; it follows from equation 5c that:

$$Z = [D''/s_r\pi] \approx [D''/\pi] \tag{5d}$$

Thus the nonwage share and saving ratio will between them determine the income level when $s_w = 0$. When $s_r = 1$, as in the simplifying hypothesis, then the average income multiplier is stark enough, depending entirely on investment income and the magnitude of the nonwage share. Although equation 5d is never 'exactly' true, the presentation conforms to eloquent theorising in the sense of delineating a relation that takes us with dispatch close to the full truth without encumbering the analysis in a morass of qualifications, many of which will scarely matter.

For those accustomed to deal in so-called 'real income', the sole requisite is to correct our money income relations in the conventional manner.

The Price Level

The price level is the prime exhibit displaying the prominence of the money wage and income distribution concepts. As I have shown many times, the basic relations can be squeezed out of equation 2a:[6]

$$Z = \Sigma PQ = kwN \quad \therefore \quad P = [kwN/Q] = [kw/A] = [w/\theta A], \tag{6}$$
where A = average product of labour = (Q/N)

Note that equation 6 accomplishes what many, brought up on Quantity Theory of Money notions of the price level, would regard as a herculean feat, namely, eliciting a price level in which the average money wage plays a crucial part while the money supply is conspicuously absent. Observe, too, that the average price markup (k) by which prices exceed unit labour costs ($ULC = w/A$), or the relative size of the wage share (θ) is a determinant of the price level.

Keynes wrote that the 'general price-level depends partly on the rate of remuneration . . . and partly on the scale of output as a whole. . . .' (*GT*, p. 294). Equation 6, which I have called the Wage–Cost Markup Equation (WCM), compresses Keynes's vision. Considering that shifts in θ, or gyrations in k, are likely to be minuscule over the short period (and substantially so over time too), and that annual improvements in productivity (A) merely creep or inch ahead rather than surging or gushing, then it must inevitably follow that a serious inflation, say of 5, 10, 20, or more per cent per annum is *simply not possible* without a corresponding escalation in the average money wage.

Economists have searched for all sorts of contorted explanations of inflation; the potency of the money wage is apt to distress them because its policy implications are inimical to wages flowing from a harmonious mechanical self-adjusting market mechanism. The implications of equation 6 would undercut the intricate, abstruse, and unwieldly tomes put out with regularity, and which attest mightily to economist's propensities for discussion and digression rather than resolution of issues which contain enormous potential for social good or evil.

The WCM equation of 6, it should be noted, refers to GBP production, or the price level of output in a *continuous reproduction economy*. The equation would not, indeed could not be, valid for nonreproducibles such as land, real estate, *objets d'art*, or financial claims as stocks, bonds, etc. Obviously, in these sectors neither the k (or θ) or *A* terms apply.

This is *not* a limitation of the theory: most of economic analysis (and certainly general equilibrium theory) is presumably concerned with events in the continuing economy of reproduction. Where, essentially, does money enter the analysis? Briefly, recalling that under the Irving Fisher Equation of Exchange (EOE) it was customary to write $MV = PQ$, and as $PQ = kwN$, then it follows that $MV = kwN$, so:[7]

$$(\Delta M/M) + (\Delta V/V) = (\Delta k/k) + (\Delta w/w) + (\Delta N/N) \text{ or}$$
$$m(\Delta M/M) \approx (\Delta w/w) + (\Delta N/N) \tag{7}$$

Equation 7 makes very apparent that if we take $m = \overline{m}$, meaning that the relative changes in money velocity are rather constant as the monetarist aver, and if $\Delta k = 0$ approximately, then any inordinate change in the average money wage not balanced by corresponding variations in the aggregate money supply, will have some rather devastating effects on jobs and unemployment rates. Elsewhere I have argued that this is the essence of the sordid stagflation sequel of the past 12 years or so.[8]

The Open Economy

To forestall the criticism that the WCM equation 6 applies only to the closed economy, we can extend it to include the prices of imported goods. This:[9]

$$P_{d+f} = (kwQ_d)/(nAQ_{d+f}) \tag{8}$$

P_{d+f} = price level of goods produced domestically and including imported content, Q_d = domestic physical content of output, Q_{d+f} = domestic and imported content and n = relative domestic value content of domestic and imported output.

Clearly, the same terms preponderate, with the Q's and the n term being new. Between them, as movements in n are likely to spark shifts in the (Q_d/Q_{d+f}) ratio, there will be some cancellation of impacts.

Further, as the value of $n = 0.9$ approximately in the United States, then a 100 per cent upheaval in world prices should affect United States prices by no more than about 10 per cent! In most other western countries m = 0.8, or somewhat higher, so that the same price disaster would compel a 20 per cent price level bulge.

It is thus something of a propensity for looseness with facts that economist stress – and exaggerate – 'imported' inflation. Practically all inflation is home-made. When price winds blow strongly through imports, they can always be neutralised by an appropriate adaptation in the average money wage, w. When imported prices are falling, a moderated income policy governing the course of w can be imposed.

The Consumer Price Level

Descending from concern with the general price level to the more specific consumer price level which is important to all of us in our household expenditure behaviour, drawing on equation 2c we can write:

$$D' = P_c Q_c = \alpha\, wN \quad \therefore \quad P_c = (\alpha\, w/A_c)\,(N/N_c) = (cw/\theta A_c)\,(N/N_c)\,(9)$$
where c-subscripts refer to the C-sector

Clearly, as before, the money wage imparts the *scale* dimension to the price level, with the other factors capable of imparting some relative wiggles up or down. Any explosive inflation, as the trebling and quadrupling of the price level in the western economies since 1968, must inevitably originate in outsized toppling movements in the average money wage. In the world of fact, and in a more stable general price level milieu, the relative size of the C-sector, or the ratio of total employment to C-sector employment, will have some influence; significance is generally exaggerated in real world phenomena for the (N/N_c) relation fails to divulge any whirling swirls. Implicit in (N/N_c), however, are some multiplier aspects. As an inflation factor its 'imbalances' have not been at the bottom of the upheavals which have marred our recent past.

IV THE REAL-WAGE

Heavy weather has been made of the theory of real-wages, involving the relation (w/P) or (w/P_c). Keynes, drawing on his Marshallian memories, tended to argue in the GT that it must fall because of 'diminishing marginal products' as employment and output increased. Later, in the face of scepticism evoked by some empirical studies (by Dunlop and Tarshis), Keynes was to express some reservations about his original hypothesis. Actually, if real-wages could rise his assault on conventional theory would be reinforced: there would be less reason, even on the part of those employed, to tolerate unemployment. More employment would benefit both the employed *and* those previously unemployed. Economically, policies to preserve the status quo, or to move slowly in restoring more jobs, would be intellectually bankrupt.

Since the dawn of marginalism, when the real-wage (w/P) was equated to the marginal product as an implication of competitive profit-maximisation, economists generally have sought to shuffle out the nearest exit when the disconcerting questions were asked, such as: (a) how the marginal product could be extracted when output was the result of a complex, interdependent, and *joint* association of productive factors; (b) how a physical product could be assigned when the end-product was a service, such as air transportation, medical care, electric power, education, government memoranda, etc; (c) the relation between physical and value productivity in monopoly-oligopoly situations; (d) estimating marginal aspects when labour is paid weekly, as in t_0, t_1, . . . and physical products and sales receipts are only realized much later in time, say 5 years hence after the physical plant or capital installation is completed, and operative. Finally, the issue that has often preoccupied me, namely, (e) of how to stabilize (or measure) the ratio of (w/P) in any serious *ex ante* fashion when $P = P$ (w. . .)? In effect, it is not *possible* to know P until w is known while marginal productivity theory, insofar as it was ever invoked to explain events in the monetised economy – and where it was not so used it was utterly futile for understanding the modern economy – did assume that the price level remained constant while the money wage altered. Thus $P = \bar{P}$, on the basis of Quantity Theory of Money conceptions, *regardless* of the average money wage. The theory committed the absurdity of positing that $P = P$ whether the average money wage was one penny per hour or \$1 billion per hour.[10]

Write, for the elasticity of prices relative to money wages:

$$(E_{pw}) = [(w\Delta P)/(P\Delta w)] \gtreqless 0$$

Traditional marginal productivity theory has assumed that $E_{pw} = 0$. I have argued generally that, in the very short period, it is apt to be approximately unity. But it can be somewhat less, or where expectations of big price moves are rife, a great deal more. If it is zero, then the usual neat neoclassical demand curve for labour can be sketched, where it is unity, as in my view, the curve dissolves into a point.[11]

On the real-wage, and its identification with 'marginal productivity theory,' economists have perpetrated many rather shocking monstrosities in attempting to make its features fit the modern economy: the feat of squaring the circle has yet to be accomplished.

Conversely, on our own methods a theory of the real-wage shakes out rather directly. Thus, from the WCM equation:

$$\text{From } P = kw/A \quad \therefore \quad (w/P) = \theta A \tag{10}$$

According to (10) the real wage is a resultant of both the average productivity of labour and the wage share. If we stipulate that the average product of labour is, over time, a more or less technological phenomenon or exogenous, from the standpoint of economics, then it would be to the determinants of the wage *share* that we would look for an explanation of the real-wage. In effect, this is what Karl Marx did in writing before the successful onset of marginalism.

The theory of the wage share thus holds the key to the real-wage. This theory, too, has unfortunately been badly evaded by economists. (cf. 'An Eclectic Theory', op. cit.)

Expressing the real-wage in terms of the prices of consumer goods introduces a mite more of complexity in the number of variables. Thus, the equation:

$$(w/P_c) = [(A_c N_c)/(\alpha N)] = [(\theta A_c N_c)/(cN)] \tag{11}$$

Average labour productivity in the C-sector emerges as critical in equation 11, along with the relative C-sector size and the association of total consumption outlay and the wage bill. In the formulation to the right, the wage share and the average propensity to consume replace the wage-bill and consumption relation.

To ascertain the likely course of the real-wage what is required, in lieu of flights of fancy into marginal productivity concepts are ideas on the course of labour-productivity and on the determinants of the wage-share, as well as the ratio of C-sector employment to total labour hire.

V   THE CONSUMPTION FUNCTION

In view of the potency of the average propensity to consume (APC)–or its coordinate partner the average propensity to save (APS) in the income or employment determination as exemplified in the multipliers – we consider the influence of income distribution on the respective magnitudes. Recalling equation 2c, involving the K–K–R generalisation of $D' = P_cQ_c = \alpha wN$, it is also possible to write:

$$D' = \alpha wN = \alpha\theta Y, \text{ where } Y = \text{GBP} = Z \tag{12a}$$

Dividing through by Y (or Z) in order to derive the average propensity to consume, then:

$$\text{APC: } c = \alpha\theta \tag{12b}$$

For the marginal propensity to consume we would ordinarily have to take into account any modifications in α and θ. If we assume that $\Delta\alpha = \Delta\theta = 0$, then:

$$\text{MPC: } [\Delta D'/\Delta Y] = \alpha\theta \tag{12c}$$

Manifestly, in relations (16a-b-c) aggregate consumption outlay rests crucially on the distribution of income, as exemplified by the wage share. It is no surprise, therefore, that income shares figure prominently in the APC and MPC.

We can also write some less familiar forms for the C-relations which point up some interesting facets on consumption data revealed from time-to-time in accounts of the economy. For example with respect to C-outlay per employee we would have:

$$(D'/N) = \alpha w \tag{12d}$$

As would be expected, the average money wage packs the outlay wallop for household disbursements. The result would be banal indeed if it were not so consistently overlooked in the recondite expositions of the consumption function, and the convoluted elaborations of the 'determinants' of purchase outlay magnitudes.

For aggregate real-consumption the relation reads:

$$Q_c = \alpha N(w/P_c) \tag{12e}$$

The real-wage (w/P_c) figures in as a determinant along with the employment volume, and of course there is the ubiquitous α.

Finally, perhaps most important of all for conveying insight into what happens to consumption outlay over time, we can write the relative movements as follows:

$$(\Delta D'/D') = (\Delta\alpha/\alpha) + (\Delta w/w) + (\Delta N/N) \tag{12f}$$

Equation 12f is revealing indeed in a time context for, say, year-to-year outlays; we would expect movements in the $\Delta\alpha$ and the ΔN ratios to be of the order of 1 to 2, or maybe 3 per cent, with the latter figure probably being outsized. On the other hand, with average money wages jumping from 5 to 10 per cent, or higher, being commonplace in recent years, it is easy to discern the major factor responsible for retail sales exploding in leaps and bounds. Trends in the pace of average money wages will be the gauge to the pace of consumer absorption.

A Visual Illustration of Income Distribution and the *C*-Function

Keynes, in one of two elusive references to income distribution, remarks after writing his consumption function in wage-units, that it depends 'partly on the subjective needs and the psychological propensities and habits of the individuals composing it [the community] and the principles on which the income is divided between them (which may suffer modification as output is increased)', (See *GT*, p. 91).

Implicitly, all that is necessary is latent in Keynes's remark; the casual reference has meant that the thought has gone literally suppressed: there are very few and sparse lines devoted to income division in the huge mountain of consumption function literature.

Figure 9.1 contains a fairly typical *C*-function of the Keynesian literature, lettered C_1. As per the usual textbook instruction it rises to the right, with the MPC < 1, according to Keynes's 'law of the marginal propensity to consume'. Implicitly C_1 *must* assume that at 'real-income' Y_1 and Y_2 the division of income is more or less the same.

Suppose, instead, that at Y_1 the real income of $10 billion was divided fairly evenly among 1 million individuals so that each had about $10 000. Suppose, however, that when income advanced to $Y_2 = $20 billion it was shared now not between 1 million individuals but among only 10 000, with each getting a $1 million income, with each perhaps now spending 0.5 so that the APC drops from, say, 0.9 to

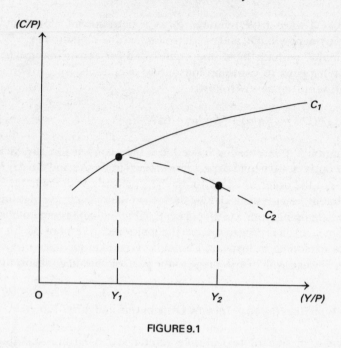

FIGURE 9.1

0.5. Hence the *total* of *C*-outlay may well decrease, as shown by the path of the broken line C_2 which now becomes the graphic portrayal of the *C*-function.

Income distribution thus becomes a vital ingredient of *C*-outlay. Economists have not attended to this fact in their prolix discussions of lesser determinants.

Another aspect inadequately explored is the proviso that as income ascends from Y_1 to Y_2 in Figure 9.1, virtually doubling, the *composition* of output must effectually stay unchanged so that, in the instance cited, *all* goods must be multiplied by two. Otherwise, if at Y_1 there is a wide assortment of *C*-items while at Y_2 there are *only* breadstuffs or washing machines, the *C*-course might well follow the path denoted by C_2 rather than C_1.

Theories of 'the' C-function which are silent about income division of Q_c-composition are lacking in vital dimensions.

VI HARMONIES AND CONFLICTS IN EMPLOYMENT GROWTH

Analysis so far has turned up no causes for disharmony or dissension on any ground, let alone economic considerations, from any growth in income and employment. On the contrary, an increase in employment and income created the potential for more individuals to have at least the same money income; real wages would depend on the (w/P) ratio which, we noted, was itself contingent on average productivity phenomena and the forces determining income shares. So far as A, average productivity, was concerned we are cognisant of the tendency of this to improve through technology as we pass into time yielding the usual complement of technological developments. In respect of θ, the wage share has tended to remain either rather stolid or to edge up, tending to improve labour's relative position. Absolute profits would move up with investment – as we shall note below. There would be no conflicts, no antinomies, no cleavage, no disharmony: events would appear to be smooth and beneficial; even Frederic Bastiat would approve.

Unfortunately, antagonisms can arise because of income redistribution accompanying employment growth. A more obvious kindling for some contention will be illustrated by appeal to Figure 9.2.

Up to this stage we have been classifying income as either W or R, as either wage or non-wage income, where the latter was a residual gross category which included all claims on the GBP beyond the wage bill, including depreciation and depletion charges. Suppose, instead, that we partition the GBP into the tripartite division so that:

$$Z = wN + F + R = W + F + R \tag{13}$$

where F = fixed payments and R = residual gross profits

Figure 9.2 draws in the Z-function, and in non-linear form so that the wage share declines and the profit share – however defined – is enlarged by more output and employment. Assuming $w = \bar{w}$ the W-function is linear as drawn; superimposed on the wage-bill are the fixed payments traced out by FF. Casual inspection suggests that fixed income recipients really walk a tightrope, eager mainly that jobs never fall below N' for then the fixed charges would not be met. On the other hand, for employment in excess of N' the fixed *share* of the rentier

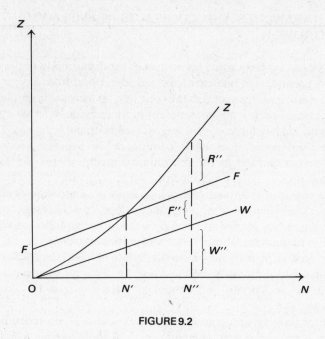

FIGURE 9.2

group *must* fall relatively and, if higher employment is accompanied by higher prices, rentier real income will be eroded. For the profit residual, total profits are perforce lifted. Likewise, the wage-bill must increase absolutely with some vagueness about real-wages (depending on the course of Z, whether linear or not; on the Figure 9.2 representation the real-wage would plunge somewhat).[12]   The following relations offer some guidance on the relative shift in income shares. Thus:

$$1 = (W/Z) + (F/Z) + (R/Z) = \theta + f + \pi \tag{14a}$$

$$\therefore \quad \pi = 1 - (\theta + f)$$

$$(\Delta\pi/\Delta N) = -[(\Delta\theta/\Delta N) + (\Delta f/\Delta N)] \tag{14b}$$

Thus the profit share will always increase by the descent in the wage share and the drop in the rentier portion. If the Z-function were linear, so that $\Delta\theta = 0$, the profit segment would always absorb the turn in the rentier slice. A definite antagonism is operative: what rentiers lose relatively profit recipients irresistably gain. Likewise, to a smaller degree, there is the same antagonism between the wage and profit *share*, between θ and π.

The analysis surrounding Figure 9.2 has been conducted on the hypothesis of the money wage constant and thus with the price level showing only small or minor percumbations. If the money wage rises (so that W is no longer linear), the rentier share would erode further, as under the thunderclap of inflation.

The shift to profits, and thus the erosion of the rentier share, would be captured through some elasticity relations. Thus:

$$(\Delta Z/\Delta N) = w + (\Delta R/\Delta N) \text{ or}$$
$$[N\Delta Z/Z\Delta N] = (wN/Z) + (N\Delta R/Z\Delta N) \tag{15a}$$

$$E_{zn} = \theta + \pi E_{rz} \text{ or } E_{rz} = (E_{zn} - \theta)/\pi \tag{15b}$$

According to equation 15b the elasticity of the function with respect to employment depends on the wage share, and the profit share multiplied by the relative profit movement compared to the relative proceeds change. The profit elasticity can also be put into terms of the same variables, as in equation 15b.

Rentiers, in brief, always find their real income and relative share diluted with an employment (and price) advance. Their vested economic interest is in an income level ample to avert widespread bankruptcy, but not too robust as to foster full employment and the optimal job climate. The rentier 'optimal' does not parallel that of job seekers.

The Entrepreneurial Stake

Contary to the rentier position entrepreneurs have the clearest and surest stake in full employment for, as the equational relations and Figure 9.2 disclose, profits are magnified as the job momentum carries the economy rightward along the Z-function. Aggregate profits are indubitably enhanced. Further, in the short period where the stock of capital is fixed, so that $K = \bar{K}$ (where the K-aggregate reflects some aggregation of subjective estimates of capital) there is the clear knowledge that the rate of profit advances directly with the employment flow.

The pure beneficiary of full employment, at least under the assumed conditions of $w = \bar{w}$, and thus of price level stability without the excesses of inflation and surging rates of interest, would thus be the entrepreneurial class, or enterepreneurs as a group. One might guess that they would thus always be in the van, devising measures and policies to promote full employment. And yet it is not uncommon to find them supporting rentier protests about an 'overheated' economy, and financial community advocacy of creating economic slack to discipline labour through pouring more recruits into what Marx called the 'army of unemployed'. There does seem to be some confusion in industrialists lending support to maneuvers which are contrary to the profit aggregate and entrepreneurial interests.

It is plausible to think that because financial opinions reflecting rentier interests are articulately expressed, and as in the conventional reporting financial news is identified with the business world, as if an utter community of interest prevailed, businessmen frequently confuse separable interests. As analytic thinking is not their forte, in their expression of a point of view they are likely to parrot the financial opinions to which they have been exposed in the press, in bank letters, etc.

It is thus less bewildering to find, from time to time, more progressive views among industrialists than among financiers: sellers of farm machinery are keenly aware that their prosperity is bound up with that of the farmers. Henry Ford, a long time ago, knew that if he was to sell autos then real-wages would have to be high enough and leisure would have to be ample. Other illustrations could undoubtedly be enumerated; a case study of progressivity in the financial versus the industrial community would seem to warrant sociological investigation.

VII LABOUR SUFFERS IN A RECESSION: THE NULL INCOME GROUP

The theory of relative shares logically focusses on those who have income, or the proportions funnelled off by the respective income categories. Lost entirely is the income underclass of those without an income base in the immediate employment situation.

The Null Income Group

Those neither receiving wages, contractual fixed payments, or residual gross profits, comprise the *null* income group in GBP. Receiving no income, their income share has to be nil. What income they do receive, by way of unemployment compensation, welfare benefits, charitable handouts, can be lumped together and given some percentage dimension compared to the GBP or GNP. But so far as the active economic process is concerned their participatory income is zero; the sums they do have available for current expenditure is in the nature of a transfer (or involves some personal dissavings, where accumulations are present).

With the relative share in GBP posted at zero, the only way to get some bearings on the importance of the null income group would be to cite numbers, as those unemployed, and those unemployable either because of mental or physical deformities or handicaps. Invariably, the group is of substantial size while their existence is too often overlooked by theorists concentrating on the positive position of income participants sharing in the production receipts by virtue of a direct claim in the market economy where labour is hired freely and where contractual commitments are honored.

As the cyclical accordion expands and contracts during the recovery and recession phases, the null income group is likely to undergo similar, but not proportionate flux. Technological improvement is likely to cut demands for labour for roughly a return to the same volume of production.

It is the fate of the null income group that largely aroused and animated President Lyndon B. Johnsons's *Great Society* welfare programmes. Traditionally, the studies have been a sociological domain though surely they fit coherently into the theory of relative shares though some concepts must be redesigned to capture the magnitudes entailed.

Labour's Share In a Recession

Fewer clichés are more timeless than the overburdened platitude that 'labour suffers in a recession (or depression)'. This would, of course, only be true if somehow *each* wage earner would find the work-week cut back about proportionately. As matters stand, it is not labour but the unemployed who suffer from the income loss and the indignity of feeling their abilities are unwanted in a business downturn. To say that labour 'suffers' is a self-serving hyperbole endorsed by labour union officials. Those who remain in employment at about the same money wage may find, as in the older business cycle, that the recession–depression phase carries lower prices so that their real-wage edges higher. It is only in respect of job insecurity that there may be more universal 'suffering,' inspired by fears of not knowing where next the axe will fall, and by imposing inhibitions upon those who were contemplating some change in jobs: the uncertainty may make the current job longer than would otherwise be wished.

To be sure, when we are told that the unemployment rate is, say, 10 per cent but that the average duration of unemployment is 'only' 5 weeks, this suggests that over the year that 50 per cent of the work force will be unemployed – each for 5 weeks! Undoubtedly this overstates the facts: the greater likelihood is that individual A is laid off for 5 weeks, called back and at work for a few weeks before being shelved again. It may be surmised that perhaps 25 per cent or so of the work-force will be hit by lay-offs during the course of the year when the unemployment rate hovers more or less indefinitely at 10 per cent.

VIII   THE ELUSIVE FULL EMPLOYMENT GOAL

Analysis thus sharpens the view that only entrepreneurs and the unemployed have an undiluted and unalloyed stake in achieving the full employment goal. Universal economic benefits from an abounding jobs situation are less tangible: a less tense social and political climate can make life easier but at some cost, as rentiers might conclude. Likewise, insofar as fuller employment carried some decline in real-wages, as Keynes hypothesised at first, those already employed would have some second thoughts about the virtues of a less clogged job market: greater hire of labour at lower real-wages would have its unsavory aspects.

The interest in full employment is thus more fragmented and splintered between important groupings in our economy than economists have generally imagined. It was generally thought that individuals of all ideological persuasions, and of all income sizes and patterns, would flock to the full employment banner. It always seemed that only misanthropes would oppose the full employment goal. But considering the diverse economic interests it becomes easier to understand the denunciation of 'starry-eyed do-gooders,' Keynes, Keynesians, liberal, or New Society programmes designed to seek the Promised Land of job abundance. Even those who might benefit are often confused in their thinking by the ideological press and politicians into some mythical fears of big government and higher taxes dredged up as alarmist hobgoblins.

Full employment can thus turn out to be a mirage when one assesses the lack of a supporting majestic consensus. Important steps to the goal are only likely to be taken against the background of an overwhelming disaster such as the Great Depression. When unemployment, say, is 25 per cent out of a workforce, say of 100 million, and when there are 3 adult family members, there are some 75 millions interested in government actions to abort unemployment. As unemployment falls to 10 per cent, the clamoring political numbers are reduced to 30 millions. When the record is improved to 6 per cent unemployment, the full employment consitituency is ground down, in our illustration, to 18 million. Others, now in jobs, are apt to react with complacency, and even to fear further measures as entailing tax impositions, or as connecting 'socialism,' nationalism, unwise government intervention, or any of the other bogeys conventionally resurrected.

Thus it is that the closer we get to full employment through public policy, the more difficult it is to go the extra mile: the more successful we are in getting close to the wall, the harder it will be to vault it. The reason: the closer the economy is to full employment, the more nearly universal the political sentiment to enjoin others to 'stop rocking the boat'. Complacency will propagate clear vested interests in the optimal outcome will find their ranks decimated.

Small wonder at the near universal support for President Roosevelt in expecting his mandate to slash unemployment in the Great Depression year 1933. Likewise, it is not surprising that the more he succeeded, the greater the opposition to further ameliorative measures: all sorts of hostile groups emerged out of the woodwork, describing themselves as Liberty Leagues, Leagues for Constitutional Government, or bound together simply by venom at 'that dictator, F.D.R'. Once Roosevelt had saved them, 'the good people', they had their usual bourbonic torpor in comprehending why he wanted to do more.

Economists have been myopic in thinking that there was a universal consensus for full employment. Acknowledging the splintered interests in achieving the job optimal, the sordid record of the last 15 years becomes more intelligable. Economic and this ideological, commitment to full employment is a pipe-dream. Full success for Keynes's vision has thus become mainly a mirage, despite its virtues and accessibility.

IX INVESTMENT AND PROFITS

Reviewing Figure 9.2 at N'' employment, the wage-bill is W'', fixed payments are F'', and gross profits are R''. Or capitalist income, combining the non-wage categories, amounts to $(F'' + R'')$. How is the total determined? Clearly, what we need are some demand notions in order to learn where N will settle. Actually, in the context of profits it is possible to rely wholly on demand concepts without injecting supply considerations, except to give determinateness to the entire equilibrium configuration.

Enormous advances have been made on the theory of profits since Keynes's *GT*, mainly through the K–K–R insights. Too, the work lends itself to quantitative assessment as compared to the historic vaguesness from Adam Smith to Alfred Marshall, and in the modern neoclassical general equilibrium theorists who, when pressed still convey vapidities by way of 'normal' profits which, in their very nature are always abnormal.

C-Sector Profits

From Joan Robinson's perceptions, honed a trifle by the K–K–R generalization, it is possible to give some direct tone to the magnitude of C-sector profits.[13]

C-Sector Output Value: $P_c Q_c = W_c + R_c$ (16a)

C-Sector Purchases: $P_c Q_c = \alpha W$ (16b)

C-Sector Profits: $R_c = \alpha W - W_c$ (16c)

On the K–K–R hypothesis that $\alpha = 1$, then:

C-Sector Profits: $R_c = W_i + W_g$, when $\alpha = 1$ (16d)

Profits in the C-sector depend rather uniquely upon the wage-bill in the I-sector and on earnings of civil service employees. Where $\alpha > 1$, the spendings of capitalists (non-wage-earners) enter to bolster the C-sector profit aggregate.

Equations 16 a–d embody some impressive results. Profits in the C-sector will be strong insofar as employment and money wages are high among capital goods and government employees.

Total Profits

To develop the aggregate profit magnitudes we will employ (for brevity) the customary notation used by those writings which deal in 'real' quantities, or nominal quantities corrected for price level changes. We can, nonetheless, interpret the total as before, as nominal magnitudes.

Value of Output Purchased: $Z = C + I + G_b$ (17a)

where G_b = private sector government purchases

Allocation of Income Earned: $Z = C + S + T$ (17b)

Income Disbursed: $Z = W + R + T,$ (17c)

where $T = tW + tR$ and t = average tax rate

Recalling that $C = \alpha W$, and then putting equations 17a and 17c in juxtaposition, it follows that:

$$R = I + (G_b - T) + W(\alpha - l) \quad (17d)$$
$$= I + D_f + W(\alpha - 1) \approx I + D_f$$

Thus, under the K–K–R hypothesis, aggregate profits are contingent upon the magnitude of gross investment and the government deficit (defined here in a special way to refer to government GBP outlays – which exclude civil servant pay – and includes only personal and corporate income taxes). When $\alpha > 1$, so that there is ample capitalist consumption, this too goes to swell the profit aggregate.

Removing all the qualifying hypotheses (as in a more detailed analysis) it would still follow that the profit aggregate will rise or fall with the investment aggregate, with the total fortified by the magnitude of the government deficit and the consumption of the rentier and entrepreneurial groups. The presence of the deficit as part of the profit aggregate must be grasped for confusion is rife on this aspect in the modern Reagan–Thatcher superfical ideological posturing era.

X THE NUMÉRAIRE

The importance of income distribution in the determination of the macro-magnitudes such as employment, income, the price level, has now been revealed: omitting income distribution leaves a significant void in the theory. Too, income shares opens the door to an understanding of events influencing the real-wage.

Beyond the integral part of income distribution in macrotheory, distributive implications illuminate some economic disharmonies that go far to explain the less than universal conviction on the merits of full employment and the imperfect consensus impairing the possible outcome. Income distribution fears thus do much to impart perspective on why full employment, on the reason the job optimum, continues to elude us, as desert mirage. We may have deluded ourselves about the consensus attributes of full employment.

Since the opening references, the analysis has detoured about the nature and significance of the numéraire, namely, Keynes's wage-unit interpreted as the average wage (w). Yet despite the lack of explicitness the average wage, or numéraire, has been a featured part of the analysis. In determining employment, as in equation 3 the money wage acts to ferret absolute numbers out of the numerator D'' where $D'' = P_i Q_i = k_i w_i N_i$ where $w_i = w$. Likewise in equations 4 and 5, in the determination of money income, the money wage is tucked away in D'': in *all* money magnitudes, it is the money wage that is ubiquitous, giving the nominal thrust to the magnitudes involved. For the various price levels, and for the money sums of consumer outlay, it is likewise the money wage that yields the price or nominal dimension.

Literally, we live in a money wage economy. Money prices come into being because money wages are paid: if wages were paid in rabbit's ears, we would have a set of rabbit ear prices. Our economy might have started out originally as a price system from the use of money in final purchase arrangements. It has, however, been converted over time into a money wage (or money income) system, and thus one in which money prices emerge.

The money wage is thus the effective numéraire, adopting the same function as the setting of the price of an ounce of gold under the old and bygone gold standard. Money wages preponderate in practically all unit costs; money wages dominate consumer purchasing power. Alter money wages, boost them skywards say, and both demand and supply forces are thrust higher.

The average money wage is thus the effective numéraire in our economy, as Keynes long ago discerned. To disclose how money fits into the scheme, affecting Q's and N's while hardly troubling the P's, entails a separate and lengthy story.[14]

NOTES

1. Cf. my indictment, and references therein, in 'Hicksian Keynesianism: Dominance and Decline', *Modern Economic Thought*, Sidney Weintraub (ed.) (University of Pennsylvania Press, 1977).

2. A small dent in monetarist misconceptions appears in the fine, if belated, article by Allan Meltzer, 'Keynes's *General Theory* A Different Perspective' *Journal of Economic Literature* (March 1981).

3. Don Patinkin thus credits me with more originality than I have claimed with respect to the Aggregate Supply–Demand concepts. See his 'A Study of Keynes' Theory of Effective Demand', *Economic Inquiry*, April 1979, p. 159n.

4. The late Harry G. Johnson, a high priest among monetarists though rarely hewing the strict doctrinaire line, denounced Kaldor, Joan Robinson and myself as what he was ideologically disposed to call 'scientific' economics by our rejection of marginal productivity theory and our espousal of incomes policy. See his 'Cambridge in the 1950s', *Encounter* (January 1974) p. 38.

5. Cf. my 'Generalising Kalecki and Simplifying Macroeconomics', *Journal of Post Keynesian Economics* (Spring 1979) and my 'An Eclectic Theory of Income Shares', ibid. (Autumn 1981). Use of some of the same concepts in another context appears in 'A Macrodistributive Model Dispelling the Econometric Fog', *Banca Nazionale del Lavoro Quarterly Review* (Spring 1983).

6. Cf. my *General Theory of the Price Level, etc.* (Greenwood Press, 1959 reprint). For the various extensions which follow, see *Capitalism's Inflation and Unemployment Crisis* (Addison-Wesley, 1978) ch. 3.

7. See my 'Bedrock in the Money-Wage-Money Supply Inflation Controversy', *Banca Nazionale del Lavoro Quarterly Review* (December 1981).

8. Cf. *Capitalism's Inflation and Unemployment Crisis*, chs 3 and 4.

9. For more discussion, ibid., ch. 3.

10. Cf. my 'The Missing Theory of Money Wages', *Journal of Post Keynesian Economics* (Winter 1978/79).

11. See, with E. Roy Weintraub, 'The Full employment Model: A Critique', *Kyklos* (1972). Reprinted in my *Keynes, Keynesians, and Monetarists* (University of Pennsylvania Press, 1978).

12. On the analysis surrounding Figure 9.2, and the general remarks on antagonisms as employment grows, see my *Approach to the Theory of Income Distribution* (Greenwood Press reprint, 1958) ch. 2.

13. On this entire section, for elaboration and references, see my 'An Eclectic Theory', op. cit., and 'Dispelling the Econometric Fog', op. cit.

14. For my own views see *Capitalism's Crisis*, ch. 4 and 'Money-Demand Motives; A Reconsideration', *Economie Appliquée* (1983). On money wages as the numéraire, see ch. 9 in the former work.

Index